African Perspectives on Adult Learning

The Social Context of Adult Learning in Africa

Other books in the Series

- *The Psychology of Adult Learning in Africa*
  Thomas Fasokun, Anne Katahoire and Akpovire Oduaran
- *Foundations of Adult Education in Africa*
  Frederick Nafukho, Maurice Amutabi and Ruth Otunga
- *Research Methods for Adult Educators in Africa*
  Bagele Chilisa and Julia Preece
- *Developing Programmes for Adult Learners in Africa*
  Matthew Gboku and Nthogo Lekoko

The Editorial Board for the Series

- Adama Ouane, UNESCO Institute for Education (Chairperson)
- Martin Kamwengo, University of Zambia
- David Langhan, Pearson Education South Africa
- Wolfgang Leumer, Institute for International Cooperation, German Adult Education Association
- Christopher McIntosh, UNESCO Institute for Education
- Mantina Mohasi, National University of Lesotho
- Stanley Mpofu, National University of Science and Technology, Zimbabwe
- Gabo Ntseane, University of Botswana (Assistant Series Managing Editor)
- Anthony Okech, Makerere University, Uganda
- Orrin F. Summerell, UNESCO Institute for Education
- Edward Turay, University of Sierra Leone
- Frank Youngman, University of Botswana (Series Managing Editor)

African Perspectives on Adult Learning

The Social Context of Adult Learning in Africa

Sabo Indabawa with Stanley Mpofu

Co-published by the UNESCO Institute for Education, Feldbrunnenstr. 58, 20148 Hamburg, Germany, and Pearson Education South Africa, corner of Logan Way and Forest Drive, Pinelands, Cape Town, South Africa, in collaboration with the Institute for International Cooperation of the German Adult Education Association, Obere Wilhelmstr. 32, 53225 Bonn, Germany, and the Adult Education Department of the University of Botswana, Private Bag 0022, Gaborone, Botswana.

First published 2006

ISBN 9282011194

Published by Rolene Liebenberg with David Langhan
Project manager: Anita van Zyl
Symbol research and selection: Sandie Vahl
Editor: Mafalda Marchesi
Book design by Graham Arbuckle
Cover design and artwork by Toby Newsome
Typesetting by Robin Taylor
Printed by Creda Communications

Contents

ADINKRA SYMBOLS

For the icons in this Series, we have chosen Adinkra symbols that are associated with learning and community in some way. These striking and expressive symbols are used by the people of Ghana and the Ivory Coast in textile and jewellery design, architecture, wood carvings, etc., and represent only one of a number of writing systems found in Africa.

	Symbol	Meaning	Interpretation
🕸	bese saka	sack of cola nuts	abundance, plenty, affluence, power, unity, togetherness
⊕	dame-dame	name of a board game	intelligence, ingenuity, strategy, craftiness
	dwennimmen	ram's horns	humility, strength, wisdom, learning
	mate masie	what I hear I keep	wisdom, knowledge, learning, prudence, understanding
	nkonsonkonson	chain link	unity, human relations, brotherhood, cooperation
	nsaa	hand-woven fabric	excellence, authenticity, genuineness
	sesa woruban	morning star inside a wheel	life transformation

To Africa's equitable development utilising adult education as a tool and to the late Sabo Indabawa's newly born child, Muhammad Mutawakkil, who should join the vanguard of making the world a better place.

The authors

Sabo A. Indabawa

Sabo Indabawa obtained his BAEd (BUK), MEd and PhD degree in Ibadan. He was a university teacher for more than twenty years and held the post of Associate Professor of Education (including Adult Education). In his career he served as Head, Department of Adult Education and Community Services, Bayero University, Kano, Nigeria; and Head, Department of Adult and Nonformal Education, University of Namibia, Republic of Namibia. He authored more than eighty scholarly works, including fifteen books in the specialist areas of adult and non-formal education, as well as in the areas of literacy and gender and education. At the time of his death in 2004 Sabo Indabawa was on leave of absence from the University serving with an Abuja, Nigeria think-tank organisation, the National Development Project (NDP), as its Director of Policy and Coordination. Among numerous local and international professional engagements, Indabawa served on the University of Manchester Higher Education Links Programme (HELP) and also held a Fellowship of the UNESCO Institute for Education, Hamburg, Germany.

Stanley Mpofu

Professor Stanley Mpofu obtained a BAdmin, MSc RUP degree in Rhodesia and a PhD degree at Michigan State University, USA. He is the Director of the Centre for Continuing Education at the National University of Science and Technology, Zimbabwe. He worked previously in the Adult Education Departments of the University of Zimbabwe (1987–1995), the University of Botswana (1995–1999) and the University of Namibia (1999–2003), where he served as Head of Department for three years (2001–2003). He has published extensively on many aspects of adult education, including distance and lifelong learning. His latest international assignments include a consultancy for the Ministry of Education, Eritrea, where he spent three months working in the Department of Adult and Media Education.

Foreword

The remedial strategy of borrowing textbooks conceived in contexts of and for students from developed countries with well-established traditions of adult education is no longer viable. The present textbook series, African Perspectives on Adult Learning, represents the outcome of a venture initiated three decades ago by the Institute for International Cooperation of the German Adult Education Association (known by its German acronym as IIZ/DVV). Bringing together non-governmental and civil society organisations, the IIZ/DVV turned this venture into a creative partnership with academia, aimed at building the training and research capacities of African universities that serve the adult education community. It has become a means of fruitful cooperation with several leading African universities, all partners being concerned with providing textbooks for university departments and institutes of adult education relevant for the African context.

The abiding interest as well as growing financial support and substantive input of the IIZ/DVV has provided a key ingredient for the success of this project, along with establishing its potential for expansion. The University of Botswana has been another major contibutor right from the beginning. Its Department of Adult Education has given the academic and institutional support needed for such an ambitious undertaking, graciously shouldering the Editorial Secretariat of the Series. The third pillar of this endeavour – and a decisive one – was furnished by the UNESCO Institute for Education (UIE), an international centre of excellence in adult learning enjoying the full backing of UNESCO and boasting extensive publishing experience in the field. UIE brought in vital international and inter-regional expertise coupled with the vision of the Fifth International Conference on Adult Education (CONFINTEA V). The Institute has also mobilised sizeable financial resources of its own, led the Series Editorial Board and assumed responsibility for managing often difficult matters entailed by such a complex venture.

The present series recommends itself through other distinctive features that reflect the unique manner in which it has come about. One of these has to do with the professional guidance and technical advice provided by the competent, sensitive and broadly representative Series Editorial Board, whose members have displayed the capability and wisdom required to steer a project of this kind. Their intellectual resources, experience and know-how made it possible for the Series to take on its actual form. We wish to express our deep gratitude to all of the members of the Editorial Board for their profound involvement and the optimism which they brought to the Series and their dedication to its successful completion.

The co-publisher with UIE is Pearson Education South Africa, which has proven to be a partner highly committed to the goals of the project, one prepared to engage in a collaboration of a different order and take risks in exploring new paths in publishing. As a full member of the Series Editorial Board, the co-publisher has offered invaluable assistance, especially in the writers' workshops and in coaching the authors throughout the composition of the chapters. The creative way in which Pearson Education South Africa has integrated the project into its work and its firm dedication to fostering editorial and authorial capacities in Africa deserve special mention. Without this sense of mission, the Series would not have seen the light of day.

The authors of the works in this Series have themselves been selected on the basis of proposals they submitted. We took pleasure in working with all of these devoted partners, and the project greatly benefited from their combination of individual conviction with teamwork and collective analysis and decision-making. We wish to thank all of the authors for their hard work as well as their adherence to a demanding schedule. Their professionalism and competence lie at the heart of this Series and were instrumental in its realisation.

Finally, and most importantly, Professor Frank Youngman, the Series Managing Editor, and his Assistant, Dr Gabo Ntseane, of the University of Botswana, who constitute the Editorial Board Secretariat, deserve special recognition. Frank Youngman initiated the idea of this Series in 2001, and the Secretariat has been in the front line at all times, carefully guiding the process, monitoring progress and ensuring the quality of the work at all stages without compromise.

This Series addresses the critical lack of textbooks for adult education and the alienating nature of those currently in use in Africa. We have sought to develop a new set of foundational works conceived and developed from an African perspective and written mainly by African scholars. An African perspective, however, is not mere Afrocentrism, although some degree of the latter is required to move beyond the reigning Eurocentrism and general Western domination of all scientific domains and adult education in particular. Injecting a dose of Afrocentrism without prejudice to universal values, elementary scientific knowledge, and other cultures, and without complacency in the face of retrograde and discriminatory values and traditions has proven to be a significant challenge. In essence, the African perspective has revealed itself to be both a renaissance of the continent and its manifold traditions, as well as the birth of its own new vision and prospects in the context of a fast-growing, ever-changing and increasingly globalised world.

For the initial volumes in this evolving series, the following five titles were selected: *The Psychology of Adult Learning in Africa; Foundations of Adult Education in Africa; Research Methods for Adult Educators in Africa; Developing Programmes for Adult Learners in Africa* and *The Social Context of Adult Learning in Africa*. We will certainly judge the success of these volumes by taking into account the reactions and responses of their users, and we will make any necessary adjustments while striving to widen the scope of the venture to cover other linguistic areas of Africa and to explore new thematic fields for deepening the African perspective. There is no question but that IIZ/DVV and UIE are committed to lending their intellectual and financial support to this endeavour. Furthermore, the University of Botswana is committed to providing the academic and administrative base for the Series, whilst Pearson Education South Africa foresees the ongoing viability of the project. In opening up new approaches to adult education and learning in Africa, the Series meets the needs of governments, non-governmental and civil society organisations, and academia in an area of great importance to UNESCO and the community of nations.

Adama Ouane
Director, UNESCO Institute for Education

Preface

It became clear during the 1990s that adult learning must be an important part of all strategies for development. In a series of world conferences between 1990 and 1996, various agencies of the United Nations addressed the issues of education for all, the environment, human rights, population, social development, the status of women, human settlements and food security. Each of these conferences recognised that progress would be dependent on adult members of society transforming their life circumstances and gaining greater control over their lives. To achieve this change, adults require new knowledge, skills and attitudes. This significant insight was highlighted by the Fifth International Conference on Adult Education (CONFINTEA V) that was organised by UNESCO in 1997. CONFINTEA V affirmed that adult learning is potentially a powerful force for promoting people-centred development. It concluded that the education of adults is a key to the twenty-first century.

The concept of adult learning articulated by CONFINTEA V is a broad one embracing formal, non-formal and informal learning processes in all areas of people's lives. This concept is relevant in African contexts, where the learning of adults takes place across their various social roles, in the home, the community, and the workplace, as well as in formal educational and training institutions. Opportunities for learning are availed by a wide variety of providers. The state has a central responsibility to promote and facilitate adult learning. In some countries this responsibility has been diminished by the impact of structural adjustment policies. But in others, the state continues to play an important role, with a wide range of government departments organising programmes that involve adult learning. These programmes are multi-sectoral, including activities as varied as agricultural extension, health education, business training, consumer education, community development, and wildlife education. Also, the organisations of civil society are significant sites of adult learning, providing their own educational programmes, as well as a context in which adults acquire new competencies through their active involvement in running such organisations. For example, in many countries the trade union movement is an

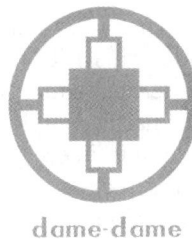

dame-dame

important source of adult learning. Increasingly, the private sector is a major provider of learning opportunities for adults. Its role has two dimensions. Firstly, companies are expanding their training and development for employees as they respond to the challenges of technological change and global competition. Secondly, there is a rapid growth of commercial educational institutions, such as colleges, academies and institutes, which are responding to market demands for learning opportunities, especially in work-related fields such as computing, tourism and business. These institutions are to be found in all the urban centres of Africa. Public and private universities also cater for many adult learners, especially through their part-time, evening and distance learning programmes. The education and training of adults in Africa therefore takes place in many settings, embraces many content areas and modes of learning, and is provided by many different types of organisations. It is a complex and diverse field of activity.

The successful implementation of adult learning policies and programmes depends in large measure on the availability of knowledgeable, skilful, and socially committed educators of adults. Because they are key agents in the realisation of adult learning, the quality of their initial and continuing training is crucial. The educators of adults in Africa work in a wide variety of organisational and social contexts, from government bureaucracies to community-based projects. They have multiple roles as programme planners, organisers, teachers, researchers and counsellors. While this diversity of situations and roles reflects the reality of adult learning settings, it presents significant conceptual and practical problems in terms of the training of those who educate adults. One example is that not all who work with adults in learning activities identify themselves as adult educators. Rather, they identify themselves as health promoters or business advisors or community workers. Nevertheless, whatever the nomenclature of a particular cadre, it is important that they are proficient in their work of helping adults to learn. The development of their expertise includes a body of knowledge, skills and values that is centred on adult education as a field of study and practice.

The professional training of educators of adults in Africa takes place in institutions of tertiary education across the continent, primarily at diploma and degree level. For example, in every country there are colleges of agriculture that prepare agricultural extension workers, health institutes that train community-based health workers and technical colleges that train vocational teachers. In particular, many African universities have departments or institutes of adult education which train personnel for fields as varied as adult basic education, prison education and human resource development. Although the areas of content specialisation vary from agronomy to literacy, the curricula of the training programmes have many common topics, such as the psychology of adult learning, programme development, communication skills and research methods. This is because all educators of adults require a common body of knowledge (such as awareness of the historical and philosophical dimensions of adult education practice) and a number of generic skills (for example, in teaching and research). A key learning resource in these training programmes is the prescribed course textbook. However, those who teach these programmes often have difficulty in finding textbooks that are relevant to the work situations and social contexts of their students.

A review of English-language curriculum materials used in the professional training of adult educators in Africa reveals that the majority of textbooks for the courses are published in the United States or the United Kingdom. The content of these books seldom reflects issues of African development or the realities of adult education policy and practice in Africa. The social and organisational contexts, theoretical underpinnings and practical examples are largely derived from the experience of adult education in the advanced industrialised countries of the West. Hence the textbooks currently being used in the training of adult educators in Africa are at best lacking in relevance and at worst actively promoting inappropriate models of adult education. Furthermore, because of the cost of these books, student access is often limited.

The post-colonial history of adult education as a field of study in African tertiary education institutions shows that very few indigenous textbooks have been produced over the years. Useful individual books, such as the *Adult Education Handbook* (edited by the Institute of Adult Education, Dar-es-Salaam, 1973) and *A Handbook of Adult Education for West Africa* (edited by Lalage Bown and Sunday Hezekiah Olu Tomori, London, 1979), have been one-off publications that were not followed up and were not widely available. When an institution in one country has consistently produced relevant materials, such as the Department of Adult Education at the University of Ibadan in Nigeria, they have been difficult to obtain in other countries. The problem of a lack of appropriate and accessible textbooks for use in the training of African adult educators remains.

There is, therefore, a need to develop relevant, affordable, and available textbooks that reflect African social realities, theoretical and cultural perspectives, policies and modes of practice. This is the need that the Series African Perspectives on Adult Learning seeks to meet. The books in the series put the African context at the centre of their discussions of adult education topics. They take into account the impact of colonialism, liberation struggles, neo-colonialism and globalisation. They show the importance to adult learning of African philosophies, indigenous knowledge systems, traditions and cultures. They demonstrate that the realities of class, gender, race and ethnicity in African societies shape the nature of adult learning activities. They provide examples of the policies and practices that characterise adult education across the continent. Whilst referring to international discourses on adult learning, their presentation of issues in adult education is Africa-centred. The series therefore contributes to the endogenisation of education within the perspective of the African Renaissance.

The books in the series African Perspectives on Adult Learning cover important subjects for the training of educators of adults in Africa. They are intended to be course textbooks that will be used in face-to-face teaching environments in a way that encourages interactive learning. Each book is designed to provide an overview of the subject, to introduce appropriate theory, and to provide discussion and examples rooted in professional practice, policies and research from African contexts. Each chapter features clear learning objectives, practical examples and activities for the reader to do individually or in a group, a summary and key points, further questions to think about and suggested readings. It is hoped that the use of the books will promote the development of relevant curricula and interactive teaching approaches in adult education training programmes across the continent.

Each book in the series provides an African perspective on an important area of knowledge and practice for the educator of adults. In *The Social Context of Adult Learning in Africa*, Sabo Indabawa and Stanley Mpofu consider how adult learning programmes are affected by their surrounding context. The book is based on the assumption that adult education is not simply a technical activity, rather it is shaped by and influences the society in which it takes place. Therefore the educators of adults need a sociological understanding of the contexts in which they work. Although it has abundant human and natural resources, Africa faces many development challenges. These include problems of race, ethnicity and religion, divisions of social class and gender, widespread poverty and national debt, weak democratic systems, health problems, environmental degradation, and increased marginalisation in a globalised world. Many of these social and economic problems affect the most disadvantaged groups of the poor, women and children. Adult education has the potential to help African countries and communities achieve their developmental goals. But to realise this potential requires adult educators who have a clear understanding of development issues. Hence the book seeks to develop a comprehensive sociological approach to the context of adult education which reflects African realities.

The aims of the book are:

- to provide a critical analysis of the concepts and theories of social change and development in the African context; and
- to provide an understanding of the major developmental issues that influence the nature of adult learning in Africa.

Chapters 1 and 2 deals with the concepts and issues of development, social change and their bearing on adult education. Chapter 3 examines the concept, practices and concerns of community development and the role of adult education in the process. Chapter 4 discusses the issues of race, ethnicity, and religion in relation to adult education. Chapter 5 clarifies the concepts of social class and gender, and examines their implications for adult education theory and practice. Chapter 6 explains the concept of empowerment and indicates how alternative adult education programmes can be used in efforts to empower disadvantaged groups in society. Chapter 7 looks at the concept of democracy and demonstrates ways through which adult education can be used to promote the practice of democracy in Africa contexts. Chapter 8 examines health and HIV/AIDS and the possible role of adult education in this regard. Special emphasis is placed on HIV/AIDS because of the seriousness of the epidemic throughout the continent. In Chapter 9, the concepts of poverty and debt are defined and their impact on adult education discussed. Chapter 10 examines globalisation and its many implications for Africa and adult education. Finally, Chapter 11 analyses the concepts and strategies of promoting environmental adult education as an important contribution to attaining sustainable development on the continent.

The tools of social analysis are very important if educators of adults are to be reflective practitioners aware of the social consequences of their work. *The Social Context of Adult Learning in Africa* provides an excellent resource for developing and enhancing this knowledge and understanding.

Frank Youngman
University of Botswana

Acknowledgements

The thought that went into writing this book, as well as the actual write-up and completion of it, is the outcome of various forms of support received from different sources. First, I give the entire credit to Allah (Subhanahu Wa Ta'ala), my Creator, for everything.

In the intellectual diaspora many people also willingly gave of their time, ideas, moral and material support. The authors of the scholarly works used (duly acknowledged under the references section) deserve my appreciation. Professor Frank Youngman of the University of Botswana, Gaborone helped in innumerable ways, and Dr Adama Ouane, Director, UNESCO Institute for Education (UIE), Hamburg, Germany, also assisted considerably. I am especially grateful to the latter for the opportunity to participate in the prestigious Fellowship Programme of the UNESCO Institute for Education. Most of the recently published materials used in generating ideas for this book were sourced from the UIE Documentation Centre. Similarly, my associates and friends at UIE, especially Professor Thomas Fasokun, Dr Christopher McIntosh, Lisa Krolak, Louise Silz and Cendrine Sebastiani gave considerable support and assistance.

Similarly, Professor Akpovire Oduaran, Head, Department of Adult Education, University of Botswana, Gaborone and Dr Hanno Schindele of the Institute for International Cooperation of the German Adult Education Association (IIZ-DVV), Bonn, Germany, offered personal support and professional input into this work. Equally, Mr David Langhan, Publishing Director, Pearson Education South Africa, as well as the participants at the Gaborone writers' workshop of August 2002 did much to shape the form and character of the book. David in particular organised the editing of the book in a most impressive and efficient style.

At home, special thanks are due to Dr Usman Muhammad Bugaje, Project Coordinator, National Development Project, Abuja (where I served as Director of Policy and Coordination between 2001 and 2003); Dr Aabdurrasheed Aderinoye, of UNESCO, Abuja; my colleagues at Bayero University, Kano, Nigeria, especially Abba A. Haladu and Dr M. B. Shitu (who read some of the draft chapters of the book), as well as all the members of my family, especially Aisha I. Husain, my wife, and Abubakar Sabo Sani, my first child. In a similar way, I am grateful to Dr Hafiz Abubakar and Dr Akilu Sani Indabawa for immense moral and material support.

For the show of rare and exceeding confidence in my ability and capacity for accomplishing daunting intellectual tasks, I appreciate the kind support and understanding of Professor Barnabas Otaala of the University of Namibia.

Finally, while expressing gratitude for the help received from many parties, I take full responsibility for any error of fact, analysis or opinion found in this book, and I am willing to make corrections where attention is drawn to any serious inaccuracy.

Sabo A. Indabawa

My involvement in this book was a result of the untimely death of Sabo Indabawa. When Sabo died, I felt obliged to complete the work he had started – just like I had extended his legacy at the University of Namibia (UNAM) when I succeeded him as Head of Department in 2001. Apart from having worked with him, two other factors worked in my favour. Firstly, the subject matter of the book was within my broad area of specialisation. Secondly, I was a member of the Series Editorial Board and, in this regard, I was beholden to the objectives of the African Perspectives on Adult Learning (APAL) project. Thirdly, I was available (at least I thought I was till I realised just how much needed to be done to complete the task).

Accordingly, I wish to pay tribute to Sabo Amin Indabawa, with whom I shared the trials and tribulations of the X-Block at UNAM. I also wish to thank the Series Editorial Board for affording me this opportunity to extend my influence in the APAL Series beyond the boardroom. I am particularly indebted to Professor Frank Youngman the Series Managing Editor, who exceeded the confines of his role as Series Editor and provided mentorship for many other scholarly activities that I have taken on in recent years.

Finally, I must thank members of my immediate family for the many sacrifices they have made on account of my career: my wife, Ntombikayise, for sacrificing her career for mine; my sons, Thembelani and Makhosini, for managing my other affairs while I carry on with my academic work; and my little girl, Buhlebethu, for giving me one more reason to go on.

Stanley Mpofu

African Perspectives on Adult Learning

The Social Context of
Adult Learning in Africa

Chapter 1

Adult education and development

OVERVIEW

This chapter defines adult education and development. A proper understanding of adult education and development will help you to see how adult education facilitates development, and how it in turn affects the provision and effectiveness of adult education in society. We also look at the formulation of the term *adult education* and how it has evolved over the years.

LEARNING OBJECTIVES

By the end of this chapter, you should be able to:

1 Explain the meaning of adult education and some related concepts.
2 Explain the meaning of development.
3 Explain the role of adult education in development.

dame-dame

KEY TERMS

adult education   Any learning or educational activity that occurs outside the structure of the formal education system and is undertaken by people who are considered to be adults in their society.

development   A process of social change in a society intended to bring about both social and material advancement for the people by allowing greater control over their environment.

Gross Domestic Product (GDP)   A nation's annual output of goods and services valued at current market prices, measured in order to determine the level of economic growth or development.

Gross National Product (GNP)   A nation's Gross Domestic Product (GDP) plus all external earnings, such as remittances and interest from investment in foreign countries.

New Partnership for Africa's Development (NEPAD)   This is a new initiative started by the heads of states of South Africa, Nigeria and Algeria, aimed at promoting the accelerated economic development of Africa based on the continent's abundant human and material resources through good governance and transparent leadership.

non-formal education   Any organised, systematic educational activity carried out outside the framework of the formal system aimed at providing selected types of learning to particular sub-groups in the population, whether they be adults, youth or children.

per capita income   The average income per person, calculated by dividing the GNP of a country by the total population.

⊞ BEFORE YOU START

Adult education has become a common term in today's society. Write down five learning activities that come to mind when the term *adult education* is mentioned.

THE MEANING OF ADULT EDUCATION

The meaning of adult education has changed from literacy and remedial education in the 1930s and 1940s to life-wide and lifelong education in the 1950s and 1960s, respectively (Mpofu and Amin, 2004).

A definition of *adult education* that reflects the literacy and remedial view of adult education was provided by Morgan in the 1930s: 'Adult education offers some who were not privileged a last chance to learn. Some feel a need for training in basic skills of learning so they enrol for work in reading, writing and arithmetic' (Okedara, 1981: 13).

In accordance with this perception, the focus of adult education at that time was to give second chances to those who, for some reason, had very little or no formal schooling at all.

The literacy and remedial view of adult education has long been abandoned. In the 1952 edition of the *International Directory of Adult Education*, UNESCO wrote that

> Adult education has been associated with teaching literacy and with such remedial measures as the night school for adults who have missed the opportunity for formal schooling. The concept of adult education has been broadened considerably so as to cover the activities of a wide range of institutions or agencies and to include a content as wide as life itself ...

Although this was still a narrow description of the term adult education, it acknowledged the life-wide nature of adult education.

The lifelong dimension of adult education did not come into being until the 1960s (Mpofu and Amin, 2004). During this period the term *lifelong education* became an increasing feature of literature on adult education. A view from this era that reflects the lifelong learning nature of adult education is provided by Professor E. A. Tugbiyele (cited in Okedara 1981: 14) as follows:

> By adult education we do not mean literacy education alone. Adult education is more than literacy or remedial education to 'fill the gap'. It is something people need and want as long as they are alive and regardless of the amount of their previous education.

Historically, the 1960s marked a turning point in adult education. It was during this time that adult education was transformed from its association with certain learning opportunities to mean all responsibly organised learning opportunities that enable people who are considered to be adults in their communities to enlarge and interpret their own living experience (Liveright, 1968). This view of adult education was carried into the 1970s by Hutchinson (1970) and Coombs and Ahmed (1974), among others. For example, Coombs and Ahmed described non-formal education, a term that incorporates the concept of adult education, as 'any organised, systematic educational activity carried out outside the framework of the formal system to provide selected types of learning to particular subgroups in the population, adults as well as children' (Uche, 1993: 1).

Later in the decade, this view was adopted and elaborated by UNESCO (cited in Titmus et al., 1979) as follows:

> Adult education denotes the entire body of organized educational processes, whatever the content, level and method, whether formal or otherwise, whether they prolong or replace initial education in schools, colleges and universities as well as in apprenticeship, whereby persons regarded as adult by the society to which they

belong develop their abilities, enrich their knowledge, improve their technical or professional qualifications or turn them in a new direction and bring about changes in their attitudes or behaviour in the twofold perspective of full personal development and participation in balanced and independent social, economic and cultural development.

This view of adult education has remained stable to date. However, many variants have emerged both in practical and scholarly circles since the late 1970s. In Europe, particularly in Britain, the 1980s marked the transformation of adult education into a welfare- and employment-orientated activity aimed at serving the needs of the economy (Griffin, cited in Peters, Jarvis et al., 1991: 265). The 1980s also saw the emergence of many explanations of adult education in a variety of contexts (Knowles, 1980; Bhola, 1983; La Belle, 1983; Hugkuntod and Lewis, 1987; and Yoloye, 1987). For example, Knowles (1980) argued that adult education should be organised around 'life application' categories and sequenced according to learners' readiness to learn, while Young (1985) saw adult education as a process whereby adults were helped to move from being less to more competent persons.

The adult education discourse continued through the 1990s and into the 2000s (Jarvis, 1990; Peters, Jarvis, et al., 1991; Garrido, 1992; Uche, 1993; Merriam and Brockett, 1997; and Walters and Watters, 2000). A notable discourse of the 1990s came from Merriam and Brockett (1997: 9) who define adult education as follows: 'Any organised learning or educational activity outside the structure of the formal education system that is consciously aimed at meeting the specific learning needs of people who are considered (regarded) to be adults in (the community) their society'.

The 1990s witnessed an increase in the use of the term *adult learning* in adult education literature. As a concept, adult learning includes adult education. It refers to all learning activities undertaken by adults throughout life. It includes non-formal learning through which adults acquire attitudes, values, skills and knowledge, through non-formally organised education. It also includes informal learning by adults from their day-to-day experiences through interaction with family, neighbours, colleagues at work, or through the mass media (Bacquelaine and Raymaekers, in Uche, 1993: 2).

Despite the various explanations of adult education, these explanations seem to have one thing in common, namely, that the purpose of adult education is to address the adult learners' educational needs outside the constraining and often discriminatory formal education system. Accordingly, for the purposes of discussing the social context of adult education, the term adult education and, consequently adult learning, shall denote any learning or educational activity that takes place outside the formal education system by adults in that society.

There is a general consensus particularly in academic circles about what adult education and adult learning entail (Mpofu and Amin, 2004). In the Western world and in most parts of Asia, the concept of adult education has been expanded to include community education as well as continuing education aimed at facilitating modernisation and development in general. In Western countries, where adult education has been a discipline for more than fifty years (Mpofu, 1998), the term adult education denotes all activities in which capacities and capabilities of people who are considered to be adults are developed for specific purposes, irrespective of the particular setting of the activity. Accordingly, learning activities in commercial, industrial, mining, governmental, non-governmental and private institutions are viewed to be adult learning, even though such activities may be termed manpower development or something else that overshadows their educational dimensions. This view of adult education has been expanded to include learning that takes place informally in places such as museums, churches and cultural festivals, where the educational dimension may not be immediately obvious to the beholder.

Similarly, in most parts of Asia adult education is viewed to be much larger than literacy education and remedial education (Hinzen, cited in Mpofu and Amin, 2004). For example, in Malaysia and Thailand adult education is considered to have a very important role in the development of human resources for all sectors of the economy. And in China, adult education is expected to facilitate national modernisation and development programmes in general.

African societies have generally remained behind in adopting this broader and more encompassing view of adult education. Although there is plenty of adult education and adult learning going on in industrial and traditional circles of Africa, there has been very little acknowledgement of the role of adult education in development in these societies. Nevertheless, resistance to the broader view of adult education is not confined to Africa. Mpofu (1998) cites Western scholars who lament the eclectic nature of adult education which, to a very large extent, is responsible for the fragmented development of the field. And Hinzen (cited in Mpofu and Amin, 2004) reports that in some parts of South Asia the status of adult education remains marginal. Be that as it may, the most acute resistance to the broader view of adult education seems to be occurring in Africa. With specific reference to Southern Africa, Mpofu

and Amin (2004) contend that adult education has been generally marginalised in most countries. From a review of relevant literature they concluded that in most African countries adult education activities lack direction and focus, and are characterised by lack of clarity and holism. Namibia is a case in point.

A recent study (Mpofu and Amin, 2004) of perceptions of adult learning involving institutional providers of adult education, among others in Namibia, revealed that the perception of adult education remains very narrow. Adult education is largely viewed as nothing more than literacy and remedial education. Namibia is not alone in this predicament. The concept of adult education remains hazy in most African countries and, consequently, there is very little commitment to the promotion of adult education activities.

A historical overview of the provision of education in Africa may help explain why most institutional providers of adult education are not aware that they are engaged in adult learning. The pattern of educational development during the colonial era was generally the same across the continent of Africa.

The colonial educational systems did not make provision for the development of institutionalised adult education in most African countries. The colonial governments were not keen on promoting a literate and numerate indigenous population, due to the general perception that an enlightened black population would become a threat to the establishment. For this reason, great disparities in educational provision existed between the white settler communities and the indigenous black populations up to the attainment of independence in these countries. Isolated efforts, particularly by non-governmental organisations through non-formal education, could not close the educational gap.

At independence, the new African governments were obliged to come up with more concerted efforts to close the educational gap. Almost without exception, the new governments launched national literacy programmes of various sorts. Examples of literacy programmes in the continent include:

- The Tanzania National Literacy Campaign, launched in 1971;
- The Botswana National Literacy Programme, launched in 1981;
- The National Mass Literacy Campaign of Nigeria, launched in 1982;
- The Zimbabwe National Literacy Campaign, launched in 1983; and
- The Namibian National Literacy Programme, launched in 1992.

The fanfare that often accompanied the launch of these national literacy programmes gave them great prominence in the provision of adult education, and the custodians of these literacy programmes became synonymous with adult learning. Given such names as the 'Division of Non-Formal Education', the 'Department of Adult and Non-Formal Education' and the 'Department of Adult and Basic Education', these government agencies have become symbols of adult learning in their respective countries. Meanwhile, the adult learning activities of the many other government departments, such as divisions of agricultural extension services and health education, and that of other providers of non-formal education, such as non-governmental organisations, as well as private correspondence colleges, seem to have done very little to correct that perception. The equivalence between government literacy agencies and adult learning has remained frozen in the minds of many (Mpofu and Amin, 2004).

Compounding this problem is the insufficiency of clearly defined policies of adult learning in Africa. This suggests that there are no proper guidelines on the coverage and on planning of parameters (Mpofu and Amin, 2004).

Nonetheless, since UNESCO's Fifth International Conference on Adult Education in 1997, an increasing acceptance and commitment to lifelong learning and the promotion of a learning society has taken off in a number of African countries. The Pietermaritzburg Declaration (2002), signed by nineteen African countries, among others, is yet another testimony of this renewed commitment to lifelong education and the creation of learning societies in Africa.

The renewed commitment to adult learning in certain parts of Africa comes in the wake of new initiatives to kick-start the African economy. A notable initiative in this regard is the New Partnership for African Development (NEPAD) whose stated goal in Africa is 'to promote accelerated growth and sustainable development' (Diescho, 2002: 13). The role of adult education cannot be underestimated in the promotion of the many development initiatives that will be brought forth by NEPAD.

ACTIVITY

1 Look at the adult learning activities that you outlined in the 'Before you start' activity at the beginning of this chapter. Do they all agree with the meaning of adult education that you derived from reading the preceding section? Explain your answer.

2 You must have heard the term *development* many times. You have also probably come across it in your everyday life. You may often wonder about

the exact meaning of this concept. You probably have your own views about the meaning of development. Take a sheet of paper and briefly outline what you understand by the term *development*. Keep the sheet of paper out of sight until you have finished reading the next section.

THE MEANING OF DEVELOPMENT

This section explores the meaning of development.

Changing views of development

Like the concept of adult education, the concept of *development* has undergone several changes in the past three decades. Up until 1970, development was seen solely as the quantitative provision of infrastructure and utilities such as potable water, electricity, schools, primary health clinics, roads, bridges and recreational facilities (Rogers, 1983). An important aspect of this view of development was economic growth characterised in terms of the Gross National Product (GNP) – a nation's annual output of goods and services valued at current market prices (Robert, 1993: 186) – and per capita income.

The quantitative approach to development was generally passive in nature in that the process of development was largely dependent on what has become known as the 'trickle down' factor – the assumption that the benefits of growth will eventually find their way to all sectors of society (Rogers, 1983). For this reason, there was no need for any form of intervention in the distribution of development benefits.

This quantitative view of development has long been considered one-sided, faulty and unrealistic (Indabawa, 1995).

It generally equates development with 'modernisation', which simply means the attainment of standards of Western technological, economic or political advancement. This view of development does not adequately explain the meaning of the concept. This is why as early as 1969, Seers argued that if poverty, unemployment and inequality have not declined but are growing in any society 'then it will be strange to call the result development even if per capita income doubled' (Youngman, 2000: 54). There is more to human development than the material (Akinpelu, 1990). For example, in many parts of Africa, the spiritual aspect of life is often seen to be more essential than the material.

The year 1970 witnessed a shift in the basic conception of development. The new view of development placed more emphasis on the person, the ultimate beneficiary of all developmental efforts (Rogers, 1983). In this view of development, the target of the development process is people, and not the material artefacts surrounding them, nor the economic growth of their country. The central concern of this conception of development is that all efforts need to be directed to meeting people's diverse needs more effectively (United Nations, 1993). Development is seen as a process of helping people change, equipping them with the skills, knowledge and attitudes necessary to conceive, plan, design and implement their own self-development. This conception of development is conceived as made up of two stages. The first stage consists of liberating people from all social, economic, political and cultural inhibitions that prevent them from realising their full potential. The second stage involves the enhancement of people's knowledge, skills and attitudes in order to boost their self-confidence, creativity and readiness to participate in all issues involving their personal development and that of their society. The envisaged end result of the second stage constitutes what Julius Nyerere (1974) and Paulo Freire (1984), among others, have described as transformation or change in consciousness.

This qualitative conception of development does not condemn the quantitative view of development. Instead, it seeks to incorporate the two views in such a manner that they complement each other. In this regard, development means transformation both socially and materially.

A survey of conceptions of development from the 1980s through to the 2000s suggests that the qualitative view of development has remained unchanged since 1970. In 1980, Christenson and Robinson, underscored the qualitative view of development when they contended that development implies improvement, growth and change, in which cultures, societies and communities proceed from less advanced to more advanced social stages.

A few years later, the qualitative view of development was reaffirmed by Rogers (1983: 121) when he defined it as 'a widely participatory process of social change in a society intended to bring about both social and material advancement (including greater equality, freedom and other valued qualities) for the majority of people through their gaining greater control over their environment'.

In 1990, an African scholar echoed the same sentiments when he contended that development is an all-encompassing concept that should be seen as the 'generation of more wealth within a nation; more equitable distribution of such wealth or at least more equitable distribution of the opportunity for access to that wealth; and the existence of political structures relevant to the promotion of the above values' (Akinpelu, 1990: 19).

In the same year, the International Bureau of Education (1990: 19) endorsed the qualitative view of development when it described development as 'a multivariate quantitative and qualitative process or product of change in the personality of the individual or the society, which is characterised by the cultivation of a distinctive self-identity and an ability to face the world with purpose and pride. It involves the integrative growth of the collective personality in the economic, social, political, cultural and spiritual as well as attitudinal realm of the nation'.

And, in 2000, Youngman provided yet another endorsement for the qualitative view of development. Youngman (2000: 5) suggests that development 'refers to the idea that deliberate action can be taken to change society in chosen directions which are considered desirable'. This means that development relates to positive changes in the life of any given society. The changes may be in any of the major spheres of its life, that is, social, economic, political, scientific, cultural, technological, industrial or even spiritual. Development could be qualitative in that it affects the improvement of the lives of individuals in society. It can also be quantitative, as is possible through the increase of society's wealth, productivity or economic prosperity.

The elements of development

Three elements of development are discernible from the qualitative view of development, namely, growth, improvement and change.

Development as growth entails economic prosperity. The most common index of economic prosperity is the Gross National Product (GNP). For example, Diescho (2002) uses findings of the Lagos Plan of Action (an Economic Commission on Africa initiative) to show that the African continent is not doing very well in this regard. From an assessment of long-term development trends for the period 1960 to 1975, the Lagos Plan of Action revealed that Africa's performance was markedly below all the targets set by the United Nations' Second Development Decade. Africa's Gross Domestic Product (GDP) growth rate per annum was 4.5%, 1.5% short of the target of 6%. The continent's agricultural and manufacturing growth rates per year were 1.6% and 6.0%, respectively, instead of the targets of 4.0% and 8.0%, respectively. At 2.8%, instead of the target of 7.0%, the annual export growth rate was undoubtedly the poorest performing sector. Conversely, during the same period, the continent's annual import growth rate was at 10.0%, 3% above the target of 7.0%, clearly showing a negative balance between imports and exports.

Development as growth is not limited to economic prosperity as shown by the GNP and the GDP. It also includes transformation of infrastructure and technology to facilitate the production of more goods and services, and the efficient distribution of those goods and services.

Whereas development as quantitative growth is concerned with economic and technological transformation, development as qualitative improvement involves social and psychological transformation (Christenson and Robinson, 1980). Social and psychological transformation essentially mean the democratisation of society. The democratisation of society entails the development of people's capacity to grow socially, culturally, economically and politically through the acquisition of new knowledge, attitudes and skills, and through participation in social and political decision-making.

Finally, development as change broadens the concept beyond growth and improvement. Development has also been described as a form of social exchange (Kim, 1980), and as such is tantamount to planned intervention (Christenson and Robinson, 1980). It does not just happen on its own. It is 'deliberate action' (Youngman, 2000) intended to bring about 'desirable' (Youngman, 2000) 'change in the personality of the individual or the society' (International Bureau of Education, 1990). Development as social change entails the purposive pursuit of particular ideologies. The deliberate pursuit of an ideology suggests 'the existence of political structures relevant to the promotion' of that ideology (Akinpelu, 1990: 19).

Together, the three elements of growth, improvement and change make up the qualitative paradigm of development. Minus one of the three elements, the qualitative paradigm of development cannot stand independently. For example, growth on its own is nothing more than the quantitative paradigm, which conceives development in terms of economic prosperity. Similarly, social transformation that fails to bring about economic prosperity cannot be termed development, because, as Sachs (1993: 253) aptly observes, development relates to achieving higher levels of 'health and demographic conditions, food and nutrition, education and literacy skills, conditions of work, employment situation, aggregate consumption and saving, transportation, housing and facilities, clothing, recreation and entertainment, social security and human freedom'.

Implied here is that basic needs such as food, shelter or housing, water, safety and security are essential components of sustainable social transformation. However, apart from basic needs, human beings have other basic needs that have to be met in order for them to become more completely human or to achieve a measure of modern development (Freire, 1974). There is a clear desire for everybody's condition, standard of living and quality of life to be improved or made qualitatively better (Omolewa and

Adekanmbi, 1994). Hence, economic growth alone is a limited view of development.

It is the last two elements, namely, improvement and change, that distinguish qualitative development from its predecessor and thus define its character. Economic growth that is not accompanied by improvement and change is passive development. Passive development occurs without the involvement of the people. The quantitative view of development evolves from what Christenson and Robinson (1980) call the 'natural-law and the invisible hand ideology', which asserts that if natural forces are not tampered with they will bring about the maximum good for all. Unlike the quantitative approach to development, which is passive, the qualitative approach is proactive in that it implies social transformation via some form of intervention.

⚏ ACTIVITY

1 Refer to the sheet of paper in which you outlined your understanding of the term *development*. Briefly explain the differences, if any, between the meaning of development you had before and the meaning you have derived from reading the preceding section.
2 Which element of development do you consider more consistent with the process of adult education? Why?

ADULT EDUCATION IN DEVELOPMENT

It is the elements of improvement and change that bring education, and *ipso facto*, adult education, into the process of development. Education is by all accounts the only ethical means at our disposal for imparting knowledge and changing attitudes, and thus ensuring durability and sustainability of development. Many claims have been made for education's role in development, namely:

■ that it is an essential factor in development in African countries (British Committee on Literacy, cited in Mpofu, 2000);
■ that basic education is indispensable to development, peace and stability in Africa (Conference of African Ministers of Education, cited in Mpofu, 2000); and
■ that it is the most basic personal skill which underlies the whole modernising sequence (Smith, cited in Mpofu, 2000).

The drawbacks of a low-level education have also been pointed out:

■ as a real counter-development factor in an emerging nation (UNESCO, cited in Mpofu, 2000); and
■ as a handicap to work performance by hampering a citizen's chances of contributing to nation-building, the family, community productivity and civic matters, and consequently slowing progress in society (Bown and Tomori, cited in Mpofu, 2000).

Bowman and Anderson (cited in Mpofu, 2000: 183) illustrate, with literacy figures, the close relationship between human resources development and economic development. They studied literacy rates in 1950, and per capita income in 1955, measured in United States dollars in 83 countries, and found that these countries could be classified in three ways:

1 Thirty poor countries with adult literacy rates of below 40%, in which 1955 per capita income never exceeded $300 (except for oil-rich Sabah);
2 Twenty-seven mixed countries in which literacy rates ranged from 30–70% and in

which incomes were virtually uncorrelated with literacy; and

3 Twenty-four rich countries with literacy rates above 70%, including twenty-one very rich countries with literacy rates of 90%, where 1955 per capita income always exceeded $5 000 (Mpofu, 2000: 183).

On the basis of their analysis, 'Bowman and Anderson concluded that a literacy rate of about 40 per cent was necessary to raise the per capita incomes to over $500' (Mpofu, 2000: 183). There is empirical support for Bowman and Anderson's conclusion (Mpofu, 2000: 183), as reflected below.

According to Bhagwat, the 1950 world mean literacy rate (calculated from available statistics in 136 countries) was 56%, and the whole of Africa (except South Africa), Asia, South East Asia, Latin Central America and the Middle East, fell below this mean. Also, according to Bhagwat, the world mean per capita income for the same year (calculated from available statistics in 96 countries) was $200. Similarly, the above areas (with the exception of Latin America) fell below the mean.

Implied here is that attempts by African countries to attain the world mean per capita income must be accompanied by efforts to raise the average literacy rates.

Bowman and Anderson were taken to task by several economists for this analysis. Notable among their critics was Blaug (1972), who argued that literacy figures are rather suspect because of lack of adequate data, especially in developing countries. Blaug also argued that incomes were calculated in terms of the exchange rates and that no attention was given to the real value of money within a given context. However, he did not deny that education facilitates development.

Also, there seems to be a significant correlation between low levels of literacy and instability. For example, most of Africa, most of Asia and South Asia, most of Latin and Central America and the Middle East have been bedevilled by wars, coups and general instability. Undoubtedly, there are other forces at work in the aforementioned regions. Literacy is just one of many interrelated variables. Be that as it may, the foregoing seems to suggest that literacy is a good index of a country's socio-economic development and stability. Although the above review contains no evidence of a direct or causal relationship between literacy and development, it shows that there is some correlation between literacy and development. This suggests that there is a parallel relationship between literacy and the major indicators of development. Conversely, this suggests that there is a parallel relationship between illiteracy and some indicators of underdevelopment, such as poverty.

UNESCO (1990) points out the problem of not recognising that the map of world illiteracy coincides with that of poverty. Lind and Johnston (1990: 45) also make reference to this coincidence when they made the following observation: 'the causal link between literacy and development remains ambiguous or unproved. There are, however, numerous examples of coincidence between advances in literacy and advances in economic and social development'.

On the basis of existing data, it seems that the best we can do is to claim that there is a positive correlation between adult education and development. Therefore, we can assert that higher levels of literacy seem to exist in conjunction with higher levels of development, and vice versa. We cannot claim, on the basis of the existing evidence, that one causes the other.

Evidence of a causal relationship between literacy and development, particularly one that shows that literacy leads to the social and economic transformation of society, would be welcome to many. Despite numerous efforts involving the Experimental World Literacy Programme (EWLP) to 'evaluate the social and economic effects of literacy' there is no basis to believe that literacy has anything to do with the economic, social and political development of a people (Lind and Johnston, 1990: 45). Wagner (1995: 345) explored what he terms the five rationales for linking literacy to development, and has concluded that there is little research as yet to suggest that literacy programmes are enabling the unemployed to obtain new jobs or to make major career changes, even though anecdotal claims abound. Furthermore, there is virtually no evidence from developing countries that adult literacy programmes lead to actual economic improvements in the lives of programme participants.

For as long as there is no conclusive evidence on how literacy affects development, it leaves open the possibility that it is actually the other way around. It could be that social and economic advancement lead to the attainment of higher levels of literacy rates. Similarly, underdevelopment could incapacitate the ability of a society to attain a higher-level literacy rate.

Although there is no evidence to directly link literacy to development, educationists have settled for what Lind and Johnston call the 'dialectic view' of the relationship between literacy and development. This suggests the existence of a symbiotic relationship between the two, in which each affects and is affected by the other. If we subscribe to the existence of a dialectic relationship between literacy and development, we must conclude that education and, *ipso facto*, adult education is an indispensable condition for sustainable development in any society. As Faundez (1991: 10) aptly puts it: 'The development process is in fact an educational process, or rather it should unfailingly be viewed as such. We cannot therefore conceive of development in the absence of education any more than education in the absence of development'.

Rogers underscores the relationship between education and development when he rejects the notion of development as the provision of technical assistance through the building of dams and the provision of tractors to farmers. With reference to education and training, Rogers (1992: 3) says: 'the process of changing attitudes as well as providing the new knowledge and skills and understandings which development programmes need is what is properly meant by education and training'.

ACTIVITY

Using your community or country as a reference point, present evidence to support or reject the notion that underdevelopment incapacitates the ability of a society to attain a higher-level literacy rate.

SUMMARY

This chapter has explained the concepts of *adult education* and *development*, and how they relate to one another. Adult education is any learning or educational activity that occurs outside the structure of the formal education system which is undertaken by people who are considered to be adults in their society, and development is deliberate action intended to bring about desirable change in the personality of the individual or the society. Adult education has long been acclaimed as an essential component of development. Although there is no conclusive evidence to this effect, there is no denying that education and, *ipso facto*, adult education is an indispensable condition for sustainable development in any society.

KEY POINTS

- Adult education is any learning or education activity that takes place outside the formal education system and which is undertaken by adults.
- Development is deliberate action intended to bring about desirable change in the individual or the society.
- Education and therewith adult education is an indispensable condition for sustainable development in any society.

❖ ACTIVITY

Summarise the role of adult education in the development process. Illustrate your answer with relevant examples.

FURTHER QUESTIONS

1 Without modernisation, qualitative development does not constitute real development, and vice versa. Do you agree? Explain your answer.

2 Adult education alone cannot bring about development in Africa. Do you agree with this assertion? Explain your answer.

SUGGESTED READINGS

Knowles, M. 1980. *The modern practice of adult education: From pedagogy to andragogy.* Eaglewood Cliffs, NJ: Cambridge.

Merriam, S. B. and Brockett, R. G. 1997. *The profession and practice of adult education: An introduction.* San Francisco: Jossey-Bass Publishers.

Peters, J. M., Jarvis, P. and Associates (eds.). 1991. *Adult education: Evolution and achievements in a developing field of study.* San Francisco: Jossey Bass Publishers.

Uche, G. 1993. *The practice of non-formal education in developing countries.* Hull: The University of Hull.

Youngman, F. 2000. *The political economy of adult education and development.* London: Zed Books.

Chapter 2

Social change and development

OVERVIEW

In our discussion of development in Chapter 1, we made reference to development as a form of social change. Social change is central to development, hence the relevance of this concept in any meaningful discussion of development. In this chapter we explore the concept and the various contemporary theories of *social change*, as well as their relevance to our understanding of development in Africa. This chapter also explores the role of adult education in social change.

LEARNING OBJECTIVES

By the end of this chapter, you should be able to:

1 Explain the meaning of social change.
2 Explain the various contemporary theories of social change.
3 Explain the role of adult education in social change.

dwennimmen

KEY TERMS

capitalism   A system whereby the economy and politics of a society are managed on the basis of the private ownership of the means of production and capital.

colonialism   The practice by foreign countries of forming and maintaining colonies in other countries in order to control their raw materials and subsequently the world markets.

communism   A system of economic and political management of society by the government based on common ownership of the wealth of society.

ideologies   Abstract explanations of the social, moral, religious, political and economic order of a particular group.

imperialism   The policy and practice of dominating the political and economic affairs of underdeveloped and weaker nations.

Organisation of African Unity (OAU)   A continental organisation that was founded in 1963 to promote the political and economic liberation of African countries. It has recently been replaced by the African Union.

social change   The transformation of society by means of changes in social behaviour and in social structure.

socialism   A system of economic and political management by the state of a nation's resources.

BEFORE YOU START

Based on your reading of Chapter 1, in which reference is made to social change, what is your understanding of the concept of *social change*?

THE MEANING OF SOCIAL CHANGE

Societies are created through the inter-action of people with each other. Social change refers to those changes in social behaviour and social structure that occur in society over a period of time (Wallace and Wallace, 1985). The changes that occur in a society and in the interaction of its members set that society in motion. For this reason, social change has been described as 'the social dynamics that reveal the laws of motion of societies' (Mitchell, 1979: 179).

Several theories have been put forward to explain social change.

Contemporary theories of social change

Theoretical explanations of social change can be grouped into four major categories, namely, evolutionary, cyclical, equilibrium and conflict.

Evolutionary theories of social change

Evolutionary theories perceive society as moving from simple, primitive communities to more complex and advanced states. Early evolutionary theories were influenced by Charles Darwin's theories of biological evolution. Charles Darwin believed that the laws of natural selection led to the survival of the fittest and consequently, the extinction of the least capable species.

A good example of an evolutionary theory was provided by Auguste Comte (1798-1857). Auguste Comte (cited in Wallace and Wallace, 1985) believed that society evolved through three stages of development, namely, theological, meta-physical and positivistic.

At the theological stage, which according to Auguste Comte reached its zenith in Europe during the Middle Ages (about AD 900), people believed that everything was a result of supernatural powers. In Africa, it is believed that this stage existed until about the end of the 1700s. During this stage, priests and spirit mediums were dominant figures in the society of Europe and Africa, respectively. It was believed that priests and spirit mediums were able to consult the supernatural powers and in this way could explain certain phenomena. In Southern Africa, there is the legendary story of Non-qause, a spirit medium and diviner, who lived in the Eastern Cape around the 1800s. One night she is said to have had a dream in which she was told by the ancestral spirits to advise everyone in the community to burn whatever agricultural produce they had and slaughter all their cattle. She told the com-munity that everyone who did this would wake up the following day to find their storage barns filled with huge quantities of agricultural produce. The people had faith in her spiritual powers and accordingly carried out the wishes of the ancestral spirits. When they woke up the following day, there was nothing in their barns, and they were devas-tated by famine.

In the metaphysical stage (which occurred in Europe between the 1300s and 1800s), knowledge was seen as a product of abstract forces of either a religious or a secular nature. Once again, priests were considered very important because they could explain abstract forces of a religious nature. However, since they could not explain abstract phenomena of a secular nature, they had to share their prominence in society with a new group of people who professed wisdom with regard to the forces of law, namely lawyers. Together, priests and lawyers were seen as leaders in European society during this period.

In Africa, the metaphysical stage took hold in the 1700s and the 1800s. Although the 'Nonqauses' retained their importance, they were joined at centre stage by wise people, mostly men who served as advisors to royalty. Although counsel to the king consisted of an advisory board made up of chiefs and other trusted people, one or two people occupied the role of chief advisor. A case in point is Mbopha (or Mopho) kaSithayi, the trusted advisor and aide to Shaka, the most celebrated Zulu king.

The positivistic stage (from the 1800s to the present) has been referred to as the scientific stage, due to the role played by scientific knowledge in this period. At this stage, laws based on proven knowledge hold the key to natural and social phenomena. Accordingly, scientists are the most important people in the positivistic stage of evolution.

Auguste Comte's analysis has been hailed as valid for the evolution and development of Europe and Western society in general. How does it fare when applied to African society? Although there is hardly any analysis in respect of how this theory applies to African societies, inferences can be drawn from sociological analyses of related issues. For example, from her analysis of African beliefs, values, customs and culture among the Ndebele of Zimbabwe, Child (1968) concludes that the average African subscribes to both Christian and traditional values. Africans go to church on Sunday or Saturday and, when required by traditional custom, participate in rituals such as traditional cleansing ceremonies. Similarly, positivistic values exist alongside metaphysical values in many African societies. The Alice Lenshina movement in Zambia in the 1960s and the Alice Lekwena movement in Uganda in the 1980s, in which divine powers were invoked to mobilise supporters against established authorities, are strong reminders that the 'Nonqauses' are still very prevalent. And the fact that almost every African country has the equivalent of the suppression of a witchcraft statute is clear testimony that spirit mediums and diviners are still very much a factor in African society.

Emile Durkheim (1858-1917) provided a two-stage evolutionary theory (Wallace and Wallace, 1985). He saw societies as moving from simple to complex entities. Simple societies were characterised by mechanical solidarity, whereby people were tightly bound together by shared values and the similarities of their everyday activities. However, due to industrialisation simple societies have been transformed from mechanical to organic solidarity, in which people are held together by business-like relationships. The jack-of-all-trades which was found in mechanical societies has been replaced by highly specialised workers in organic societies. In the organic society, no single individual is capable of producing all the necessities for survival. Instead, workers perform specialised tasks for which they are paid wages that they use to purchase the products of other equally specialised workers. Durkheim used the term 'anomie' to describe the organic society. Anomie means 'normlessness'. It refers to a situation whereby people are uncertain about the norms of society and where they have no common shared values.

Most traditional African societies are consistent with mechanical society, while urban centres possess the attributes of organic societies.

Ferdinand Tonnies (1855–1936), in yet another evolutionary theory, distinguishes between *Gemeinschaft* and *Gesellschaft* societies (Wallace and Wallace, 1985). *Gemeinschaft* societies are characterised by personalised face-to-face relationships such as those that occur in the family and in rural societies where relationships are intimate. Most traditional African societies can be described as *Gemeinschaft*. In contrast, *Gesellschaft* societies are characterised by formal impersonal relationships which occur for the purpose of achieving some end, normally some economic end. These are utilitarian types of relationships that occur mostly in urban places in the form of business transactions.

Although they may vary, evolutionary theories have several things in common. Firstly, they view change as unilinear, meaning that it follows one line of development and, as such, progresses naturally toward a better world.

Secondly, they are passive in approach. In this regard, the evolutionary explanation of social change is not different from the quantitative or the modernisation view of development. The quantitative view of development is premised on the principle of non-intervention. It is based on the assumption that the benefits from the betterment of society will eventually 'trickle down' to all sectors of society. The evolutionary view of change is consistent with a limited conception of development. Consequently, this view of social change has limited application to the explanation of development in our societies today.

Evolutionary theories have been used to explain modernisation. Evolutionary theorists believe that industrialised nations such as the United States, Canada, Britain, France, Germany and Japan are where they are today due to a process of evolution. And they believe that sooner or later, poor countries in Africa, Latin America and Asia will eventually become modernised through the process of evolution. However, as suggested in Chapter 1, on its own, modernisation does not constitute development. Similarly, evolution alone cannot account for all the development we see in our societies.

Cyclical theories of social change

In contrast to the evolutionary theorists, who see change as continuous progress, the cyclical theorists view change as a circle of growth and decline. A well-known cyclical theorist is Oswald Spengler (1918), who defines five stages in the life of a society, namely, birth, childhood, maturity (the golden age), decline (old age) and death (Wallace and Wallace, 1985). The early stages are characterised by rapid growth, whereas the later stages are retrogressive and materialistic. From a study of eight previous civilisations, Spengler concluded that the present form of civilisation will eventually die and be replaced by a new society. History abounds with accounts of thriving societies that eventually collapsed. Notable examples include the Greek and Roman societies in Europe; the Mesopotamian civilisation in the Middle East; the kingdoms of Zululand, Hausaland, Yorubaland and Benin; and the Ashanti and the Baganda in parts of Africa. You will be familiar with biblical accounts of earlier kingdoms and the great civilisations of Egypt in Africa as well as China in the Far East, all of which were highly developed before they crumbled.

Arnold Toynbee (1962), another cyclical theorist, studied developments in 21 societies and concluded that societies are constantly challenged by their environments and neighbouring societies (Wallace and Wallace, 1985). If a society successfully deals with its challenges, it lives on. Conversely, if the society fails to successfully deal with its challenges, it perishes and gives way to another. The examples given above to illustrate Spengler's theory are equally applicable here. Each and every one of those societies collapsed because they could not successfully deal with their challenges. For example, the African kingdoms of the Zulus, the Hausas, the Yorubas and the Bagandas failed to ward off the invading Europeans in the nineteenth century.

Consequently, these kingdoms perished and became part of European colonies. One after another African kingdoms were colonised by European countries such as Britain, Germany, France, Portugal and Belgium. The exception, which proves the rule, is Abyssinia (present-day Ethiopia). Abyssinia defeated the Italian invaders in 1929 and survived as an independent nation.

The European colonies in Africa began to crumble in the middle of the twentieth century when they could not successfully deal with anti-colonial challenges mounted mainly by enlightened African elites. Beginning in Egypt and Ghana in the 1940s, struggles for independence spread to Kenya, Uganda, Nigeria, Tanzania, Botswana, Zambia, Algeria and Tunisia in the 1950s; to Angola and Mozambique in the 1970s; to Zimbabwe and Namibia in the 1980s; and to South Africa in the 1990s. The struggles for African independence took many shapes, for example, in the form of negotiation as in the cases of Ghana and Nigeria, and through armed guerilla warfare as in the cases of Algeria, Angola, Mozambique, Zimbabwe, Namibia and South Africa.

Although change is the common feature of the two cyclical theories examined here, there is a major difference between the two. While Spengler believed that all societies will eventually die, Toynbee believed that those who could adequately deal with their challenges would survive. History seems to lean towards Toynbee's view. The fact that it took Africans more than a century to totally free themselves from colonial rule and domination is clear testimony that colonial rulers were able to ward off early anti-colonial agitations. In each African country, the struggle for national liberation and democratic rule began much earlier than the actual granting of independence.

For example, more than a century elapsed between the collapse of the Ndebele rebellion in the late 1800s (one of the early forms of resistance to colonial rule in Zimbabwe) and the advent of independence in 1980. Similarly, in South Africa, resistance to colonial rule dates back to the battle of Isandlwana (1879) and beyond. Colonial countries mounted counter-resistance efforts of one kind or another and thus prolonged their hegemony in Africa.

The cycle of change has continued in post-independence Africa. The most visible changes have arisen from forceful take-overs of governments through military intervention. This has been the case in most nations of Africa, including Egypt, Sudan, Libya, Niger, Nigeria, Ghana, Côte d' Ivoire, Burkina Faso, Liberia, Uganda, The Gambia, Sierra Leone, Togo, Benin and the Democratic Republic of Congo. Without a doubt, all these are examples of social change or the motions of the transformation of societies that came about due to the failure of these societies to counter forceful military takeovers.

The challenges that face societies are not limited to armed struggles and military coups d'état. For example, the former Union of Socialist Soviet Republics (USSR) collapsed in 1991 when it failed to successfully deal with the political and economic reforms that were introduced by President Mikhail Gorbachev. The political and economic reforms called *perestroika* and *glasnost* opened up the hitherto closed Soviet economy to the outside world. The challenge proved too much for the USSR and it collapsed, giving rise to many 'independent republics' including the Russian Federation, Georgia and the Ukraine. In Africa, examples of regime changes that came about due to the introduction of political reforms include the departure of Kenneth Kaunda (1991) from Zambia and of Hastings Kamuzu Banda from Malawi (1994). In Zimbabwe, the wave of political reforms that affected the other former members of the Federation of Rhodesia and Nyasaland were countered largely through a very controversial land programme, thus saving the Mugabe regime from collapse.

Equilibrium theories of social change

Equilibrium theories of social change are sometimes called functional theories because they view society as made up of parts that are functional in sustaining the social system (Parsons, cited in Wallace and Wallace, 1985). Equilibrium theorists see society as made up of sub-systems that are constantly moving in unison towards stabilising and maintaining the system. A change in one part of society leads to compensatory changes in other parts, until the entire social system approximates stability or equilibrium. This type of change has been termed the 'billiard ball' type of change (Wallace and Wallace, 1985). Those of you who are familiar with the games of billiards, pool and snooker, will know that almost every time you strike a ball, it affects the positions of the other balls on the board. However, the changes in the positions of the balls are generally minimal. These minimal changes strengthen rather than weaken the chances of each player in the game. The changes bring about a state of equilibrium to the whole game. The same phenomenon is at work in social change. The various changes that took place after the establishment of colonial rule in Africa will serve to illustrate this point.

In order to serve the best interests of the colonial administration, a new system of education and training was introduced in most parts of Africa. For the 'natives', the system emphasised the acquisition of basic skills of reading, writing and numeration. These basic skills were considered adequate for the purposes of employment as cheap labour in mines, agricultural plantations and factories. The colonial rulers could not see the need for higher levels of education in the colonies. The educational opportunities were not only provided at a very rudimentary level, they were also provided very selectively. Opportunities for this basic level of education were limited to a few, mainly sons of local chiefs known variously as *indunas, emirs, obas,* or *obis.* The purpose of this type of education was twofold. Firstly, it was designed to generate workers with limited skills with the minimal amount of training. Secondly, it was meant to instill conformity among the 'natives' so that they would accept rules, regulations, orders and the payment of taxes.

Changes in education brought about changes in other aspects of life, thus reinforcing stability in the new order. A completely new value system exists in Africa today due to Western education. For example, colonial rulers introduced completely new systems of law and order as well as in the administration of society. In some cases, such as in Anglophone African countries, an indirect rule system (a system of rule through the local structures or community leaders or those they had chosen) was used. In others, like Francophone Africa, a direct system of 'assimilation' (a system that considered citizens of French-speaking African countries as equal in status with those of France) was introduced (Gann and Duignan, 1970; Okafor, 1981). These legal and administrative systems were inherited with very little amendment by independent Africa. Also, the nuclear family system and individualism are supported by the Western education system. Together with many others, these values have been fostered and nurtured through schooling. Similarly, Western education facilitated the introduction and the spread of Christianity. Islam, which came to Africa from the Middle East around about the fifteenth century through scholarship and commercial links, has spread rapidly in recent years. The ability to read the Qur'an has played a significant role in the spread of Islam in Africa. Similarly, the ability to read the Bible has had a significant hand in the growth of Christianity in Africa.

Conflict theories of social change

Conflict theorists of social change view tensions within society as the driving force behind social change. They see society and social groups as made up of parts that are in a constant state of conflict. The conflict perspective of change can be traced back to Karl Marx (1867). According to Marx, inequality is the single source of conflict in society. Although many oppressed people view their inferior position as the will of God and, as such, do nothing about it (Lamb, 1987), some make an attempt to improve their position by taking from those who have plenty. Accordingly, conflict theorists see society as the scene of a power struggle among various groups, each competing with the other for autonomy or dominance.

Modern-day conflict theorists include C. Wright Mills, who introduced the concept of the 'power elite'. According to Mills (1956), the power elite consists of a tiny minority of government, military and business people. Each nation has a power elite that controls the affairs of the country for their own good. Education plays a very significant role in how the power elite manipulates the affairs of a nation towards the promotion of their interests over those of the general population (Collins, 1974).

Nowhere in the world has conflict between different interest groups been more visible than in Africa. Since 1960, the African continent has had more coups,

attempted coups and counter-coups than any other continent. No African region has been spared the ignominy of a military coup. In North Africa, countries that have experienced military coups include Egypt and Libya. West Africa in particular has experienced more coups (namely, Niger, Nigeria, Ghana, Côte d' Ivoire, Burkina Faso, Liberia, The Gambia, Sierra Leone, Togo and Benin, among others) than any other part of Africa. The Central African region is second only to West Africa in this respect, with military takeovers having taken place in Chad, the Central African Republic, Gabon, the Republic of Congo and the Democratic Republic of Congo. East Africa has had its fair share of military takeovers as well, namely, in Sudan, Ethiopia, Somalia, Rwanda, Uganda and Burundi. Even relatively calm Southern Africa has not been spared the shameful experience of a military takeover, for example, in the kingdom of Lesotho.

To date, the coup d'état has been the norm rather than the exception with regard to changing governments in Africa. Rarely do governments change from one group or party to another without the use of armed force. In those very rare circumstances where the gun is spared, other forms of conflict such as mass protests (Zambia and Malawi) have been used to bring down long-standing regimes.

The conflict perspective of change is applicable beyond the military coup. It has been used to explain changes in many other social spheres, such as business, commerce, mining, schooling and family life, to mention but a few. For example, the many struggles that occur between organised labour on the one hand and industrial management on the other have been instrumental in bringing about very significant changes to the industrial landscape. In addition, organised labour has had a lot of say in the political affairs of nations. The Movement for Multi-party Democracy (MMD), which toppled Kenneth Kaunda's government in Zambia, was at the time nothing more than an association of organised trade unions. The Movement for Democratic Change (MDC) which opposes the Zimbabwean government to its knees, is for all intents and purposes the political wing of the Zimbabwe Congress of Trade Unions (ZCTU). The Congress of South African Trade Unions (COSATU), a key ally of the ruling African National Congress (ANC) of South Africa, is a very influential power broker in the politics of that country. In the same manner as organised labour has triggered change in the industrial and political landscapes, school riots and protests have forced changes in the educational landscape. Jean Bedel Bokassa of the Central African Republic had to abandon his decision to get school children to wear school uniforms from his factory, following strong resistance from school children (Lamb, 1987). And, seemingly, simple family life has not escaped the trauma of conflict. The family, as a social unit, can be understood in terms of dominance and power (Collins, 1974). In almost all African societies, the family is controlled by adults, particularly adult males, who have created certain advantageous situations for themselves. In male–female relationships, the males have appropriated the best occupational roles, and have given menial labour roles to the females. In Africa, it is mostly men who control wealth in the family, and in some societies polygamy is acceptable. In adult–child relationships, adults determine what children will eat, what movies they may watch, when they must go to bed, with whom they can play, and so forth.

Women have been resisting male domination for the past two decades. The many gender-related agencies in Africa are testimony of just how serious this issue is.

Together with those of other human-rights organisations, the efforts of these agencies have brought about significant changes in male–female relationships in Africa. Women have moved out of the kitchen and have become members of boardrooms in both the public and the private sector. Also, the concept of family has changed markedly in the past decade. The family unit is no longer considered to be made up of mum, dad and the children. Today, a single parent family is considered as much a family as the mum, dad and the children unit. Divorce, the culmination of conflict between husband and wife in the family, has played a significant role in the transformation of the family unit, thus bringing about a new conception of family altogether.

⌗ ACTIVITY

Which of the four major contemporary theories of social change best explains current social changes sweeping across Africa today? Explain your answer.

MAJOR REASONS FOR SOCIAL CHANGE

From the broad array of theories on social change it is evident that the causes of social change are many and diverse. Two such causes are prominent, namely, ideologies and individuals.

Ideologies

Ideologies are abstract explanations of the social, moral, religious, political and economic order (Wallace and Wallace, 1985). Ideologies have been used to bring about change in two ways. Firstly, by highlighting the negative aspects of the existing order and, secondly, by clearly articulating the prospects of the proposed new order based on a new ideology.

Two ideologies have been remarkably instrumental in bringing about social change in Africa, namely, Protestantism and communism.

Max Weber (1904) believed that Protestantism was the ideology behind the development of capitalist economies, whose offspring 'imperialism' laid the foundation for colonialism and neo-colonialism. The term 'imperialism' is a derivative of the word 'empire'. Accordingly, imperialism is the policy and practice of forming and maintaining colonies in order to control raw materials and world markets (Hunt and Sherman, 1981). Imperialism can be achieved either by the establishment of colonies or by dominating the political and economic affairs of underdeveloped and weaker nations.

During the fifteenth century, the developing capitalist economies of Europe became so big that they could not be sustained without additional resources and cheap labour (Hunt and Sherman, 1981). In order to sustain their massive economies, European countries embarked on a systematic process of expansion in search of resources. Between the fifteenth and nineteenth centuries they acquired land in all the other continents whose inhabitants were less developed at this level and, as such, less advanced militarily and economically. In the course of five centuries, the Europeans had shared, among themselves, the continents of America, Asia and Africa. For example, in 1914, France held 40% of Africa, Britain controlled 30% and the remainder was divided among Germany, Belgium, Portugal and Spain (Hunt and Sherman, 1981). The Europeans plundered and enslaved their colonies in order to extract the maximum from their subjects. Within a short period they destroyed very successful local industries and replaced them with European industries that were designed to serve the interests of the colonialists.

The colonialists exploited the colonies, contributing to their underdevelopment by investing in extractive industries that exported raw materials to the imperial country. In the imperial country, the cheap raw materials were profitably turned into manufactured goods. Some of the manufactured goods were exported back (tariff free) to the colonial country. The purpose of exporting finished products tariff free into the colonial country was to destroy that country's local manufacturing industry, if any, or to destroy enterprise among the locals since it was cheaper to buy imported goods.

Charles Bettleheim (1968) uses the story of the Indian textile industry to illustrate how Europe underdeveloped the colonies. At the end of the eighteenth century, India was still an exporter of manufactured textile products. However, from 1815 to 1832, India's cotton exports dropped by 92%. And by 1850, India was buying one quarter of Britain's cotton exports. This marked the ruin of India's traditional trades and crafts. A similar pattern followed the exploitation and the underdevelopment of African countries. The deliberate colonial policy of developing only the primary sectors of the economy meant that the colonies became importers of finished products that were made from their own natural resources.

In order to ensure the total exploitation of the colonised, colonialism was characterised by extreme ethnocentrism – the emotional attitude that one's own ethnic group, nation or culture is superior to all others. African customs, languages, religious practices and skin colour were viewed very negatively by the Europeans. And so began a systematic process of suppression and oppression that saw Africans lose their languages, their customs, their religious practices and their names. Accordingly, within a short period the ancient and culturally advanced civilisations of Africa were largely destroyed.

The oppression of African culture took place at two levels, namely, at the level of content and the level of techniques (Kabuga, 1982). At the level of content, European education stressed the empire where the sun never set, and suppressed the great Sudanic kingdoms. The Europeans highlighted the greatness of Napoleon Bonaparte and the Duke of Wellington, and the barbarism of Shaka the Zulu. Such teachings grossly devalued and demoralised the accumulated knowledge and experiences of the African. Consequently, Africans lost the content of their lives and with that went their pride, their languages and their names. Today, many Africans are more proficient in French and in English than they are in their languages and they are proud of it. European names are still very fashionable in most parts of Africa. Take a minute to reflect on this. Think about your lecturers and tutors. Think about the current crop of African heads of states. Think about government ministers in your country. How many of them have African first names? Our estimates suggest that at least six out of every ten African people aged fifty and above have European first names. Lastly, Africans have developed a penchant for lightening their skin colour. Skin lightening creams have become a huge industry in Africa.

At the level of techniques, oppression has destroyed African technology. Africans have completely lost their ancestral skills. They have lost much of their culture, their religious practices and their songs. There is a religious song in Zulu entitled *Nansi Indaba Engesiyo Yomkhonto* (Here is a spearless tale). The song is a Christian version of a Zulu/Ndebele war song entitled *Nansi Indaba Yomkhonto* (Here is a spear tale), a song that was sung by the Ndebele warriors to motivate their rank and file for battle or to celebrate success in battle. The missionaries converted it, because in their view, it symbolised the barbaric act of killing other people with spears.

Communism is the other major ideology that has driven some of the major changes that have swept through Africa in the past six decades. As an ideology, communism can be traced back to Karl Marx's (1867) analysis of society. Social class is the basic unit of Marx's analysis of society. To Marx, a person's social class is determined by the relationship that person has to the means of production, namely, tools, machinery and raw materials. Marx makes a distinction between two social classes, namely, those who own the means of production (the capitalists) and those who do not (the proletariat or working class). The capitalists own the means of production, and members of the proletariat must sell their labour to them in exchange for wages.

Conflict is inevitable between the two social classes due to their different interests. On one hand, the capitalists are typically driven by the desire and passion for more and more profit. To this end, they seek to exploit the worker by increasing production, lengthening working days, and reducing wages to subsistence levels. While the capitalists become richer, the working class becomes impoverished, laying the foundation for conflict. Compounding this potentially volatile situation is the decline in the rank and file of the capitalist class. As competition for profits increases, some capitalists are driven out of business and forced to join the working class, therefore swelling the numbers of the proletariat. As the number of capitalists begins to dwindle and the proletariat begins to grow, the latter realises that their interests will be served best through the destruction of private property, control of the means of production and the elimination of the capitalist class, hence the eradication of the capitalist system. In this way, the revolution of the proletariat would culminate in the formation of a classless or communist society.

In its ideal form, a communist society would be characterised by public ownership of resources and the means of production, coupled with the distribution of goods and services according to need (Hunt and Sherman, 1981). A society like that has never materialised. However, communism as a set of ideas or an economic system has been used to mobilise and rally the people of Africa to rise and drive out the colonialists. Almost each and every nationalist movement in Africa preached communism as a better economic system than the capitalist system, which was blamed for the many woes of the African. Together with socialism, a watered-down version of a classless society, communism has been the driving philosophy behind African nationalism and the eradication of colonialism from Africa. As a concept, socialism means public ownership and the payment of wages according to work done. In its purest form, socialism has never materialised. However, there have been attempts by several African governments to paint themselves in socialist colours. In their early days in power, the Tanzania African National Union (TANU), the government of Tanzania; the Front for the Liberation of Mozambique (FRELIMO), the government of Mozambique; and the Zimbabwe African National Union Patriotic Front (ZANUPF), the government of Zimbabwe, were very proud to be associated with socialism.

Although there have never been and probably will never be any communist or socialist societies in Africa, the changes that occurred across Africa in the past six decades are to a very large extent attributable to the ideas that constitute communism and socialism. Using the same tactics that were used by the colonialists, African nationalists discredited the capitalist system in the eyes of the people and promised a communist or socialist system in its place. Implied here, however, is that an ideology on its own cannot bring about change. Individuals play a big role in the promotion of an ideology.

Individuals

Imperialism and colonialism were driven by individuals. The history of colonialism in Africa cannot be written without such names as David Livingstone, Henry Morton Stanley, Cecil John Rhodes, Robert Moffat, Queen Victoria (England) and King Leopold II (Belgium). These are the people who exhorted their fellow citizens to rally behind colonialism. They promoted the destruction of African cultures and customs, and the systematic plunder of Africa's resources. They condemned African customs as barbaric and in this way persuaded Africans to abandon their way of doing things. At the same time, they showed Africans their more 'advanced approach' and persuaded them to adopt this new way of life. An example is the French colonies' direct system of 'assimilation'. In the English colonies, an indirect system of 'assimilation' offered better opportunities to those who were quick to conform to the values of the English.

The legacy of the people who drove the process of colonialism in Africa is evident from the many institutions and sites that still bear their names. Notable among these are Lake Victoria in East Africa, the Victoria Falls in the Zambezi River, Rhodes University in South Africa and the city of Livingstone in Zambia.

In a similar fashion, African nationalism was driven by individuals. Through European education, the African elite became conscious of the oppressive and divisive nature of colonial administrations, and what could be done to bring them down.

And so began a process of condemnation and enlightenment.

The condemnation of colonialism entailed reminding the African people of how the Europeans had humiliated their ancestors and forcibly removed them from their land; how they had pitted Africans against one another through a calculated policy of division and rule; how they had exploited Africa's resources for their own benefit; and how they had used education as a means of oppression rather than empowerment. Condemnation laid the ground work for enlightenment, which entailed portraying how post-colonial African governments could be just and fair. Slowly nationalism gathered the necessary momentum that eventually led to the demise of colonial administrations through negotiation or by means of armed force. Behind the various forms of resistance that constituted the struggle for independence in each country were many people whose names have now become synonymous with the liberation of their country. The list of such people includes Gamal Abdul Nasser of Egypt; Kwame Nkrumah of Ghana; Leopold Senghor of Senegal; Sekou Toure of Guinea; Amcar Cabral of Guinea Bissau; Jomo Kenyatta of Kenya; Julius Nyerere of Tanzania; Patrice Lumumba of the Democratic Republic of Congo; Augustinho Neto of Angola; Kenneth Kaunda of Zambia; Hastings Kamuzu Banda of Malawi; Samora Machel of Mozambique; Robert Mugabe of Zimbabwe; Sam Nujoma of Namibia; Seretse Khama of Botswana; and the legendary Nelson Mandela of South Africa.

The list of Africans who have contributed tremendously towards political change in Africa is not confined to heads and former heads of states. It includes many others such as Oginga Odinga of Kenya, Eduardo Mondlane of Mozambique, Joshua Nkomo of Zimbabwe, and Oliver Tambo and Walter Sisulu of South Africa, to mention but a few

prominent nationalists who did not become heads of state. Also, the list is not limited to men. They are many women who deserve to be mentioned alongside the men above. One such woman is Winnie Madikizela Mandela of South Africa. Further, since social change in Africa has not been limited to political change, there are many other men and women who will not be mentioned here, but who have helped bring about change in the many other aspects of human life, that is, economics, education, art and culture, and so forth.

⌗ ACTIVITY

Explain the changes that have taken place in your community over the past ten years, paying particular attention to the ideologies and the individuals that guided them.

SOCIAL CHANGE AND DEVELOPMENT IN AFRICA

From the foregoing, it is evident that in less than 200 years Africa has undergone tremendous transformation, from kingdoms that were ruled by kings to colonies of European countries and recently, to independent states with all the trimmings and trappings of modern nations. Ironically, it is these twists and turns that seem to be responsible for the backwardness of Africa today.

The days of open colonialism are over, but the pattern of trade that characterised colonialism remains the same. The deliberate policy of colonialism to develop only the primary sector of the economy continues to haunt Africa today. The refining and the manufacturing sectors of the economy of the majority of African countries were deliberately underdeveloped by the colonialists, in order to protect European economies from competition. This has ensured that former colonies remain dependent on the former colonial masters (Diescho, 2002) for finished products such as equipment and machinery. The precious minerals that are mined in Africa are very rarely processed and refined in Africa. They have to be sent to Europe for refinement and for the manufacturing of jewellery.

The underdevelopment of African economies was a deliberate ploy to secure rich resources for the imperialists and to ensure that the colonial countries did not develop whole and independent economies. In other words, colonialism held back the growth of the colonies and fostered that of the imperialist nations. Today, most African countries still export their unfinished products to the former colonial masters and import most of their finished products. Clearly, political independence has had very little impact on the economic pattern that was put in place by the colonialists. Foreign investments still dominate African industries.

The uneven balance of economic development that we have today is referred to as neo-colonialism because it is a legacy of the colonial era. Whereas colonialism means both political and economic domination, neo-colonialiasm only means economic domination. Whereas the benefits of colonialism were limited to the colonialists, the benefits of neo-colonialism have been extended to countries like Japan and Switzerland – countries that never held colonial power over any underdeveloped country, at least in Africa. Although Japan and Switzerland did not have a hand in the creation of the present pattern of trade and investment, they have exploited its existence to the full (Hunt and Sherman, 1981). For example, Japan has heavily invested in Africa, particularly in the motor and electronics industry.

While colonialism grossly exploited Africa's natural resources and thus reduced the continent's capacity to grow, communism and socialism have failed to uplift the economies of Africa in any substantial way and, in some cases, can be blamed for making matters worse.

Many post-independence African leaders have advocated a socialist or democratic humanist model of development rooted in the culture and traditions of the African people. Some have called it African socialism. Advocates of this model include the late Kwame Nkrumah of Ghana; Julius Nyerere of Tanzania; Kenneth Kaunda of Zambia; the late Sekou Toure of Guinea; the late Leopold Senghor of Senegal; Amicar Cabral of Guinea Bissau; the late Samora Machel of Mozambique; and Robert Mugabe of Zimbabwe. These countries and many others that have considered and practised socialism rank among the poorest nations in the world today. African socialism, if we can call it that, lacks a reasonable theoretical interpretation and is therefore incoherent. It has furthermore produced a new breed of capitalists, the most resistant type that seems to thrive in very difficult economic conditions.

It is generally accepted that today most African countries are worse off economically than they were at the time of independence. Joseph Diescho (2002: 3) writes:

In Africa, 340 million people, or half the population live on less than US$1 per day. The mortality rate of children under 5 years is 140 per 1 000, and life expectancy at birth is only 54 years. Only 58 percent of the population has access to safe water. The rate of illiteracy for people over 15 is 41 percent. There are only 18 mainline telephones per 1 000 people in Africa, compared with 146 for the world as a whole and 567 for high-income countries.

Compounding the economic underdevelopment of Africa has been the machinations of African leaders, the very individuals that were at the forefront of the fight for independence. As Diescho (2002: 8) aptly observes, 'the independence leaders' of Africa have been 'invariably ... preoccupied with their own positions of power, tenure and material well-being, more often than not at the expense of their African citizenry'. He goes on to say:

Almost all African leaders, be they civilian or military, ran Africa into the ground as they believed that their names were synonymous with the names of the countries they liberated. They became Perfect Men and tin-box dictators, the consequence of which was a pillaging of African resources, human and material, by the developed world. In the end, political independence meant what it was meant to be only to a small handful of people and those blindly loyal to them.

The rule of law and good governance have long been considered an essential component to economic development in Africa. Accordingly, the African leaders, under the auspices of the Organisation of African Unity (OAU), adopted the African Charter on Human and People's Rights on 23 October 1986. The Charter declared that 'Every individual shall have the right to assemble freely with others ... Every citizen shall have the right to participate freely in the government of his country, either directly or through freely chosen representatives' (Diescho, 2002: 9).

The record of human rights violations in Africa has worsened since 1986. It is difficult to imagine that the perpetrators of these human rights violations are the same leaders who signed the Charter to protect human rights in Africa (Diescho, 2002). As Diescho (2002: 8) aptly observes: 'The ideals of the rule of law, good corporate governance and human dignity [in Africa] were left hanging on the scaffolding, with overt and covert assistance by the developed world'.

Development initiatives in Africa

Since 1980, several strategies have emerged to put Africa on the right footing with regard to development. Some of these efforts are (Diescho, 2002):

- The Lagos Plan of Action for the Economic Development of Africa, 1980–2000 and the Final Act of Lagos (1980).
- Africa's Priority Programme for Economic Recovery (APPER), 1986–1990, which later became the United Nations Programme of Action for Africa's Economic Recovery and Development (UN-PAAERD) (1986).
- The African Alternative Framework to Structural Adjustment Programme for Socio-Economic Recovery and Transformation (AAF-SAP) (1989).
- The African Charter for Popular Participation for Development (1990).
- The United Nations New Agenda for the Development of Africa (UN-NADAF) (1991).
- The World Bank's Sub-Saharan Africa: From Crisis to Sustainable Growth (1989).

Each of these efforts set forth urgent measures that were needed to put Africa on the path to economic recovery. By the year 2002, Africa still fell short of the Millenium Development Goals (MDGs) and the 7% annual GDP growth rate (Diescho, 2002: 1). There was clearly need for something new. Accordingly, two new initiatives have emerged to advance development in Africa. The first is the African Renaissance initiative, which stresses the need to resuscitate all the good values that made Africa great in the past. President Thabo Mbeki of South Africa is currently leading this initiative. The second is the New Partnership for Africa's Development (NEPAD), which is the brain-child of Presidents Thabo Mbeki (South Africa), Olusegun Obasanjo (Nigeria) and Abdelaziz Bouteflika (Algeria). NEPAD seeks to emphasise the need for the economic development of Africa based on the continent's abundant human and material resources, through good governance and transparent leadership supported by the international community, especially Europe and America. The goals for NEPAD are as follows (Diescho, 2002: 13–14):

- To promote accelerated growth and sustainable development (i.e. enrol all children of school-going age in schools by 2015; make progress towards gender equality by empowering women and eliminating gender inequalities in schools by 2015; reduce infant and child mortality ratios by two-thirds by 2015; reduce maternal mortality ratios by three-quarters by 2015; increase access to reproductive health services by 2015; and reverse the loss of environmental resources by 2015).
- To eradicate widespread and severe poverty (reduce poverty by half by 2015).
- To halt the marginalisation of Africa in the globalisation process (i.e. implement national strategies for sustainable development by 2005; and reverse the brain drain).

Education is integral to the stated goals of the African Renaissance and NEPAD. A culture of adult learning is without any doubt essential for the successful implementation of efforts that will lead to the attainment of the objectives of these latest initiatives for the development of Africa. It is perhaps too early to judge the African Renaissance and NEPAD. Time will be needed to allow for an objective assessment or evaluation of their impacts. However, it is worth noting

that many have already expressed doubt about the possibility of NEPAD's success (Ahmadu, 2002).

⊞ ACTIVITY

1 Between the legacy of colonialism and poor governance, which do you consider most responsible for the underdevelopment of Africa today? Explain your answer.
2 Any development initiative in Africa (e.g. NEPAD) is bound to fail. Do you agree with this assertion? Explain.

SUMMARY

This chapter has explored the concept of social change, particularly various contemporary theories of social change and their relevance to our understanding of development in Africa. Social change refers to transformations in the behaviour and structure of a society that occur over a period of time. Theoretical explanations of social change can be grouped into four major categories, namely, evolutionary, cyclical, equilibrium and conflict. Evolutionary theories see society as moving from simple primitive communities to more complex and advanced states. Cyclical theories view change as a circle of growth and decline. Equilibrium theories of social change view society as made up of sub-systems that are constantly moving in unison towards stabilising and maintaining the system. Conflict theories see society and social groups as made up of parts that are in a constant state of conflict. There have been two major causes of social change in Africa, namely, ideologies and individuals. Two ideologies have been remarkably instrumental in this regard, that is, Protestantism and communism. Protestantism is the ideology behind the development of capitalist economies, whose offspring 'imperialism' laid the foundation for colonialism and neo-colonialism. Communism advocates a society which is characterised by public ownership of resources and the means of production coupled with the distribution of goods and services according to need. Both ideologies, however, were driven by individuals. Similarly, African nationalism, which has brought about political independence in Africa, was driven by individuals. Names like Kwame Nkrumah, Julius Nyerere, Kenneth Kaunda and Nelson Mandela have become synonymous with the fight for the liberation of Africa. The political liberation of Africa has not been followed by economic development. The major explanation for this is the inability of African nations to eradicate the trade patterns that were set up by the colonialists in favour of their own countries. The other reason is the lack of good leadership in Africa. Many development initiatives have come and gone with little impact on the development of Africa. The latest development initiative, NEPAD, may well go the same way unless education, particularly adult education, is made part of its process.

KEY POINTS

- Social change means the transformations in the behaviour and structure of a society that occur over a period of time.
- Theoretical explanations of social change can be grouped into four major categories, namely, evolutionary, cyclical, equilibrium and conflict.
- Evolutionary theories see society as moving from simple, primitive communities to more complex and advanced states.
- Cyclical theories view change as a circle of growth and decline.

- Equilibrium theories view society as made up of sub-systems that are constantly moving in unison towards stabilising and maintaining the system.
- Conflict theories see society and social groups as made up of parts that are in a constant state of conflict.
- Ideologies and individuals have been two major causes of social change in Africa.
- Two ideologies have been remarkably influential in bringing about change in Africa, namely, Protestantism and communism.
- Similarly, individuals such as Kwame Nkrumah, Julius Nyerere, Kenneth Kaunda and Nelson Mandela have been instrumental in bringing about change in Africa.
- Political liberation has not been followed by economic development in Africa.
- Although the pattern of trade that was set up by the colonialists is largely responsible for underdevelopment in Africa, bad governance in Africa has contributed significantly to the underdevelopment of the continent.
- Many development initiatives have come and gone with little impact on the development of Africa.
- The latest development initiative, NEPAD, is likely to fail unless education is made an integral part of its process.

▨ ACTIVITY

Unless adult education is made an integral part of NEPAD, it will fail in its aims in the same way as many other development initiatives before it. Do you agree with this assertion? Explain.

FURTHER QUESTIONS

1 Do you think Africa would be better off
   if it had not been subjected to colonialism? Explain your answer.
2 In your opinion, what needs to be done
   to counter underdevelopment in Africa?
   By whom?

SUGGESTED READINGS

Wallace, R. C. and Wallace, W. D. 1985.
   Sociology. Boston: Allyn and Bacon, Inc.

Chapter 3

Community and adult education

OVERVIEW

Development, social change and learning take place within a social environment or community. Therefore, adult educators as change agents need to know what a community entails. We also need to know about community development. Further, it is essential to know about the adult educational needs of communities and ways of assessing them. The educational needs of today's communities are dynamic and diverse. What can government agencies, community-based organisations (CBOs) and non-governmental organisations (NGOs) do to deal with the complex educational needs of today's communities? These are the key areas of concern of this chapter.

LEARNING OBJECTIVES

By the end of this chapter, you should be able to:

1 Define community and community development.
2 Identify and discuss the adult educational needs of communities in Africa and the strategies for responding to them.
3 Briefly describe the roles of the government, CBOs, NGOs and donor agencies in promoting community education programmes.

KEY TERMS

adashi   A Hausa word used to refer to a local cooperative savings practice that is widely used in various African communities.

community   A group of people living together in the same area, sharing the same language, culture, tradition, religion and bound by a common legal and administrative system or authority.

community development   Deliberately planned and organised efforts aimed at improving community life or solving particular problems in a community.

cooperative practices   Collaborative economic efforts with particular emphasis on savings and informal banking.

kibbutz   A type of small community in Israel.

needs   Something required by someone or a society for meaningful survival, for example, food for the human person. There are basic or primary needs and secondary needs.

secular   Non-religious; not connected with or controlled by a church or a religious authority.

sharia   Islamic legal system which binds every Muslim. It is also a description of the total way of life of Muslims far beyond its legal meaning.

▨ BEFORE YOU START

What do you understand by the word *community*? Write your answer to this question on a piece of paper. Keep the piece of paper out of sight till you have finished reading this section.

THE MEANING OF COMMUNITY

This section discusses the concept of community. Suitable case studies to help in the understanding of this concept are also provided.

Defining community

Simply put, a community is a place where people live together for many reasons. Although the reasons for living together may differ from one community to another, there are certain features that are common to most communities. For example, community members normally have a common language and share common ways of doing things. They normally share common norms such as hard work, kindness, care or respect for elders, women and children. Also, a community may have common leaders such as traditional or religious leaders. In addition, community members may share the same purpose, goal and vision. Nevertheless, no two communities will be exactly the same.

In a classic book on the subject of community, Warren (1978) reviews several perspectives on the community and concludes that it can be viewed from any one of four perspectives, namely:

1 Community as space – this refers to the distribution and the clustering of people in space.
2 Community as shared institutions and values – this refers to the common human interests and needs that lay the foundation for a common way of life.
3 Community as interaction – this refers to the social processes that take place in a community, such as conflict, cooperation and competition.
4 Community as a social system – this refers to the processes that go on within

and outside the community, and within and between the structures of the community.

A more or less similar view of community comes from Oduaran (1993). From a review of several definitions, Oduaran suggests that a community can simply be described as a social, ecological, geographical, legal, political and administrative unit, which is the equivalent of a society. It is an ideal mental entity as well as a process.

From the above, it can be seen that community refers not only to the place, but also to the people who reside in that place, and the common features that distinguish them as a community. In other words, a community is defined by its people and the way they live, the environment, the land, its laws and regulations and the way it is organised, led or ruled. In this regard, a group of people living in a particular place such as a neighbourhood or a district constitute a community. Similarly, people who live in a particular ecological or geographical area such as the Cape Peninsula can be considered to be a community. Furthermore, people who share the same culture and have a common language, common values, norms, beliefs and customs make up a community. In the same way, people who belong to the same clan constitute a community, as well as people who belong to the same religion or who share common leadership in the form of traditional, legal or administrative authorities.

Traditionally, the most common denominator for African communities is ethnicity. People who belong to the same ethnic group share a common culture and view themselves as distinct from other ethnic groups. Such communities include the Hausa, the Ibo, the Yoruba, the Urhobo, the Nupe and the Ibibio of Nigeria; the San of Botswana and Namibia; the Bamangwato and the Bakalanga of Botswana; the

Kwanyama and the Herero of Namibia; the Zulu, the Xhosa, and the Afrikaner of South Africa; the Kikuyu and the Luo of Kenya; the Arabs of Libya; the Tuaregs and Fulani of Mali, Niger and Senegal; the Nuer of the Sudan; the Saros of Liberia and Sierra Leone; the Shona and the Ndebele of Zimbabwe; the Lozi of Zambia and Namibia; and the Bemba of Zambia. Although they are distinct communities, each of these peoples are just one such community in the countries to which they belong. Together with other equally distinct groups they constitute that country's community. Therefore, we can talk of the South African community as composed of the various distinct groups in South Africa. Whereas the Zulus may share a vision which is different from that of the other ethnic groups in South Africa, as South Africans they share a common vision with the many other ethnic groups that make up the South African community. Similarly, the Yorubas share a common identity, but as Nigerians they share a common identity with the Hausas, the Ibos and the many other ethnic groups in Nigeria. This analysis can be taken a step further. While the citizens of each African country constitute a community in respect of being Batswana, Kenyans, Ethiopians, Angolans, Zimbabweans, Libyans, etc., when grouped together with other African countries they become part of the larger African community. Similarly, there are broader communities of the peoples of America or Europe or Asia which are made up of a number of their own different communities.

Unlike traditional societies, modern societies are more cosmopolitan and as such tend to be heterogeneous. There are very few communities that are made up entirely of people from the same ethnic group. Nevertheless, these heterogeneous societies are communities in their own right, because, in any unit, there will always be some attributes and characteristics that bind most members together. In this regard, the whole world constitutes 'one global human community' with shared problems, challenges, hopes and aspirations. Although peoples of the world may be different and diverse, they share the broader common identity and attributes of, first and foremost, being human. Globalisation is discussed in detail in Chapter 10.

Members of a community have a sense of belonging to a particular group as differentiated from other groups. For example, residents of a particular neighbourhood may share a common vision for the progress of their area. Similarly, citizens of a particular country may subscribe to a common vision in respect of the development of their country. The attainment of a community's vision may demand that the community cooperate with other communities. Regional and international cooperation blocks, such as the Southern African Development Community (SADC) and the Non-Aligned Movement (NAM), respectively, are examples of how countries cooperate among themselves to attain common interests. In some cases, the attainment of a particular community's vision may compromise the advancement of others, leading to some conflict between two or more communities. Nations have resorted to both legal and military warfare in order to protect national interests. The dispute between Namibia and Botswana (1999–2000) regarding the ownership of the Sedudu island (an uninhabited islet in the middle of the Chobe River) had to be settled by an international court in The Hague. Similarly, in 1998, Ethiopia and Eritrea took up arms to settle the matter of the disputed boundary between them. That war, which lasted until 2000, killed an estimated 70 000 people. At the micro-level, Christians and Muslims in some Nigerian cities, particularly Kano and Kaduna, have killed one another in recent years over the issue of which religion is more righteous.

It should be noted that a common territory is not always necessary for a group of people to be considered a community. For example, members of a religious community may live apart in diverse places such as in a region, country or across nations.

CASE STUDY: THE KANO COMMUNITY

In this case study, you will find a description of one large community, Kano, an ancient pre-colonial city in the northern part of Nigeria.

Kano is one of the thirty-six states of Nigeria. The name of the state is also the name of its capital city. It is located in the northern part of the country. By 2002, its population was estimated to be about seven to eight million people. The indigenous people speak a common language called Hausa. In terms of numbers, Hausa is the largest indigenous language in West Africa.

On the African continent, non-indigenous people who come from other places speak English, which has been the official language of communication in Nigeria since independence in October 1960. Kano occupies a land area of 20 680 m², and the dominant economic activities are farming, commerce and trade. Almost all the local inhabitants are Sunni Muslims.

Kano has both traditional and modern leadership structures. The traditional leadership structure is headed by an *emir* (who is also called *sarki,* or king). He is followed in hierarchy by *hakimai* (singular: *hakimi,* also known as district head) who preside over 50 districts scattered around Kano. Next to the *hakimai* are the *dagatai* (singular: *dagaci)* who provide leadership at village levels. The last tier of leadership is made up of the *masu unguwa* (singular: *maiɫunguwa,* or ward head) who are in charge of wards.

In the modern hierarchy, there are two structures, that is, at state and local government levels. The chief executive of the state is the governor, assisted by a deputy, commissioners responsible for ministerial affairs, permanent secretaries and directors in charge of various organs of government. There is also an elected state House of Assembly, with a speaker and members responsible for the legislative functions of the government. Currently, Kano is led by a government formed under the People's Democratic Party (PDP), the largest political party in Nigeria, and perhaps in Africa.

There is also a judicial arm of government headed by the state chief judge and the grand *khadi,* assisted by other secular or *sharia* court judges at the high courts, *sharia* courts, magistrate courts and area courts spread across the Kano community. This arm ensures the implementation of the rule of law through the application of common law and Islamic law.

At the local level, there are chairmen of local government councils who are assisted by their deputies, elected councillors and civil servants manning the various organs of government at the local level.

Kano has numerous urban towns, rural villages and hamlets. It has several markets, most notable of which are the Kurmi, Sabongari, Rimi, Kwari and Dawanau markets. These are urban outlets through which the community's commercial and trading activities are conducted, making Kano the centre of commerce in the northern part of Nigeria.

Kano also has modern industrial estates located in the Bompai, Sharada and Challawa areas, where modern manufacturing activities are conducted. Kano is the largest industrial state in the northern part of the country and the second largest, after Nigeria's commercial capital, Lagos.

Kano has more than 5 000 primary schools, 44 area coordinating offices supervising the provision of adult basic education, more than 500 junior and senior secondary schools, three colleges of education, one polytechnic and two universities – Bayero University in the city of Kano, and Kano State University of Technology, located at Wudil, a fishing town 40 km east of the city of Kano. Also, there is in Kano a network of Qu'ranic, Ilm and Islamiyya schools offering an opportunity for the acquisition of varying forms and degrees of Islamic education to the young, old, male and female members of the community.

Hospital services for basic health care are available in most towns and villages and are directly linked to the Murtala Mohammed Specialist Hospital and the Aminu Kano Teaching Hospital, located in Kano city.

Kano is considered an economically prosperous community and a land full of vibrant and politically conscious citizens who actively participate in Nigeria's national life. Kano city is an example of a large ancient African urban community found in most parts of the continent.

▦ ACTIVITY

1 Refer to the piece of paper on which you wrote the meaning of *community*. Briefly explain the differences, if any, between the meaning of community you had before and the meaning you have derived from reading the preceding section.
2 Identify three communities nearest to you and for each:
   a. Name the place and the language of communication.
   b. Name two things that bind the people of this community together.
   c. Briefly describe their culture in respect of their values, norms and beliefs.
3 Identify two characteristics common to all three communities.
4 Identify one trait that differentiates the three communities from one another.
5 State what you think makes your own community different from the ones identified above.

TYPES OF COMMUNITY

There are several types of community. Communities are often classified on the basis of location, size or complexity. Below, ten types are listed and briefly outlined.

Urban community

This is a type of community that is located in cities or towns. Generally, when compared with rural communities, urban communities have the following attributes:

- Large population size, running into millions in some instances (for example, Kano mentioned in the case study above).
- More enlightened inhabitants in terms of education and awareness of social issues and problems.
- Less homogenous – there are differences in language, culture and even food.
- Less intimate in terms of social relations. Relationships are loose and weak, and can be broken easier than is the case in rural communities.
- More flexible and open to change.
- Less compliant in terms of obedience to law and order and the maintenance of social security.
- More open to deviant behaviours and violence.
- Often agitative in respect of demands

for the rights of individuals and groups, especially with regard to social services and amenities from public or government providers.

■ More active in collective, civic and popular actions.
■ More likely to be engaged in diverse occupational activities to meet different community needs, aspirations and expectations.

Rural community

This is a community type that is found in remote or rural settings. The people in these types of communities exhibit the following tendencies:

■ Live mainly off the land, often on a seasonal basis. Livestock raising and farming are the most common means of economic survival.
■ Patient, persevering and compliant to civil authorities.
■ Homogenous in terms of ethnic composition, language, culture, religion and social relations.
■ Less violent and more tolerant of oppressive measures, laws and regulations.
■ Closely knit, usually through kinship networks and relationships.
■ Generally resistant to change and innovation in common life skills and practices.
■ More religious and committed to common belief systems.
■ More prone to illiteracy, disease and poverty, superstitious beliefs and practices.
■ Less likely to adopt modern practices like family planning, savings and technical innovations applicable to local trades and occupations such as farming, hunting and fishing.
■ Likely to be engaged in common vocational and occupational activities to meet

mainly minimal and monotype needs.
■ Lower expectations and demands on services from government or its agencies.
■ More likely to undertake community development projects to help solve local problems and issues.

Small community

As the name suggests, a small community is small in all respects, that is, in terms of space, population, needs and aspirations. Small communities are usually identified as villages or hamlets, or as units of larger communities. Most small communities exhibit characteristics typical of rural communities. Good examples include the village systems in most parts of Africa, the kibbutz system in Israel and the communes in China or Russia.

Medium and large communities

Medium and large communities are the bigger versions of the small community. They occupy more land space, have larger populations and demand more services and goods to meet different needs. The populations of the large types of communities can run into millions. These communities are very diverse in their needs and expectations, and are more complex than small communities. In many parts of Africa, such communities are exemplified by towns.

Religious community

In religious communities, religion is the main binding factor. Such communities are characterised by a strong belief system. Religious communities are places where people fear and obey their God. Typically, religious communities are well established and ancient in nature. Examples of religious communities include those whose inhabitants are adherents or believers of Jewish,

Islamic, Christian or African traditional religions. It is common to find believers of major religions all over the world forming one universal religious community. For instance, all Muslims believe that they are one *ummah* or community. Similarly, the Roman Catholics believe that they are one family or community. Religious beliefs prescribe codes of behaviour and guidelines for life for their members. Believers accept their religions as a 'complete way of life'. However, a major issue of concern in these types of communities is their reluctance to accept or accommodate non-believers or believers of other faiths. This is a potential threat to peaceful co-existence and harmonious living, and possibly explains the many persistent religious crises in different parts of the world, including Africa.

Secular community

This is a modern concept of community. A secular community either takes the form of one in which diverse belief systems are acceptable or one in which no particular belief system exists. Most constitutional states of Africa are secular in that citizens are at liberty to pursue religions of their choice. Although the government cannot ignore religion as an essential institution in society, it does not adopt any one religion as a state religion.

The tradition of secularism originated in Europe. In this tradition, the state (or structures of governance) is separated from religion. One of the problems of a secular community is that those who wish to live according to the dictates of their religious beliefs often find it difficult to do so. There is also a tendency to deny religious rights in some secular communities. This often leads to social crises and conflicts in society.

Ethnic community

An ethnic community is one in which ethnicity is one of the most important and popular bonds of solidarity. The people of these communities live together because they come from the same ethnic group. Many ethnic communities tend to be discriminatory. In this regard, they hardly admit others into their folds, nor accept other ethnic groups or their ways of life. This is largely due to primordial sentiments and lack of exposure to outsiders. This is, however, changing rapidly as most communities now admit and accept outsiders and their cultures. Migration, the effects of globalisation and the ever-increasing cases of inter-marriages have undermineds the existence of the purely ethnic community (Kristeva, 1990).

Racial community

A racial community is similar to an ethnic community since it is defined by its racial composition. Although such a community could have more than one racial group, their co-existence is governed by the laws of the land. For example, until 1994, the Republic of South Africa was run as a racial community with white settlers ruling through the discriminatory policy of apartheid. This rule divided the people of the entire country into groups governed through discriminatory and apartheid laws. The society was characterised by violence perpetrated by both the oppressive white regime and the oppressed non-white groups fighting for their liberation until the apartheid system was destroyed. It was then replaced by the current non-racial order whose first president, Nelson Mandela, had been a victim of racial imprisonment for 27 years. Racial communities are hostile to outsiders and to insiders who do not belong to the ruling race. More details on racism are provided in Chapter 4.

Vocational/occupational community

A vocational community is one in which members live together because of the common pursuits of a particular occupational practice. Examples of these are fishing, dyeing, blacksmithing, hunting, trading and farming communities. Like racial communities, these types of communities are exclusive and have tended not to allow others into them until recently. Vocational communities may be incorporated into larger communities. However, even then, they are largely inaccessible to outsiders. There are many such types in Africa. However, these communities are gradually transforming and becoming less exclusive and more tolerant, allowing new entrants and becoming more accepting of others.

Economic community

Since the end of World War II in 1945, the increasing need for regional integration in order to face common challenges, crises and problems, as well as to promote economic growth and development, has led to the emergence of regional economic communities. These are essentially groups of countries coming together due to monetary, business and trade interests. The most familiar include the West African Economic Community (ECOWAS), the East African Economic Community (which has not been functional for some time), the Southern African Development Community (SADC), the New Partnership for Africa's Development (NEPAD) and the European Union (EU). These communities seek to promote trade, security and good governance within each of the member nations, between member nations and with other economic blocks around the world. They seek to integrate their own economies for the general good of the peoples of their various member countries.

⊞ ACTIVITY

For each type of community outlined above, identify one such community in your country or region, and briefly explain why you think that community fits into that type.

COMMUNITY DEVELOPMENT

It has been shown that a community essentially contains four major elements, namely, the people, the place (or environment), the shared values and the social processes. These elements are dynamic and, as such, are changing all the time. There is a need to ensure that the transformation of these elements is positive at all times. The positive outcome of qualitative and quantitative transformation of people, their environment, values and social processes can be described as *development*. Therefore, community development implies qualitatively and quantitatively transforming people, their environment, values and social processes. This leads us to ask the question: by whom? The simple answer is that it is by the people, perhaps with the help of others from within or outside their environment.

In what has turned out to be a landmark analysis of the concept, Sanders (1958) presented a fourfold typology of community development, namely, as a process, a method, a programme and a movement as elaborated below:

1 Community development as a process involves progression from one condition or state to the next. It lays more

emphasis on the improvement of the people, both socially and psychologically.

2 Community development as a method is essentially community development as a 'process' which is managed in a certain way in order to bring about a specific result. In short, community development as a 'method' is a process that is guided to serve a particular objective.

3 Community development as a programme is a combination of method and content, where method refers to a stated set of procedures, and content means a list of activities. The emphasis in community development as a programme is on the programme activities rather than on the people involved in the programme.

4 Community development as a movement is a programme plus emotional dynamics. In this regard, community development is a crusade and a cause to which people become emotionally attached. Unlike community development as a process, community as a programme is not neutral; one either supports it or is against it.

The Sanders typology has formed the philosophical backbone of virtually every conception of community development since 1958. Consider the following definitions and the points they raise:

> a planned and organized effort to assist individuals to acquire attitudes, skills and concepts required for their democratic participation in the effective solution of as wide as possible, a range of community problems in an order of priority determined by their increasing levels of competence (Meziro, cited in Oduaran, 1994: 8).

Although there is a hint of community development as a programme (planned and organised effort), this definition largely describes community development as a process designed to enhance the abilities and capabilities of the people so that they can effectively deal with their problems. Again:

> the induction and educational management of that kind of interaction between the community and its people which leads to the improvement of both (McCuskey, cited in Oduaran, 1994: 9).

Unlike the Meziro definition, this definition places more emphasis on community development as a method. The emphasis here is on three of the four vital components of the community, namely, the social processes (interaction), the place (environment), and the people. Like community development as a process, community development as a method is basically concerned with the improvement of the environment and its people. However, community development as a method is broader in that, unlike community development as a process, which is confined to the problems of the people, it seeks the development of the entire community. Once more:

> the process by which the efforts of the people themselves are united with those of governmental (and perhaps non-governmental) authorities to improve the economic, social and cultural conditions of communities, to integrate these communities into the life of the nation, and to enable them to contribute fully to national progress (United Nations, 1963: 4).

This definition embraces community development as a process and community development as a method. It incorporates the four major elements of the community, namely, the people, the shared values (implied in 'efforts of the people'), the social processes and the place. And, like the McCuskey definition, it seeks the development of the entire society (nation). Finally:

> something involving the enacting of a set of procedures in the [effort] to achieve a goal [such that] emphasis is shifted to how specialties such as health, welfare, agriculture, industry, recreation, among others could be integrated to promote the development of people and their communities … [Hence,] it requires a special type of programme that needs promise and total commitment (Oduaran, 1994: 10).

This definition describes community development as both a programme and a movement. As a programme, community development is said to be a sequence of activities that make up a community development programme. Community development programmes are institutional and, as such, use institutional structures. In addition, they are managed by professional planners and experts who put in place procedural arrangements in order to achieve the ideal goals of the community. As a movement, community development is characterised by passion and emotion, and requires total commitment by the community members.

A definition that seems to incorporate and synthesise many elements of the definitions presented above and thus incorporates all four perspectives of community development and the four major components of a community is provided by Christenson and Robinson (1980: 10). They define community development as (1) a group of people (2) in a community (3) reaching a decision (4) to initiate a social action process (i.e. planned intervention) (5) to change (6) their economic, social, cultural or environmental situation.

Although they vary in emphasis, the above definitions suggest that community

development is about people, their environment and their collective efforts aimed at addressing particular social, economic, political and cultural problems. It seeks to raise the quality of life for the people and to improve their conditions for the better. Community development is a joint and collective undertaking. Although community development is the responsibility of the people, the process can be positively aided or supported by governmental and non-governmental agencies.

The following case study is an illustration of a collaborative community development effort in Africa.

CASE STUDY: WOMEN'S CENTRE IN GONGORE, REPUBLIC OF GUINEA

Gongore is a small community of 8 000 inhabitants, situated 359 km northeast of Conakry, in Guinea. In 1988, forty women in Gongore formed the Guilintico group to carry out income-generating activities for themselves. The women identified adult illiteracy as one of the major problems of the community. To address this problem, they mobilised the whole community to participate in the building of a literacy centre.

Three main parties were involved in the project and each contributed part of the resources and efforts required to accomplish the task. The German Adult Education Association (DVV) contributed 35% of the materials needed in the form of cement, corrugated iron sheets, timber and bricks. Another non-governmental organisation called CENAFOD helped with 10% of the materials needed, while the Guilintico women's group provided 55% of the other necessary components, including sand, gravel, blocks of stone and water. The

Guilintico group also provided accommodation and food for four craftspeople and labourers. In addition, the group bore the daily expenses for the services of the construction of the centre for the entire two-month construction period.

From this collaborative effort there emerged a literacy centre which provides the following facilities on a permanent basis: (1) a fully equipped literacy class; (2) a workshop; (3) a shop; (4) an office; and (5) a toilet or rest room.

These facilities serve the interests of the members of the women's group and others in the community who use them for literacy sessions and meetings. The centre is also used as a special place where important visitors to the village are received or welcomed. The literacy centre solved the immediate community problem of the lack of a suitable literacy centre that could accommodate other community activities, and in this way facilitate the empowerment of the women's group and other members of the locality.

Cooperative practices

Community development undertakings and cooperative practices in Africa are very similar in nature. Both seek the positive improvement of the life of their members. The only significant difference between them is that cooperative practices involve collaboration in terms of economic group practices with particular emphasis on savings and informal banking. For example, occupational groups gather together and agree on minimum terms for keeping money and similar properties for the common good of all.

In Nigeria, this savings practice is called *asusu/adashi* in Hausa, and *esusu* in Ibo. The names of savings practices may differ across communities in Africa, but the methods and the ends served are usually the same.

When people save together, there is usually an agreed sum that all subscribers pay into a group savings scheme. There is a timetable that defines when individual subscribers take their subscriptions back together with any dividends thereof. The duration could be as short or as long as members wish. The executive members of the cooperative societies or savings clubs are also entitled to some cash reward, payable by individuals or by the group as agreed. Sometimes, the keeper of the money uses it in a revolving business. This is usually with the express permission of the subscribers, since risks are likely to be high in such ventures. It is of paramount importance that once a subscriber is to be paid, no default is expected, nor entertained. Often, conflicts arise from failure to pay. Community elders or leaders are often called upon to settle these sorts of conflicts amicably, without recourse to formal courts of law. There is evidence that this practice is gender sensitive, as both male and female members of the community engage in it. Significantly, these cooperative efforts are more likely to last longer when females are involved, while cases of default and criminal intent to cheat are more likely with male groups (Salau, 1990).

Based on this practice, more modern cooperative initiatives have been introduced in many African communities with varying degrees of success. However, newer capitalist values are eroding the importance of these types of practices. Formal banking alternatives are gaining acceptance in many rural African communities, with varying degrees of success and failure. The Peoples Bank system in Nigeria initiated by the military government in 1989 seems to have failed, and has been discontinued because, being a government initiative, loan beneficiaries saw it as a way of getting their own 'free share of the national cake'. Similarly, the alternative system of Community Banks was also inefficient due to the lack of trust among partners who operated them.

⊞ ACTIVITY

Identify a cooperative practice in your community or country. With reference to a particular cooperative or club, outline the following:

1 The administrative structure and membership.
2 The subscription and payback system.
3 How you would improve the cooperative practice, and why.

COMMUNITY EDUCATIONAL NEEDS

The adult educational needs of African peoples are as varied as the different types of the communities they live in. These needs arise from a combination of local challenges and those posed mainly by modernisation. Typically, these are economic, scientific and technological challenges.

Whatever the situation, adult education can improve the life of individuals and groups through the provision of skills, competencies and the modification of behaviours, values, attitudes, mores and beliefs so as to fit the dynamics of change.

All human needs and problems have implications for education. In this regard, their solutions can be acquired at school, at home, in the market, at mosques, in churches, on the battlefield or from the larger community. All people need to acquire knowledge, skills and competences that are necessary for everyday life. Similarly, all people need to be able to modify or adapt their behaviour to changes and new challenges. We all want to learn about our religion, culture, and new ways and means

of improving the quality of our own lives, and that of our families and relatives. We also wish to learn about these important things as they relate to other people and communities.

Although human needs are normally built on a hierarchy or order of importance (Maslow, 1970), they also complement one another. For example, the basic need for food cannot be satisfied without some security in the environment. In other words, farming activities cannot take place during wars.

Therefore, in developing adult education programmes, efforts must be made to cater for all the needs of the people, beginning with the most urgent ones, and building on them in the order of priority (Indabawa, 2000).

In order to ensure that there is a match between the community's educational needs and the efforts that are used to address them, the community members must play a leading role in the determination of their educational needs and the best possible ways of tackling them. Usually mistakes are made when the educational problems of a community or group of people and the solutions thereof are solely determined by someone else, such as a government official or a programme provider. In such cases, when proper consultation does not happen, the programmes provided may not meet the learners' needs or achieve the expected outcomes. This results in a waste of time and resources.

It is also important to note that the adullt educational needs of one community are not necessarily similar to those of others.

Roles of the state, CBOs, NGOs and others

As suggested earlier, community members must play a major role in the planning and implementation of community education programmes. However, they cannot do this without some assistance from elsewhere. This assistance normally comes from government, community-based organisations (CBOs), non-governmental organisations (NGOs) and donor agencies.

Below is a brief outline of what each of these forms of assistance entail. A more comprehensive description of the work of these agencies is provided in *Foundations of Adult Education in Africa* in this series (Nafukho, Amutabi and Otunga, 2005).

State or government agencies

Generally, there are two to three levels of government. In some cases, the levels include federal and regional governments. In others, there are federal and provincial governments. And yet in others there are federal, state and local governments.

One of the legal-constitutional responsibilities of government at any level is the provision of education for the people. This is so because education is considered 'a tool par excellence' for the development of human beings and communities (Federal Republic of Nigeria, 1989). Usually, the Ministry or Department of Education is vested with the power of managing the entire education system, including adult and non-formal education.

However, adult education is instrumental to the work of many other government departments and agencies, hence virtually all government departments are involved in the provision of adult education in one way or another.

CBOs or NGOs

Community-based organisations (CBOs) are small voluntary bodies that provide services at local community level. They differ from larger non-governmental organisations (NGOs), which may be local or international and that usually seek wider coverage in terms of the provision of their services. Both provide educational programmes or projects on their own, but they are usually guided by government policies in this regard. This is essentially because educational practices, the quality of programmes and standards are expected to be the same within any given community or country of Africa.

However, in Africa the work of CBOs and NGOs has been fraught with controversy for two reasons. Firstly, they rarely provide unconditional assistance. For example, they may choose to support certain adult educational activities such as gender awareness and HIV/AIDS programmes, as opposed to others such as bee-keeping and basket-making. This way, they set trends in adult education irrespective of whether those trends are on target or not. Secondly, they are more accountable to their donor agencies outside the country than to the governments of the countries in which they operate. This has created a lot of tension between them and dictatorial governments in Africa that are suspicious of anything they have no control over.

Donor agencies

Donor agencies are essentially bodies that provide different forms of support to help improve communities in various areas such as education, health and professional training or services, among others. They may be governmental or non-governmental, multi-lateral, international, national or local. Sometimes these agencies are called development organisations. Examples of some of the most widely known ones in Africa include the United Nations' agencies such as UNESCO, the United Nations Development Programme (UNDP), the United Nations Children's Fund (UNICEF) and the International Labour Organisation (ILO).

Other notable agencies include the United Kingdom's Department for International Development (DFID), the United States Agency for International Development (USAID) and the German Adult Education Association (DVV).

These agencies are normally the funders of the work of CBOs and NGOs and, likewise, their work is fraught with controversy for the same reasons.

ACTIVITY

For each form of assistance outlined above, identify one such agency and briefly explain the community development role of the agency. Give suggestions on how the services of each agency could be improved.

SUMMARY

The term *community* describes a place and the people who reside in that place, and the common features that distinguish them from other communities. Community development is about people, their environment and their collective efforts aimed at addressing particular social, economic, political and cultural problems. Although community members must play a key role in the planning and implementation of community development and educational programmes, they need assistance from other interested parties such as government, community-based organisations, non-governmental organisations and donor agencies.

KEY POINTS

- Community refers to the place and the people who reside in that place, and the common features that distinguish them as a community.
- Communities are often classified on the basis of location, size or complexity.
- Community development is about people, their environment and their collective efforts aimed at addressing particular social, economic, political and cultural problems.
- Cooperative practices involve collaboration in terms of economic group practices with particular emphasis on savings and informal banking.
- The community members must play a leading role in the determination of their adult educational needs and the best possible ways of tackling them. Otherwise, scarce resources may be wasted on programmes that are unsuitable for the people's needs and expectations.
- Although community members play a key role in the planning and implementation of community education programmes, they get assistance from other interested parties such as government, community-based organisations, non-governmental organisations and donor agencies.

ACTIVITY

A community development programme that is planned and implemented solely by the community is bound to fail. Do you agree? Explain your answer.

FURTHER QUESTIONS

1 Do you think the process of community development can be affected by the size of the community?
2 Can development (as explained in Chapter 2) take place without community development?

SUGGESTED READINGS

Nyirenda, J., Indabawa, S. A. and Avoseh, M. B. M. (eds.). 1999. *Developing professional adult education programmes in Namibia.* Windhoek: DANFE/UNAM.

Oduaran, A. B. 1994. *An introduction to community development.* Benin: University of Benin Press. (Read especially pages 1–37, dealing with the concept of community development, modern community development and the purpose and scope of community development.)

Chapter 4

Race, ethnicity, religion and adult education

OVERVIEW

Issues of race, ethnicity and religion are some of the most significant and influential aspects in the life of any society. This is because human beings belong to groups based on these social categorisations. Although these factors have the potential to help create harmony in society, conflicts and misunderstandings often arise as a result of their interplay. This chapter examines the meanings of race, ethnicity and religion and how adult education can be used to enhance the positive aspects of these factors and therefore help improve peaceful co-existence among diverse groups in a community.

LEARNING OBJECTIVES

By the end of this chapter, you should be able to:

1 Explain the meanings of race, ethnicity and religion.
2 Give suitable illustrations of your own understanding of race, ethnicity and religion in Africa.
3 Explain how adult education can be used to enhance the positive aspects of race, ethnicity and religion in Africa.

nsaa

KEY TERMS

African traditional religions   Modes of worship that are based on oral traditions, expressed through myths, legends, stories, folktales, songs and dances as well as rituals, proverbs, adages, and riddles. In traditional religions, ancestors or their spirits are invoked to influence current events and situations.

Buddhism   A religion prevalent in East and Central Asia based on the teachings of Gautama Buddha.

Christianity   A religion based on the Holy Bible and the teachings of Jesus of Nazareth. It is premised on the principles of one eternal truth and one universal salvation.

ethnicity   A sense of group identity based on a common history, culture, language or religion.

Hinduism   The main religion in India, which includes belief in destiny and reincarnation.

Islam   A religion based on the teachings of the Qu'ran as brought forth by the Prophet Muhammad.

Judaism   A religion based on the Torah.

race   An exclusive group identified by distinct physical attributes, including colour.

racism   The practice of using race (colour) as an instrument of discrimination.

religion   A unified system of beliefs and practices pertaining to sacred things, particularly ways through which human beings relate to what they believe to be their creator.

tribalism   The practice of using ethnicity as an instrument of discrimination.

▨ BEFORE YOU START

What do race, ethnicity and religion mean to you?

DEFINING RACE AND RACISM

Race implies social divisions according to colour of the skin and other physical characteristics. Wallace and Wallace (1985: 309) define race as 'a population that shares visible physical characteristics from inbreeding and which thinks of itself or is thought of by outsiders as distinct'.

Although there is consensus on what race means, there is very little consensus on the number of races in the world and on the characteristics that distinguish them (Wallace and Wallace, 1985). Anthropologists generally recognise three major categories of race, namely, Caucasoid (the 'white' race), Negroid (the 'black' race), and Mongoloid (the 'yellow' race). However, as Wallace and Wallace aptly observe, there has been a great deal of gene exchange among the peoples of the world, to such an extent that it would be folly to talk of a 'pure' race. However, this has not stopped others from splitting races into many more categories. For example, Rushton (1995) divides the people of the world into the black race, white race, African race, Asian race and the European race.

To some, race is a biological concept, meaning that it is something that has to do with one's body, birth and development. To such people racial groups are different, therefore 'people often claim that other races are temperamentally different, biologically inferior, less moral, and lacking or showing certain traits, from having rhythm to being very clean' (Wallace and Wallace, 1985: 309). However, the many claims for the existence of such differences among races have no basis. Humanity is the central element in all humankind. As such, people share the same or similar biological, physical, emotional, social and other characteristics or traits (Rushton, 1995; Youngman, 2000; Grubach, 2002). Available evidence suggests that all people are 'in a biological sense, virtually the same, our genetic make-up hardly differ at all, although human beings do vary strikingly in a few highly visible characteristics, such as skin colour, eye shape, hair type, body and facial form' (Grubach, 2002: 1).

Clearly, there are no fundamental differences between human beings which predetermine the superiority or inferiority of one race in relation to another. Where there seem to be variations between races, for example in intelligence (defined as the general mental ability to reason, plan, solve problems, think abstractly, comprehend complex ideas and learn), this is largely due to the cultural bias in the tools that have traditionally been used to assess this trait (Van der Zanden, 1972; Williams, 1974; Loehlin, Lindsey, and Spuhler, 1975; Wallace and Wallace, 1985). Although most differences that are attributed to different races are myths, they are nevertheless very significant myths, in that they often form the basis for discriminatory practices towards certain races. In this regard, race is seen as a social construct, that is, an attitude and behaviour acquired through interaction with people. It is also seen as a cultural concept and practice learnt through group behaviour, beliefs, imitation and practices. Many consider race as a political concept that has do with power and power relations between people (Rose, 1974).

As adult educators we are not interested in the biological differences among the various races of the world. Instead, we are more concerned with the social consequences of the many myths that surround race. In this regard, we are interested in the conception of race as a process of racialising and constructing the other, as well as that of structuring and explaining the world. Defining the other means 'creating an image of the self as a positive reflection of the other, thereby generating a binary opposition where the other represents the negative side of the self' (Hall, 2000: 14). This has created what has often been described as 'negative characteristics of a second order' (Potter and Wetherell, 1987: 24). For example, during the Middle Ages, a variant of the Christian religion created a colour bar to focus attention on the colours black and white. Thereafter, the colour black was associated with everything negative, especially evil, darkness, sin and Satan, while the colour white was taken as the positive opposite. Building on this symbolism, black people were subsequently considered as wicked, abnormal, inhuman and associated with the devil (Miles, 1999: 25). Similarly, slavery, particularly in America, was racially motivated. Being black was synonymous with being a slave. And, although colonialism was, as explained in Chapter 2, built on conquest, it thrived on racial discrimination. The last bastion of separatist rule, apartheid in South Africa, used race as justification for oppression (Miles, 1999: 23). Racially discriminatory practices create barriers in understanding and can lead to conditions of disharmony, rancour or violence. The feeling of superiority of one race over another is considered to be the most common cause of racial disharmony in society. For instance, a deliberate racial policy to exclude a group of people from opportunities to develop certain skills, values and attitudes may result in significant perceptible differences in culture, behaviours, attitudes and beliefs, among people of different races living in the same community. Race then becomes the instrument for defining one's cultural traits, such as values, beliefs, behaviours and attitudes. These perceptible differences are then used to justify and therefore perpetuate the feeling of superiority that initially led to the deliberate policy of exclusion.

There are many other discriminatory practices in society that can be characterised as racist. When race is used as an instrument of discrimination it brings about what is referred to as racism. Zerger (1997: 73) defined racism as a phenomenon that 'comprises ideologies and forms of practice based on the construction of groups of people as communities of descent or origin, to whom certain collective characteristics are ascribed. Those characteristics will be rated implicitly or explicitly and are interpreted as hardly changeable or not transformable at all'.

According to Allport (1971), Heckmann (1992), Zerger (1997), Miles (1999) and Hall (2000), racism can manifest itself in the following ways:

- Allocation of meaning to a group of people is linked to power strategies meant to deny them access to symbolic or cultural resources.
- Philosophy that is rooted in the ideology of exclusionary practice.
- Construction of self as a dual opposite to the other.
- Polarisation of the world into two opposite parts meant to be used as a powerful tool for manipulating people.
- A structurally divisive problem that separates people in order to unify one group against the other.
- A form of prejudice as an attitude resulting in discriminatory actions involving the individual and society.
- Construction of community according to descent or origin, not just on the basis of other people as biologically different.

In recent African history, the negative application of race is exemplified by the apartheid era of white minority rule in southern Africa, particularly in Namibia and South Africa. Apartheid was built around the belief that white people were superior over other races, particularly the majority black population. In Namibia and South Africa, apartheid, which was the official state racial policy until 1990 and 1994, respectively, discriminated against other races in all aspects of life, that is, social, economic and political. For example, non-white races were denied opportunities for education and training, employment and participation in politics. This meant that non-white people were not allowed to:

- Join the army, police or immigration services. In situations where few such opportunities were given to non-whites, they were not allowed to rise beyond a limited rank.
- Seek or be given opportunities to enrol in institutions of higher learning to earn higher academic or professional qualifications.
- Vote in an election.
- Stand to be elected in an election.
- Seek or obtain employment in the government or the private sector beyond limited, non-management positions.
- Seek or obtain loans for housing, car or self-employment business undertakings.
- Shop together with white people.
- Gain access to whites-only banks, hotels or hospitals, as well as other important government institutions.
- Be treated equally in a court of justice with the white population.
- Own landed properties in cities, or enjoy the social amenities located only in white areas.
- Live together with white people.

Windhoek, the capital city of Namibia, provides a very good illustration of the policy of physical separation between the white and the black populations. Whereas the white population lived in whites-only areas such as Eros and Klein Windhoek, the black population lived outside the city in a township called Katutura. And, the so-called coloured population, people who are neither black nor white, but mainly off-spring of mixed parents or people of Asian origins, lived in another area outside the city known as Khomasdal. Similar arrangements existed in all thirteen political or regional headquarters of the country, or in major towns (Wilmot, 1979). Sadly, more than ten years after independence some of these divisions still exist in parts of Namibia and South Africa.

The effects of apartheid will take many years to reverse. The majority black populations of these two countries have been systematically disadvantaged for decades. This state of affairs has created wide disparities between the rich minority white and the poor majority black populations. It has also resulted in a lot of mistrust and disharmony between racial groups.

The new democratic governments have sought to harmonise and defuse the situation through reconciliatory measures designed to create conditions in which all past injustices are forgiven or forgotten. The new governments have also sought to correct the injustices of the past through affirmative action policies that are designed to favour previously disadvantaged black people.

However, the majority of black people have yet to taste the benefits of these new policies, and are likely to continue languishing in poverty for many decades to come.

▨ ACTIVITY

1   List the names of all the racial groups in your country.
2   Can the problems of racism be eliminated completely in any community?
3   How can adult education help in this regard?

THE MEANING OF ETHNICITY

The word *ethnicity* comes from the Greek word *ethnos* which means people or nation (Gordon, 1964). A definition that is consistent with this view of ethnicity comes from Wallace and Wallace (1985: 308), who state that 'an ethnic group thinks of itself as a people or nation or is viewed by others as culturally different. Ethnicity is a sense of peoplehood or nationhood'. They go on to say that 'members of an ethnic group feel themselves set apart from other groups by a sense of belonging together, usually due to shared customs, beliefs, language or religion (1985: 308). A similar definition is provided by Macmillan (2000: 433), who defines ethnic identity as 'people … having a shared set of values and customs deriving from a common history, culture, language and religion'.

In accordance with this perception of ethnicity, sociologists refer to ethnic Albanians, ethnic Lithuanians, ethnic Romanians etc. to describe people who view themselves as such because they were culturally socialised that way. Rarely do you come across this broad application of the concept of ethnicity in Africa. In Africa, ethnicity is linked to the idea of a tribe, which implies 'a social or tribal group, smaller than a nation' (Longman, 1995: 1163). It relates to 'the social divisions arising from cultural distinctions between groups in society' (Youngman, 2000: 163). Accordingly, anthropologists describe the Hausa, the Ibo, the Yoruba, the Urhobo, the Nupe and the Ibibio of Nigeria; the San of Botswana and Namibia; the Bamangwato and the Bakalanga of Botswana; the Ovambo and the Herero of Namibia; the Zulu and the Xhosa of South Africa; the Kikuyu and the Luo of Kenya; the Tuaregs and the Fulani of Mali, Niger and Senegal; the Nuer of the Sudan; the Saros of Liberia and Sierra Leone; the

Shona and the Ndebele of Zimbabwe; the Lozi of Zambia and Namibia; and the Bemba of Zambia, as distinct groups with very little in common.

Most scholars believe that tribalism was deliberately created by the various colonial states in Africa to sow divisions among the various ethnic groups, as part of the 'divide and rule' strategy. Unlike ethnicity, tribalism places more emphasis on distinctions between groups. More often, the idea of 'tribe' tends to promote negative assumptions or misleading stereotypes about groups of people. Yet, most ethnic groups are bound in more ways than they are differentiated. In other words, there is more commonality between Africa's ethnic entities than differences (Hutchinson and Smith, 1996).

Whereas race is defined by distinct physical characteristics formed by inbreeding, ethnicity is defined by customs and traditions that are culturally transmitted. Like race, ethnicity per se is not a concern of adult educators and other social scientists. What is of concern to them are the social consequences of ethnicity. Recent African history abounds with negative manifestations of ethnicity. Notable examples include the Nigerian civil war (1967–1970) which was sparked by the Ibo tribe's desire to secede from the Federal Republic of Nigeria, and to form a new country called Biafra (Lamb, 1987). This war cost Nigeria more than one million lives and resulted in the destruction of billions of dollars worth of property and equipment. Recently, in 2000, Lagos (the commercial capital of Nigeria) witnessed ethnic clashes between the Yoruba and the Hausa tribes, resulting in the loss of many lives and the destruction of millions of dollars worth of property.

No region, and perhaps no nation in Africa, has been spared the negative consequences of ethnicity. In the mid-seventies, Idi Amin of Uganda ordered the killing of thousands of villagers belonging to the Lango and Acholi tribes. Entire villages populated by these tribes were wiped out (Lamb, 1987). In Southern Africa, Zimbabwe is a typical example. In the 1980s, thousands of Ndebele people in Matabeleland and the Midlands provinces were killed by the Fifth Brigade of the army as part of the government's efforts to flush out dissidents from those parts of the country.

Perhaps the worst social consequence of ethnicity is what is referred to as ethnic cleansing. This is essentially an attempt by one ethnic group to exterminate another ethnic group. Memories of the Serbian genocide after the collapse of Yugoslavia in 1990 are still very fresh in people's minds. Slobodan Milosevic, the alleged mastermind behind that dark episode of Serbian history, was placed on trial in The Hague.

In Africa, the Rwandan crisis of 1994 shows just how devastating ethnic cleansing can be. Following the assassination of the country's president, the majority Hutu tribe (about 85% of the population) attacked the minority Tutsi tribe (representing about 14% of the population). More than 850 000 Tutsi people (representing 75% of the tribe) were killed by the majority Hutu tribe within just 100 days of the crisis (Yusuf, 2003). To date, instigators of the Rwandan genocide are still being tried for crimes against humanity in the The Hague and in Dar es Salaam.

It can be inferred from the above social consequences that a major cause of ethnic crises in Africa is the competition for power, influence or access to wealth among the educated and other elites, including traditional, civilian and military leaders. As Youngman (2000: 153) aptly observes 'ethnic … hierarchies have an impact in terms of differential access to economic resources, political power and social status: they are influential in the composition of the state, and affect the nature of development policies'.

The multiplicity of ethnic groups in Africa reinforces the prospects for ethnic conflict in the continent. For instance, in Nigeria alone, there are well over 350 ethnic groups, each with its distinct identity, language and culture.

Negative manifestations of ethnicity are anathema to national solidarity and work against nationhood and nationalist aspirations. Also, nations that go through such experiences lose the opportunity for rapid socio-economic progress, as scarce resources and human lives are wasted, and social life and physical infrastructure are destroyed.

The social consequences of ethnicity are not all negative. Ethnicity can have positive implications for peace, harmony and solidarity in society in the following ways:

- Unity of purpose within a particular group.
- Protection of common group interests.
- Promotion of a unique culture and tradition.
- Enhancement of popular local or vernacular language and the symbolism that accompanies it.
- Collective security of life and property.
- Collective solidarity so as to gain from wider national benefits.
- The sanctity of a social way of life within a community, keeping out undue external (negative) influences.

The African Renaissance, whose ultimate aim is the revival of the greatness of Africa, will benefit tremendously from a holistic evocation of the harmony, solidarity and other positive social consequences that are found within the many ethnic groups in the continent.

ACTIVITY

1 List the names of all the ethnic groups in your country.
2 From the list of ethnic groups above, identify any two groups and indicate three ways in which they are similar and three ways in which they differ.
3 Do you see any role for adult education in the reduction of ethnic conflicts in Africa? Explain your answer.

THE MEANING OF RELIGION

Religion can be described as a vehicle used to denote the various ways through which human beings relate to what they believe to be their creator. The creator is believed by many to be a Higher or Supreme Being with omnipotent power and authority to create and sustain the earth and all its living and non-living things. From this perspective, human beings are believed to be the highest, and perhaps the best form of creation in the animal world, that is, those beings or creations that have body and soul. This is so because human beings are reasoning social animals with codes of behaviour and networks of relationships through which they socialise with members and non-members alike (non-members include immigrants and strangers, who do not originally belong to a particular group).

A widely accepted definition of religion comes from Emile Durkheim, who describes religion as 'a unified system of beliefs and practices related to sacred things … things set apart and forbidden – beliefs and practices which unite into one single moral community… all those who adhere to them' (Wallace and Wallace, 1985: 439).

Durkheim considered 'sacredness' as the fabric of any religion. Sacred things are those aspects of a culture that are perceived to be above the ordinary routine experience of daily living. Each religion has set aside a number of objects that are considered sacred, and which are highly regarded by all members of that religion. For example, cows are highly respected by Hindus, yet are considered ordinary by Christians and most African religions.

To Durkheim, every religion has three elements, namely, beliefs, rituals and symbols. Beliefs are shared ideas that explain the sacred objects, while rituals are sacred acts which represent religious beliefs. Furthermore, symbols are objects, images and words, which take meaning from the sacred things that they represent, and which may become sacred themselves after repeated association with the sacred. For example, the Seventh Day Adventists consider Saturday to be sacred. Accordingly, they observe certain rituals on the day such as going to church to pray and worship, and avoiding doing anything that could be construed to be work. The symbols of this faith include the hats or head dresses that women wear to church and the absence of jewellery in their attire. These symbols have become sacred themselves due to their association with the Sabbath.

From Durkheim's concept of religion, we can conclude that religion has four major components: (1) the people; (2) a belief system; (3) duties or activities undertaken to translate the beliefs into practice; and (4) signs that distinguish members of that faith.

Clearly, for every religion there are believers, that is, those who accept its principles and are guided by its prescribed codes of behaviour, norms or practices. The believers may belong to one ethnic group or race or a combination of them. Whatever the case, believers will have a common link that shows unanimity of purpose and the acceptance of distinct beliefs and the performance of rites or practices. Believers may answer to a common name, for example, Muslims or Christians. These commonalities affect the everyday life of members and non-members alike, and in the course of interaction conflicts may arise within or between groups.

In Africa, there are many types of religious belief systems. However, since the early part of the fifteenth century (that is, between the years AD 1400 and 1500), many African communities have accepted external religions such as Islam and Christianity. Those who spread the new religions were traders, scholars, explorers and missionaries. The new religions changed most of the cultural and traditional practices of the peoples of Africa (Asimeng, 1989). Some consider this development as positive, while others consider it as negative. However, this development can generally be seen as a natural process, since religion itself is said to be 'a natural growth of the human society' (*Encyclopedia Britannica*, 1973: 592).

⊞ ACTIVITY

1 Describe any two religions you know that exist in Africa.
2 State any two key similarities and differences between the two religions.

ABOUT RELIGIONS

There are many religions and religious beliefs in the world today. Some are considered divine, that is, God-sent, and are characterised by the existence of revered books such as the Bible and the Quran. Others are created by humankind through human ingenuity and creativity. An example of such a religion is Buddhism. Siddhartha Gautama, the founder of Buddhism, developed a new religion inde-

pendent of the Brahman priests who had traditionally dominated ancient Indian spiritual life. He preached a way of salvation through ethical behaviour and through the cleansing of the mind and desires. His emphasis on the virtues of patience and compassion helped make Buddhism one of the gentlest and most tolerant of religions.

All religions have varying numbers of believers. However, one common attribute of all religions is commitment to and acceptance of the existence of a Higher or Supreme Being, described or called by different names such as God, Allah, *Chineke*, Omega, *Modimo*, *uMlimu* and *Mwari*. Similarly, all religions seek a 'common good' either for all of humanity or for their members.

Africa boasts all the major religions of the world, such as Christianity, Judaism, Buddhism, Hinduism and Islam. It is important for adult educators to appreciate the meaning, doctrine and focus of the major religions that are active in a community and the roles they play in the lives of the people of that community. The most prominent religions in Africa are African traditional religion, Christianity and Islam; hence they have been chosen for elaboration here. However, as indicated earlier, many other religions exist in African communities, and adult education programmers and community developers can only ignore them at their own peril.

African traditional religion

Traditional religions are known to have existed in most parts of the world since time immemorial. They came before the religions of Judaism, Christianity, Buddhism, Hinduism and Islam (Ajayi, 1981). In Africa, traditional religions exist in different forms. They are mainly based on oral traditions, expressed through myths, legends, stories, folktales, songs and dances as well as rituals, proverbs, adages and riddles. Generally, African traditional religions relate to a belief in a Higher or Supreme Being, that is, a supernatural power behind the universe. To Africans, however, this Being is located in the immediate environment. Therefore, believers of traditional religion often worship gods identified with rivers, such as the god of iron, Ogun, in south-west Nigeria; the sun and the trees, as in some parts of East Africa; thunder and stones, as in ancient Egypt; domestic animals, such as cattle and goats; self-made objects; and humans, such as those who believe that the late Emperor Haile Sellassie of Ethiopia was a god.

In traditional religions, ancestors or their spirits are invoked to influence current events and situations. Members belong to a religious bond and seek common protection for their lives, properties, customs and traditions. Most African traditional religions are usually practised in shrines located in remote parts of the community. Believers are usually accused of practising cultist rites involving sacrifice of agricultural produce to the gods. To outsiders, the practices of some traditional religions may seem repulsive and unacceptable. However, believers in traditional religion do not accept such charges and strongly object to the use of derogatory terms such as 'paganism, idolatry, fetishism, animism, polytheism, ancestor worship and juju' (Ajayi, 1981: 2), to describe their ritual practices. Presented below is a description of an African traditional mode of worship in Yorubaland, Nigeria.

CASE STUDY: AN AFRICAN TRADITIONAL RELIGION

The mode of worship described here occurs in Yorubaland. Worship may be done daily, weekly or annually. It is done to find solutions to problems or solicit the protection of the deity over the affairs of individuals or society. Annual worship is done at a central shrine in the community, but individuals can worship there too as they wish.

In worshipping Ogun (the god of iron), the person on behalf of whom the worship is done comes with materials such as a covered calabash containing kola nuts, a sacrificial victim (usually a dog, but some say even a human being), a piece of roasted yam, a bottle of palm oil and a gourd of palm wine for the offering. The worship begins by pouring libation of water or palm wine, holding it by the head and striking the emblems of the divinity, thus producing some ringing notes. This is followed by the invocation by the priest, repeatedly saying 'Attend to us, O Ogun, He who is in control all over the world, Chief of the divinities, He whose eyeballs are rare to see, support behind the orphan, the owner of the innumerable houses of heaven'. The worshipper is then asked to state the reason for coming to Ogun. The priest then pronounces to Ogun that 'Your child has come before you with materials of offering for you, she is barren, she has no one to carry in her arms; Ogun grant that she may have children'. The priest then pours the palm wine and the kola nut; the dog is slaughtered with a sharp knife and the dripping blood is smeared around the whole of the shrine. Thereafter, parts of the dog are shared with those witnessing the events, including the worshipper. The priest thanks Ogun for accepting the sacrifice, while asking the worshipper to hold a hammer (stretched out), who now says 'The blessing rests upon me'. She becomes blessed, and a solution is found to the problem.

The attitudes of believers in traditional religions towards believers in other religions range from tolerance to open hostility or rejection, although they also believe that other people have a right to belong to other belief systems. There is a general complaint among traditionalists that the spiritual and cultural values or practices of traditional religions are being eroded by Christianity and Islam. However, there are indications that many Africans who may have embraced Christianity or Islam have not abandoned their traditional religious beliefs and practices (Child, 1968). Nevertheless, they tend to be secretive about their traditional religious beliefs and practices. Whereas they practise Christianity and Islam openly, they tend to be discreet when it comes to traditional religions. The major reason for secrecy in respect of traditional religious practices is that Islam and Christianity are generally not tolerant of other religious practices.

Christianity

Christianity is an ancient religion. It is a divine religion based on a revealed book called the Holy Bible. It is based on the principles of 'one eternal truth and one universal salvation'. Christianity has a population of more than two billion followers in the world today. Believers are known as Christians, although many would prefer to be identified with their type of denomination or church such as Roman Catholics, Protestants, Methodists, Anglicans, Baptists, Pentecostals and Seventh Day Adventists. Christians are found in most parts of the world.

Christianity is marked mainly by the doctrine of the Trinity of God, that is, the Father, the Son and the Holy Spirit. The key symbol of Christianity is Jesus Christ who, it is believed, was crucified on the cross to atone for the sins of all in the world. Christianity is rooted in the belief of universal love. It is practised in churches of various denominations, although there are also

several ecumenical or joint cooperative practices binding them.

In Africa, Christians live together with believers of other religions, although some churches attempt to evangelise and convert others to their own faith. Like Islam, Christianity subscribes to the view of the existence of the Day of Judgement or the hereafter and in salvation and the bliss of heaven (for those who have done good deeds), and in the torment of hell (for those whose deeds are judged to be bad or evil). There is also a belief in the mercy and forgiveness of God Almighty to all humankind. Generally, Christianity shares common moral and ethical values with Islam. Both reject what appears to them to be the pagan nature of African traditional religion. However, there are other ways through which Christianity differs from Islam, especially with regard to the concept of God and the place of Jesus. Sometimes, this creates some misunderstandings between the two religions.

Islam

Islam is a religion that originated through the agency of Prophet Muhammad in about the seventh century AD. More than one billion people around the world believe in this religion today. Believers are known as Muslims (or Moslems) and they are guided by a holy revealed book called the Qu'ran and the traditions of the holy prophet known as the *sunnah*. Islam is a complete way of life for all those who believe in it, but its message is universal to all humankind. Muslims are found in different parts of the world, especially in the Middle East, Asia and Africa. Islam is marked by the doctrine of One God known as Allah. Muslims also believe in the existence of other divine religions such as Christianity and Judaism. The five pillars of the religion include: (1) Acceptance and belief in One God and

His Messenger and Prophet, Muhammad, as the last messenger on earth; belief in other prophets, including Jesus, and in angels; in the Day of Judgment or the hereafter; and belief in predestination, good or bad. (2) Performance of obligatory prayers (or *salat*). (3) Performance of fasting during the month of Ramadan (or *sawm*). (4) Undertaking pilgrimage to the holy city of Mecca (or *hajj*) for those who are able. (5) Payment of the poor (or *zakkat*) due by those who have the means.

Another important mark of Muslims is the obligation to always commend the doing of good deeds (*malaruf*) and the prohibiting of bad conduct (*munkar*). Muslims worship in mosques or wherever possible and are required to offer five daily prayers, especially in congregation.

In many parts of Africa, Muslims live with believers of other religions who, in their view, are unbelievers. Some negative notions of *jihad* (struggle for the sake of God) and fundamentalist practices portray Muslims as violent. Also, due to conflicts between modern and some orthodox Islamic practices, the Western world tends to think that the religion is as backward as are some of its adherents. Although this point of view may not be correct, it influences how others see Muslims in the world today.

In Islam, as in Christianity, there is a belief in the existence of a blissful heaven (*aljannah*) or paradise for good doers and a tormenting hellfire for evildoers. However, Muslims also trust that God Almighty is forgiving and merciful to humankind regardless of their circumstances. Islam, like Christianity, rejects African traditional religion, particularly on account of its mode of worship, which is seen by Muslims as 'fetish or pagan'. Islam differs from Christianity in respect of the unity of God. God (Allah) is one (proclaims a prominent Qu'ranic verse). In contrast, orthodox Christianity

is built on the doctrine of the Trinity, and, whereas Islam accepts Jesus (Isah) as one of the most esteemed prophets of God, Christianity considers him the Son of God or God. The mode of worship also differs remarkably between the two religions. This is a contentious issue that sometimes creates misunderstanding and conflict between Muslims and Christians.

⌘ ACTIVITY

1 Identify any two Christian denominations and describe their key features.
2 Indicate two similarities and two differences between the two denominations.
3 Describe the act of worship in your religion/denomination and show how you could teach that to a group of fifteen adults who are visiting your community.

RACE, ETHNICITY, RELIGION AND ADULT EDUCATION

However viewed, adult education has definite links with race, ethnicity and religion. These links can be positive or negative depending on who is involved. For example, during the period of apartheid in South Africa, adult education was used by the state as a tool to show that there was nothing wrong with the system. In other words, the content of whatever was taught in state-sponsored adult education programmes tended to legitimise the existence of apartheid. At the same time, the African National Congress (ANC) used adult education as a weapon against apartheid, teaching people about the inhumanity of the system (Walters and Watters, 2000). However, on a global scale, the field of adult education as a discipline, practice or programme seems to have 'been silent on the issues of race and ethnicity' (Johnson-Bailey, 2001: 89). This may be due to the lack of adult education research into such important social issues and problems. Perhaps such research may help to explain why so little emphasis is placed on these issues in adult education programmes. The following section is an attempt to explain the important role that adult education can play in our understanding of the issues of race, ethnicity and religion in Africa.

Adult education and race

With respect to race, adult education can play the following roles:

- Adults can be taught about the origin and nature of the different races of the world, especially the black and white races whose co-existence has been plagued by so much controversy in recent history. This could be done in non-formal lessons, courses and programmes delivered in classroom settings or via informal education modes such as radio, television and other media.
- Adults can be taught about the commonality of humanity irrespective of race. All people are human beings and as such experience many similar challenges.
- People can be taught about the potential dangers of racial discrimination, giving examples cited in this chapter where racial and ethnic inequality and intolerance instigated hostility among various population groups.
- Adults can learn about strategies of racial harmony, understanding and co-existence by learning together, living together, working together and sharing common concerns and challenges, as exemplified by post-racial societies in Africa, especially those of Southern Africa. Harmony can be achieved by placing more emphasis on those aspects of diversity

that serve as a basis for unity.
- Adults can learn about multi-racial concepts, practices, issues, challenges and concerns in non-formal education programmes. This would help to build understanding, mutual trust and tolerance of one another among the various races and thus foster peaceful co-existence among them.

Adult education and ethnicity

As with race, adult education can relate to ethnicity in many positive ways. The content of adult education programmes can focus on the following essential aspects:

- Cultures and distinct identities of other ethnic groups, including their economic, social and political way of life.
- Religions and spiritual beliefs of other ethnic groups within or outside a society.
- Accepted behaviours and prohibitions of other ethnic groups.
- How people can relate, co-exist and cooperate with other ethnic groups.

CASE STUDY: ADULT EDUCATION AND CULTURAL DIVERSITY

Botswana is a multi-cultural society. More than twenty languages are spoken. About 80% of the population is dominated by Setswana speakers. Their hegemony was strengthened during the immediate post-colonial era through an ideology of national unity which regarded any assertion of cultural identity by other ethnic groups as divisive. This policy fostered the marginalisation of other ethnic groups in several areas of national life. The impact of this policy was felt in the education sector, where Setswana was imposed as the sole language of instruction. The National Literacy Programme was affected adversely by the policy, especially since other mother tongues were ignored. The Department of Non-formal Education had difficulty in attracting and keeping non-Setswana speakers, that is, speakers of minority languages in the programme. Although churches such as the Evangelical Lutheran Church of Botswana, the Botswana Christian Council and the Reformed Church made efforts to run literacy classes in the mother tongue, this did not change the situation drastically. However, in 1998, the Department of Adult Education at the University of Bostwana started a pilot and capacity-building 'Literacy in Minority Languages' project with the financial support of the UNESCO Institute for Education (UIE). The project is being implemented in partnership with two non-governmental organisations, the Kamanakao Association and the Society for the Promotion of Ikalanga Language. The project focuses on promoting adult literacy in the Shiyeyi and Ikalanga languages. In the long run, the project seeks to meet the adult literacy needs of marginalised ethno-linguistic groups and promote the use of adult literacy for the enhancement of positive cultural diversity in Botswana. In contrast, Nigeria, which is another multi-cultural society, has more than 300 diverse language groups. Although English is the official language of communication, the national language policy provides that educational activities be promoted through the additional use of three national languages, namely, Hausa, Yoruba and Igbo. However, for purposes of instruction in basic education programmes (including adult literacy), the policy provides that the mother tongue or 'the language of the immediate community' can be utilised. Therefore, the national adult literacy programmes of the colonial era and those of the period 1982–1992 and 1995–2000, which were supported by the UNDP, adopted a multi-lingual approach in order to enhance national unity and offer an opportunity for adult literacy education for minority groups.

Adult education and religion

To foster religious harmony and understanding among existing religions, adult education programmes in Africa should seek to teach adult learners about:

- The meaning of all the religions in Africa.
- Basic knowledge and rudiments of each religious practice.
- Basic norms and behaviours.
- Ways of living together amongst different believers, citing examples of intermarriages between or across religions which have become common practice in Africa.
- Ways to avoid, resolve or manage conflicts among different believers.
- Ways of inter-religious dialogues and discussions on common issues, problems and challenges of communal living.
- The freedom to worship or not.
- The advantages of diversity in religion.

In Africa, adult education providers will have to meet the additional challenge of the diversity of learners. Particular attention has to be paid to the unique needs of each group. In cases of mixed groups, a balance must be created in terms of what is taught to allow each group's interests and needs to be addressed as far as is practical, without compromising those of others. In Muslim societies where there are cultural restrictions with regard to the mixing of male and female persons, separate provisions should be made for each group. The Kano State Women's programme is a case in point. Here, at basic and post-literacy levels, classes are opened separately for males and females. In most cases, instructors of female classes are women, while those of male classes are male (Indabawa, 1991).

In Africa today, most of the modern laws (or constitutions) governing the lives of people are secular, meaning that a government does not consider or impose any religion as its own since the people belong to different religions. The importance of this is that people are at liberty to worship (or not to) as long as they do this in ways that do not impinge upon other people's choices.

⌗ ACTIVITY

Indicate two ways (six altogether) in which adult education relates to: (1) race, (2) ethnicity and (3) religion.
Discuss your answers with your colleagues.

SUMMARY

This chapter has explained the concepts of *race* and *racism*, *ethnicity* and *religion*. Race denotes division according to skin colour and other physical characteristics, while ethnicity arises from cultural differences between groups in society. Religion is a system of beliefs and practices that serve as a set of guidelines in respect of how a group of people relate to sacred things in their lives. The chapter also outlined the three major religions found in Africa, namely, African traditional religion, Christianity and Islam. Further, the chapter sketched out the role that adult education can play in mitigating the negative social consequences of race, ethnicity and religion. For example, adult education programmes can sensitise people to other races, other cultures and other religions, in order to minimise misunderstandings that could deepen into conflicts.

KEY POINTS

- Adult educators, like other social scientists, are more concerned with the social consequences of race, ethnicity and religion, than the differences between races, ethnic and religious groups.
- Adult educators need to know and understand the racial, ethnic and religious mixes of their communities so that they can recognise harmonising variables and potentially divisive issues and thus address them accordingly.

⌗ ACTIVITY

How can adult education be used to improve inter-racial, inter-ethnic and inter-religious understanding in your community? Illustrate your answer with examples.

FURTHER QUESTIONS

1 Why do you think there are more inter-ethnic conflicts than inter-racial and inter-religious conflicts in Africa?
2 What can be done to stop inter-ethnic conflicts in Africa? By whom?
3 Reflect on the racial, ethnic and religious composition of your community. What common factors are shared by these groups and how could these be used to improve relations among them? What are the potentially divisive issues among the various groups and how would you counter them?

SUGGESTED READING

Giddens, A. 2001. *Sociology*. Cambridge: Polity.

Chapter 5

Social class, gender and adult education

OVERVIEW

This chapter deals with the issues of social class and gender, and the possible roles of adult education in tackling problems associated with these issues, such as access. In a way, class and gender are similar in meaning since they both refer to differentiation among people in society. However, while class essentially deals with broader socio-economic distinctions, gender is mainly concerned with diversities between people that result from sexual and socio-cultural differentiations. Class and gender do mix in many ways. For example, women may face double oppression both as women and as poor people (Stromquist, 1986; Indabawa, 1994). This chapter focuses on the interface of the two concepts. It also offers suggestions on remedial measures for solving the problems that the interplay of gender and class may pose for people or society.

LEARNING OBJECTIVES

By the end of this chapter, you should be able to:

1 Explain the concepts of *social class* and *gender*.
2 Identify and describe some problems of access to adult education programmes that are class and gender related.
3 Suggest possible remedies to solve class and gender-related problems.

sesa woruban

KEY TERMS

class   A large group of people who are similar in terms of wealth, power and prestige.

EFA (Education For All)   A global initiative that commenced with a declaration to provide opportunities for basic education (including adult education) for all persons by the year 2000, adopted by more than 130 United Nations Member States at Jomtien, Thailand, March 1990. The Declaration was renewed in 2000 at a World Education Forum in Dakar. The new target is now set for 2015.

equity   Fairness, especially in terms of the way people living in different social groups in society are treated.

gender   The social differences and relations between men and women, based on learnt sexual roles.

gender bias   A display of discrimination in favour of or against males or females in society based on sexual role differentiation.

gender equity   The act of ensuring fairness in treating males and females in society, especially in terms of access to or benefit from opportunities, policies and programmes.

gender roles   Those roles that men and women are expected to play according to society's definitions of masculinity and femininity.

sex   The biological differences between men and women.

BEFORE YOU START

1   **What do your experiences of class and gender tell you about these concepts?**
2   **Do you think there are similarities between the two terms?**
3   **Do you think there are any differences between the two terms?**

SOCIAL CLASS

In your own community, people can be differentiated in many ways. They can be differentiated on the basis of wealth, power and prestige. The concept of *class* has been used to explain a form of stratification in which people are ranked into categories on the basis of their economic status. A class ordinarily means a group (Grandreams, 1996). Marx uses the term 'class' to refer to those who share a common position in relation to the means of production. Accordingly, Marx divided industrial societies into two classes, that is, the owners of the means of production and the workers. Similarly, Weber (1925) uses economic position (though somewhat differently) to define a class. He defines a class as a group of people who have similar amounts of wealth or income. However, unlike Marx, Weber does not perceive society as made up of two classes. Instead, he sees society as made up of an indefinite number of classes, each distinct from the other on the basis of their wealth. A definition of class which seems to incorporate key points from both Marx and Weber comes from Lenin, a very well-known disciple of Marx. Lenin defines class as large groups of people differing from each other by the place they occupy in the social system of production; by their relation to the means of production; their role in the social organisation; and the dimensions of the share of social wealth of which they dispose and the mode of acquiring it. They are groups of people, one of which can appropriate the labour of another, owing to the different places they occupy in the social economy (Lenin, cited in Ekwekwe, 1986*).*

From Lenin's definition of class, Ekwekwe (1986) concludes that there are four basic identities of class, namely, (1) the producer and non-producer or the exploiter and the exploited; (2) ownership and non-ownership of the means of production; (3) producer as labourer and producer of surplus value; and (4) wealth or income and how it is acquired. Two other basic identities of social class can be inferred from Lenin's definition, that is, (5) power and (6) prestige. Accordingly, we can define class as a large group of people who regard themselves or are regarded by others as similar in respect of wealth, power and prestige.

Although there are many classes, there are essentially two broad categories of classes in society, that is, the rich (owners of the means of production and distribution of wealth in society) and the poor (those that only take part in the production of wealth as labourers or workers). The two categories are also referred to as the bourgeoisie and the proletariat, respectively. Although there are variations, due to political and cultural factors, the bourgeoisie are similar across the world. Similarly, the proletariat possess similar characteristics irrespective of geographical location.

As shown in our discussion of capitalism in Chapter 2, relations between the two broad categories are supposed to be functional. This means that each class has its unique roles in the running of society. In contrast, in a socialist system, the relationship between the two is perceived to be that of continuous conflict. As explained in Chapter 2, Marxists expected that class conflicts would eventually lead to the victory of the working class over their exploiters. However, this has not happened, and the collapse of communism in the former USSR in the 1990s has significantly weakened this thesis.

Any discussion of social classes is incomplete without reference to the middle class, who are neither poor nor rich. Members of this class are differentiated by their social, educational or technical attainments. Whatever the number or the composition of social classes in society, adult education has a definite role with regard to improving their conditions either collectively or distinctly as groups. Adult education programmes can also be designed to play a mediating role between classes and thus minimise areas of conflict and disharmony.

⊞ ACTIVITY

Divide your community according to classes, and explain the basis of your classification.

GENDER

Whenever *gender* is mentioned, what usually comes to the minds of many are 'women and their issues'. Gender is much more than this. It refers to 'the social differences and relations between men and women, which are learnt, [and] vary widely among societies and cultures, and change over time' (UNESCO, 2003: 2).

From the above definition, it can be seen that the term gender cannot be substituted for the word sex. *Sex* refers to the biological differences between men and women. This difference is natural and can hardly be changed. Evidently, sex roles are different from gender roles. Sex roles refer to the different roles that men and women perform in reproduction and sexual activity. On the other hand, 'gender roles are those roles that men and women are expected to play according to society's definitions of masculinity and femininity' (Wallace and Wallace, 1985: 346). Whereas sex roles are prescribed, gender roles are acquired. In other words, sex roles are determined by biological differences, while gender roles are learnt. Clearly, as a concept, gender is used 'to analyse the roles, responsibilities, constraints of and needs of women and men in all areas and in any given social con-

text' (UNESCO, 2003: 2). Accordingly, policy makers and international organisations advocate concepts such as gender equality (equal treatment without regard to whether one is male or female); gender equity (fair treatment of individuals regarding their needs without regard to their sex); and gender mainstreaming (which refers to a strategy of catering for the concerns of men and women in policies and programmes).

Instead of sex differences, stereotypes or biases, a gender perspective emphasises the role and location of role players in a social context. For instance, women constitute about 50% of the population of the world and play very significant roles in the social and economic life of societies. For example, more than 70% of the work pertaining to food production, processing, fuel and water supply is done by women (Assimang, 1990).

Similarly, women bear the brunt of the six major family roles, that is, human reproduction (pregnancy is solely born by women); parenting (care and socialisation of children is often the responsibility of women); domestic production (food production, processing and preparation); intimacy (women display enduring and deep affection towards their kith and kin); kinship (caring for family dependants such as the handicapped, the sick, the infirm and the elderly is the responsibility of women because they are assumed to be compassionate); and community assistance (women tend to be more sympathetic to community affairs, hence community activities in which they dominate are often long lasting).

Although women are at the centre of human, social, economic, cultural and political development (Sadik, 1988), they are generally assigned a second-class status in most traditional societies, especially in Africa. Also, women suffer all forms of discriminatory disadvantages both on account of their sex and class (Assimang, 1990;

Imam, 1990; Opeke, 1991; and Indabawa, 1994). In addition, there are indications that 'women earn less than men globally, experience more unemployment, are two-thirds of the world's more than one billion adult non-literates and comprise (together with children) more than 80% of the world's refugees and displaced persons' (UNESCO, 2003: 28).

From the above account, it is clear that women suffer double oppression: as women and as the poor of society. Perhaps this explains why any discussion of gender is considered to be that of women's issues and problems. Whatever the case, adult education can serve as an instrument for mitigating women's disadvantaged social class status. For example, the acquisition of certain knowledge, skills and competencies or attitudes can serve as a source of empowerment for women.

However, if not properly managed, adult education can unwittingly serve to perpetuate women's marginalisation in society. In many situations, the type of education women receive is domesticating, in the sense that it only allows them to learn about what is considered to be good for women; the type of education that will make them good wives or mothers or both (Freire, 1972).

Yet, like their male counterparts, they are capable of learning all the modern skills that will give them opportunities for employment, and are capable of rising to higher levels of the social or political ladder in society (Indabawa, 1994).

⊞ ACTIVITY

List five main roles that women perform in your community and show how they differ from those of men.

SOCIAL CLASS AND ADULT EDUCATION

Three broad types of social levels emerged from our discussion of social classes, namely, the upper class, who are usually rich and who occupy the higher social ladder in society; the middle class, who are mainly educated or traditional elites and are identified with technical, managerial, bureaucratic or leadership skills; and the lower class or the poor, (also known as the masses, disadvantaged or socially excluded). Each of these classes has distinct needs and expectations. Members of these classes live in societies and are engaged in various forms of interactions that are not confined to their class level. Through the intra- and inter-class interactions, harmony or conflict may arise; this may not necessarily be because of antagonistic relationships, as Marxists would argue. Different social classes co-exist harmoniously in many different parts of Africa. Evidently, the relationships are not necessarily antagonistic all the time.

The three classes tend to have differential access to various educational programmes. The upper class tends to have greater access to all educational programmes at basic, upper and higher levels. This is essentially because they can afford the best education available both locally and abroad. They also appreciate the value and advantages of receiving the best education. In fact, educational attainments are some of the key factors that help them to excel in their occupational and social activities and in life generally.

The upper class and adult education

In terms of adult education, the upper class in Africa can be divided into two groups. Firstly, there is the highly educated group that generally needs two types of adult education, that is, the refresher type that will update and upgrade their skills as and when required; and the liberal type of educational experience that will help them optimise their leisure time. Most members of this group already have adequate basic educational experiences that provide them with skills and instrumental values. All they need are top-ups as demanded by their occupations and lifestyle. Secondly, there is the equally rich but poorly educated group. It is not uncommon in Africa to find rich people who have not had the benefit of modern higher education. In many parts of northern Nigeria, Niger, Ghana, Mali and Senegal, there are numerous rich merchants that have not attended any type of Western school. Similarly, in East Africa the *mafuta mingi* are wealthy but very poorly educated businessmen. Given the dynamic nature of modern life, these rich people are slowly realising the need for modern education as a tool for sustaining and expanding their business empires. It is also dawning on them that basic education will enable them to extend their hobbies and leisure to new heights. In Ghana and Nigeria, there are numerous cases of individualised lessons for the rich.

Broadly, the *mafuta mingi* may have very little need for adult educational programmes for themselves. Apart from leisure activities they are not likely to pursue occupational related educational programmes. However, they could become involved in occupational adult education in other ways. For example, they could send their workers for relevant refresher courses as an effort to increase the competitiveness of their businesses. Generally, their investment in adult education tends to be minimal, since the programmes they sponsor are usually on a small scale in both size and scope. To some extent, this applies to the upper class in general. Owners of industry (means of production) generally rely on pre-service

training, as the costs of re-training will only add to the overall cost of their goods and services and thus reduce their profit margins. Some upper class members may support community literacy programmes. This is an exception rather than the rule as most believe that it is actually the obligation of government to provide such educational programmes. However, where the rich are involved in commonweal organisations, they could make a greater contribution to adult educational programmes delivery. This is often done to take advantage of government tax incentives. Unfortunately, it is not easy to determine the overall quantitative and qualitative impacts of these types of interventions in adult education by the rich. What seems clear is that they often support adult education in so far as it furthers their business and class interests.

CASE STUDY: AGRICULTURAL EXTENSION EDUCATION IN BOTSWANA

Programmes separately called Co-operation Demonstration Plot Scheme and Pupil/Master Farmer Scheme were introduced in 1946 and 1962, respectively, during the colonial period. They were meant to consolidate the position of the rich peasants who owned substantial agricultural resources and employed labour. The schemes offered both the cognitive benefits of skills and knowledge, as well as the provision of material assistance through access to the means of production, credit and marketing facilities. In 1966, a total of 2 165 mainly rich farmers (and a small fraction of poor peasants) participated in the Pupil/Master Farmer Scheme. In 1973, the programmes were reviewed to make them more broadly based, reaching all farmers instead of a few. In spite of this development, the programmes still remained more beneficial to the rich peasants owing to the unequal distribution of agricultural resources. Therefore, it was reported that even when poor farmers participated in these farmer adult education programmes, they still lacked the necessary resources to put into practice most of what they had learnt. Therefore, while agricultural extension clearly brought material benefits to particular classes, other programmes more indirectly served to reproduce the class hierarchy, for example, the National Literacy Programme that commenced in 1980.

The middle class

Like the upper class, the middle class needs little adult educational experience. They may, from time to time, need continuing professional educational experience to help them improve their career status, upgrade their skills or increase their efficiency and professionalism. They may also need liberal types of adult education programmes to assist them to become more enlightened about social, economic or political issues and problems. Overall, their adult educational needs, though greater than those of the upper class, are not as much as those of the lower class.

The lower class

The lower class needs adult education programmes and experience for many reasons. Generally, a significant proportion is excluded for one reason or another from basic or initial education opportunities. They or their children constitute the majority of non-completers of primary education. They also miss opportunities for secondary and tertiary education on account of failure in the examinations or inability to pay the cost of such education.

Besides the prohibitive costs of education, many poor parents have to contend with what is known as the opportunity cost (the need to generate income within the time available). For these reasons, many poor parents, particularly in rural Africa, prefer to engage their children and themselves in farming and other agricultural and family income-generating activities rather than seek opportunities for modern education (Evans, 1994).

Clearly, the time and resources available may not be adequate for formal education, especially since the value of that education is not so obvious. For example, many products of African schools end up unemployed either because they have acquired minimal skills or because they have received irrelevant training that does not suit them for jobs in society (Akinpelu, 1987; Yahya, 1992; and Indabawa, 1993).

An additional burden of modern schooling in Africa is that the values transmitted (apart from being in conflict with local ones) usually generate non-conforming attitudes and personalities who neither fit modern cultural norms nor the traditional ones. These students remain a social burden to the community, from which they run to cities and urban centres in order to seek modern lifestyles for which they do not have the means, the skills nor the abilities (Imaogene, 1990). Consequently, many parents resist sending their children to school because the promise of employment does not always materialise. Many prefer to seek other opportunities because as an old African adage says, 'seeing from the example of others is enough deterrence to a wrong act'.

Clearly, because of the many problems generated for the lower class by formal schooling, their only option to attain modern education is via adult education. What type of adult education do the poor need? Can they take full advantage of programmes offered or are there constraints limiting their participation?

✕ ACTIVITY

1 Describe the socio-economic characteristics of two social classes that you can identify in your community.
2 List the types of schools and educational programmes they and their children attend.

THE ADULT EDUCATION ALTERNATIVE

Adult education programmes can be planned and delivered to meet the needs of people in different social classes. For example, the majority of people in the lower class category may need basic education or vocational education based on particular objectives, while most of those in higher classes may engage in adult education for compensatory reasons, that is, to meet a particular deficiency that may arise. Similarly, adult education programmes can respond to gender-related needs. For example, men may be more inclined to enrol in agricultural programmes that focus on animal husbandry, while women may need to enrol in those that focus on crop farming.

Adult education programmes can be delivered within the walls of formal schools or outside in other locations. A general principle applicable to all adult education programmes is the need for flexibility in terms of content and method or technique, in accordance with the needs of the specific clientele. Content describes what is taught (also known as subject matter), while method refers to the approach to teaching adults (that is, persons who are fifteen years

and older). The content has to be suited to the interests and expectations of the particular adult learners, be they middle class business executives or peasant farmers. Most of the time, programme planners or delivery agents miss the opportunity to provide suitable content for adult education programmes because of the approach they adopt in the planning of such programmes.

The dominant approach is to decide on behalf of the learners what is in their best interests. A related approach involves deciding that what is suitable for one group (for example, fathers) is suitable for another (for example, mothers). The problem with these approaches is that planners develop and design programmes without knowing exactly what the actual learners' needs are. Unless they consult directly with the learners, there is no way planners would figure out exactly what the learners need. Many curriculum planners argue that it is impossible to contact all learners. While this may be true of a large population of learners, it is possible to consult key representatives. Some form of consultation will always be better than none, because the learners are more likely to own the process and product of learning in which they are consulted. Consulting the learners is likely to make learning more enjoyable and in turn this will help to get the adult learners to stay on to complete the expected cycle of the programme (Indabawa, 2000).

The method or technique should also be made flexible and suitable to the autonomous nature of the adult learner. In particular, the facilitator must 'be warm, loving, caring and accepting of the learners; must have high regard for the learners' self-planning competencies and use them at all times; see himself/herself and the learners as participating in dialogue between equals; always be open to change and accept new experiences as well as seek to learn to improve for better results' (Brookfield, 1994: 63). As you have, undoubtedly, often heard, an important maxim for effective adult learning is: Do not treat adult learners as children for they will not stay on or enjoy the programme. Such behaviour is likely to lead to a waste of the scarce resources, time and effort used to put together adult education programmes. Coupled with the need to respect the adult learner, there is the need to fine-tune the techniques in accordance with the finer aspects of the particular clientele at hand. The finer techniques of a business management programme for business executives are different from the finer techniques of a similar programme for members of a rural based women's cooperative.

Clearly, adult education programmes, irrespective of the social class or the gender of the target clientele, will only succeed in attaining the set objectives if they are provided within the general principles of adult learning and, as such, are designed to respond directly to the clientele at hand. For the principles and more on adult learning, refer to *Foundations of Adult Education in Africa* (Nafukho, Amutabi and Otunga, 2005) in this series.

⊞ ACTIVITY

How would you go about consulting adult learners before deciding on the content of their programme?

RANGE OF PROGRAMMES

The range of programmes in adult education is large. However, two broad categorisations can be used to differentiate them. There are programmes that seek to offer equivalents of the types of programmes offered in formal education, namely, basic (primary, lower and upper), secondary and tertiary. The mode of delivery here tends to be classroom, regular face-to-face or distance and open learning. These programmes are often called adult primary (or adult basic education), adult secondary or adult tertiary. They normally share the same content with the equivalent formal education programmes and also face problems similar to those experienced in formal education.

The second category is that of adult non-formal education programmes. These are generally open in content, methods and techniques, with wide opportunities for learner participation at every stage. They seek to meet the immediate needs of the adult learners.

There is an ongoing debate about which programmes will suit the poor. The alternatives from providers often seek to meet their own organisational objectives. However, the preferred types (discussed in more detail in Chapter 6) include those that are empowering, awareness-raising, functional, meet needs and generate skills and income (Freire, 1972; Stromquist, 1986; and Indabawa, 1991).

Nevertheless, as with content, method and technique, the decision as to which programme will suit who should be left to the person or group. This does not prevent providers from guiding learners on what is best for their needs from among available programmes. For example, the poor may need programmes that will equip them with the skills and knowledge that will enable them to cope with their everyday challenges and thus deliver them from their present problems.

⊞ ACTIVITY

Which types of adult education programmes would you recommend for the poor in your community and why?

PROBLEMS OF ACCESS AND PARTICIPATION

Access and participation vary according to social class and gender. The general access pattern in Africa is that adult education opportunities are more accessible to the upper and middle classes than they are to the lower class. The simple explanation for this is that the majority of adult education opportunities are found in the cities and towns where most members of the upper and middle classes live. Conversely, such educational opportunities are scarce in the rural and remote areas where the majority of the poor live. Also, it has been generally found that the higher the level of initial education that a person has, the higher the likelihood that such a person will take advantage of available adult education opportunities. Conversely, the lower the initial level of education that a person has, the less the likelihood that such a person will enrol in adult education programmes. For the poor, the same reasons that adversely affected their participation in initial schooling, such as costs of programmes and lack of awareness of the importance of participating, apply here. Between men and women, the overall picture suggests that adult education opportunities are more accessible to men than to women. The simple reason for this is that the employment pattern in Africa still favours men. Therefore, more men than women live in towns and other commercial centres where most adult education opportunities are found. For women the opposite is true. More women than men live in rural areas where educational opportunities are fewer. For the same reasons, men are more likely to make use of adult education opportunities than women. However, a cautionary note is needed here. Men have more access than women to employment-based and employment-related educational oppor-

tunities. Accordingly, they are far more likely to participate in such programmes than women. Conversely, women are more likely to participate in personal, social and community-oriented programmes that do not necessarily lead to employment. Whereas men will make use of vocational and on-the-job training opportunities, women are likely to participate in literacy programmes to enlighten themselves. In fact, the African continent abounds with literacy programmes that are dominated by women (Lind and Johnston, 1990). Apart from the obvious reason that literacy programmes in Africa are more visible in the rural areas where most women live, and less visible in commercial centres where most men are, there is a very interesting anecdote that has been used to explain the absence of men in literacy classes. Most men in Africa (including those that are illiterate) describe themselves as literate. For such men, enrolling in literacy classes would be tantamount to blowing their cover; therefore they stay away.

There are many other factors that affect access to and participation in adult learning. They have been broadly classified as situational, institutional and dispositional. Below is an outline of some of these factors.

Situational factors
- Lack of money for tuition, books, and child care
- Lack of time
- Domestic responsibilities
- Job responsibilities
- Lack of child care
- Long distances to places of learning
- No study facilities at home or nearby
- Lack of support from relatives and friends

Institutional or programme factors
- No part-time programmes on offer
- Length of programme

- Inconvenient class schedule
- No information about programme offerings
- Strict attendance requirements
- Relevant courses not on offer
- Too many problems with getting enrolled
- No entry requirements
- Dead-end programmes

Dispositional factors
- Too old to go back to school
- Lack of confidence due to past experience
- Not enough drive to learn
- Do not enjoy studying
- Tired of school and classrooms
- Do not know what to learn or what it would lead to
- Do not want to appear too ambitious

Although these obstacles are not confined to a particular class or gender, they seem to affect the poor and women more than they affect anyone else. For example, by their nature, situational obstacles, such as lack of money to pay the necessary fees, lack of time, job responsibilities and home chores, lack of child minders, and lack of support from relatives discourage women and low-income people from participating in educational programmes.

Similarly, institutional barriers such as lack of information on what is on offer and lack of entry requirements mostly affect people with poor educational backgrounds, which in Africa generally means the poor and women. Dispositional factors such as lack of confidence and the reluctance to seem too ambitious are generated by poor educational backgrounds, suggesting that these apply more to women and the poor than to other groups. The situation with regard to women deserves special attention.

ACTIVITY

1 Identify ten poor people in your community and request each of them to indicate three adult education programmes they need.
2 Rank the programmes in descending order according to frequency.
3 Go to a community literacy class and ask ten learners to give you three important factors that are adversely affecting their participation in the programme. Compile the list and compare it with factors on the outline discussed. Do you find any similarities?

GENDER AND ADULT EDUCATION

The preceding section raises general issues and problems of access and participation that apply to both men and women in society. However, as suggested above, these issues seem to affect women more than they affect men. Therefore, in order to build gender balance in society, special attention should be focused on adult education programmes for women. Firstly, this is necessary because women, as a social group, face far more problems than their male counterparts. For example, while women constitute the greatest portion of adult illiterates in the world (especially in Asia and Africa), their overall participation in literacy programmes is lower than that of men (Sweetman, 1998).

Secondly, even though men and women participate in more or less the same type of literacy programmes, women's specific needs are hardly catered for. It is often wrongly assumed that women will be empowered through programmes designed for them, rather than programmes determined by them. In women's programmes, the so-called income-generating activities are limited by cultural choices. For example, women are generally taught skills that will make them better mothers, tailors or cooks.

As already pointed out, there are many constraints that inhibit specifically women's full participation. For example, certain situational obstacles such as lack of child minders, home chores and lack of support from relatives solely apply to women. Child care and other domestic chores take up all the time that women have. Women are generally discouraged by their parents and husbands from pursuing higher levels of education that would take them away from home. Even in the more strictly formal system of education, women are not encouraged to pursue careers in science, technology and mathematics education.

Although in some Muslim parts of Africa, women are provided with separate adult education programmes, these programmes usually lack adequate staff, facilities and instructional materials. The shortfall is largely due to the fact that these programmes are not considered priorities by the authorities concerned. Examples of the extent of the neglect of women's centres are shown by Indabawa (1994) in a study of women's education centres in Kano and some parts of Oyo state in Nigeria.

Based on the above, it appears necessary that women's adult education be prioritised and perhaps treated separately. Women should be involved in determining the content, form and delivery mode of their programmes. They should benefit from a package that will guarantee them quick recovery from the many problems they face in society. The content should reflect the reality of women's lives and be focused on knowing and doing (Chlebowska, 1992: 27-28). It should seek to

increase their output and earnings, provide for the welfare of their families and enable them to obtain credit more easily; [assist them to perform their] roles as wives and mothers while contributing as equal partners in social, [political] and economic efforts; and give priority to child concerns relating to health, nutrition, child's education; [offer] provisions for subjects bound up with the social and political roles of women and their civic rights.

In order to promote full participation, women's programmes should be free of any financial charges, particularly the initial phases of the programmes. Their husbands should be mobilised to support their involvement in educational activities. Where necessary, laws compelling husbands to offer assistance in this regard should be enacted, especially since democracy in Africa will benefit from this process, given that more women will qualify to contest elections and occupy positions of responsibility in society.

⌗ ACTIVITY

1 Explain how you would improve women's participation in adult education programmes in your community.
2 Suggest five special incentives that could be used to persuade husbands and families to support the education of their wives and daughters.

SUMMARY

This chapter has explained the concepts of social class and gender. Social class is the differentiation of people in society on the basis of wealth, power and prestige, while gender means the differences and relations between men and women that are socially acquired. There are three distinct social classes in society, namely, the upper, the middle and the lower classes. Each class has distinct characteristics that differentiate it from the others. Accordingly, each class has distinct learning needs that are different from those of the other two classes. This suggests that the content, methods and techniques of adult education must be adapted to the preferences of each group. Similarly, adult education programmes need to be sensitive to the needs of both men and women.

However, women deserve special attention in terms of the type of adult education programmes they need, given that they suffer several disadvantages that need to be compensated for or rectified so as to create the desired condition of equity in society.

KEY POINTS

- Social classes are not determined by gender, since both men and women belong to all three social classes.
- In planning and designing adult education programmes for a group of people (irrespective of their class or gender) deliberate steps should be taken to consult them, for they know best what their priority needs are.
- Women in Africa constitute the majority of the poor, therefore, some of the problems they face are due to their social class and the fact that they are women.
- Women constitute a special group that deserves special attention. They should be provided with special adult education programmes that will respond to their needs, and thus improve their performance in the many roles they perform as human beings, mothers, workers and members of the larger society.

ACTIVITY

1 Which social classes should constitute the major clientele for adult education programmes? Why?
2 Women suffer double oppression as women and as the poor of society. Do you agree with this assertion? Illustrate your answer with relevant examples.

FURTHER QUESTIONS

1 What are some of the parameters that you would use to determine the social classes in your community?
2 Who should take the responsibility to provide special adult education for women in the community and why?

SUGGESTED READINGS

Bown, L. and Okedara, J. T. (eds.). 1981. *An introduction to the study of adult education: A multi-disciplinary and cross-cultural approach for developing countries.* Ibadan: University Press Ltd.

Chleboswka, C. 1992. *Knowing and doing: Literacy for women.* Paris: UNESCO.

Indabawa, S. A., Oduaran, A. B., Afrik, T. and Walters, S. (eds.). 2000. *The state of adult and continuing education in Africa.* Windhoek: Department of Adult and Nonformal Education, University of Namibia.

Indabawa, S. A. 2000. *Teaching methods and techniques I, II and III.* Windhoek: Centre for External Studies, University of Namibia.

Oduaran, A. B. 1996. *The essentials of adult learning.* Ibadan: Ibadan University Press.

Youngman, F. 2000. *The political economy of adult education and development.* London: Zed Books.

Chapter 6

Adult education and empowerment

OVERVIEW

To empower is simply to enable someone to perform a task, achieve a goal, or meet a particular need at a personal or social level. Disempowered people are not able to do these things due to personal, social or systemic problems or deficiencies. For example, a poor rural woman may be unable to meet the basic needs of her family and pay the medical or education fees of her children because she does not have the money or the means to do so. Lacking the money or the means may be due to many different reasons. Perhaps she has had no education from which to acquire employable skills or competencies. Or, she has no income, land or property from which to gain some surplus so that she can meet her children's health, education or basic needs. Furthermore, if the children do not have basic health or education and their basic needs are not met, it is likely that they may grow up to become similarly disadvantaged. How can adult education enable people like these to achieve and so break the cycle of poverty

and disempowerment in their lives? And what type of adult education will be most suitable to help the particular individual in this regard? These are the issues that will be discussed in this chapter.

LEARNING OBJECTIVES

By the end of this chapter, you should be able to:

1 Define empowerment in simple and broad terms.
2 Indicate the empowering potential of specific adult education programmes and activities.
3 Explain the factors that may adversely affect the process of empowerment through adult education programmes and activities.

bese saka

KEY TERMS

distance education   A system or mode
of education in which the learner is
separated by time and/or location from
the more typical face-to-face learning
environment. Instruction normally
takes place through open modes such as
printed course materials, radio or television programmes, video conferencing
and the Internet.

empowerment   The ability people have
to take effective control of their lives
in terms of being well-informed and
equipped with regard to education,
finance and relevant skills that will
enable them to make the choices they
want, follow the careers they desire and
achieve the goals they set for themselves.

⌗ BEFORE YOU START

Identify five different groups of people in
your community who need empowerment.
State the reasons for your choices.

THE MEANING OF EMPOWERMENT

Generally, empowerment is considered to be a person's ability to 'take effective control of one's life in terms of being well informed and equipped with education, finance and relevant skills to take decisions without any external influence' (Johns Hopkins University, 2002: 13). In this sense, empowerment has four basic elements, namely, control of one's life; access to information and education; access to finance; and access to skills for decision-making related to one's situation. Collectively, these elements can enable a person to become empowered. In other words, empowerment enables people to make the choices they want, follow the careers they desire and achieve the goals they set for themselves.

Empowerment connotes people's demands to be recognised, consulted and valued. In a narrow sense, empowerment describes a wide range of efforts aimed at enhancing the power of individuals, groups, and organisations in society. Fundamentally, empowerment is the process of changing the balance of power in favour of those who were kept out of the mainstream of economic, social and cultural activities as a consequence of deliberate policies such as colonialism and apartheid. Empowerment is the process of enhancing feelings of self-efficacy in communities through identification and removal of conditions that reinforce powerlessness. In this regard, empowerment involves the four ever-changing processes of seeking access to economic or public resources; awareness-raising with regard to rights, especially across gender lines; equity and fairness in terms of access to public resources and their management; and action in order to effect changes or to modify the situations, circumstances and social relations in which people find themselves (Stromquist, 1988).

In Chapter 5, it was pointed out that traditionally women are among the most disempowered groups. Therefore, efforts aimed at empowering people normally involve or target women and other disadvantaged people like street children, the elderly, the orphaned, the handicapped, the rural and urban poor, minority ethnic groups, refugees, victims of epidemic diseases such as malaria and HIV/AIDS, and non-literate adults. This is necessary in order to create a more just world in which the needs of diverse groups are attended to. Of particular importance is the empowerment of women because they are considered to be at the centre of sustainable development. (Stromquist, 1988). According to Bhasin (1992: 19-20), women's empowerment means among other things 'the recognition of their contribution and knowledge, helping (their) self-respect and dignity, enabling them to become more economically independent and self-reliant, reducing their burden of work, especially at home and promoting their qualities of nurturing, caring and gentleness'.

⊞ ACTIVITY

Name the four ever-changing processes involved in the empowering of people.

EMPOWERMENT THROUGH ADULT EDUCATION

In generic terms, adult education refers to all education that takes place outside the formal constraints of formal schooling. It is for people who are biologically (at least fifteen years of age) and socially (can take responsibilities in the family or the community) recognised as adults. Such people may have missed the opportunity for initial education while they were young and, for this reason, need some form of compensation. They may need to extend their knowledge or learn a trade, a recreational or a leisure-time activity, or just acquire more knowledge for its own sake (Omolewa, 1981; Okedara, 1983; and Lindeman, 1989).

Given this description, and the large scale of people who are excluded or pushed out of the mainstream of formal education, adult education can no longer be only for people who are adults in absolute terms. It is also for the young, the unserved or under-served adolescents as well as the unreached children who live on the streets of African cities and townships. This new perspective has become current since the World Declaration on Education For All (EFA) taken at Jomtien, Thailand in March 1990, and renewed at the Dakar World Education Forum of April 2000. Adult education is meant to meet the basic learning needs of all in a lifelong form, promoting learning to know, learning to do, learning to live and learning to be, as well as living to learn (Delors, 1998; Youngman, 1998; Muller, 2000; and Oduaran, 2002).

Therefore, in the process of empowering people, adult education is a viable instrument that can be used at all times and in all places. In fact, there is a growing worldwide consensus that 'literacy and adult education are a means for people to overcome poverty and exclusion, establish and reinforce democracy, achieve justice and comprehensive peace, enhance economic and social well-being and improve health and ensure food security. Adult education helps to prevent and eliminate gender and racial disparity, and other social problems such as violence against women, drug addiction, environmental destruction and HIV/AIDS' (ICAE, 2000: 10).

In short, adult education is a tool for enhancing people's empowerment with the guarantee of helping to create the necessary conditions and opportunities for sustainable human development. This is especially relevant in Africa where inequities hinder optimum progress. What type of adult education will suit the diverse groups of people needing empowerment in Africa?

Types of adult education

There are as many types of adult education programmes and activities as there are varieties of clientele needing them for various purposes. The type of adult education programme that any one person or group will need is best determined by them. However, people may be assisted to ensure that they make the right choice. Usually, experts and providers of adult education programmes are best suited to assist those who need adult education programmes.

The providers of adult education programmes vary widely. In Africa, government or its agencies (sometimes identified as the state) is a major provider of adult education programmes. The range of deliverable and active adult education programmes (Omolewa, 1981; Okedara, 1983; Oduaran, 1991; and Indabawa, 1991) includes:

- literacy, at basic and post-literacy levels
- remedial
- income-generating/vocational
- continuing
- extra-mural/coaching
- leisure
- liberal
- agricultural extension
- distance/correspondence
- workers/labour education
- higher/tertiary

Each of these is briefly outlined here.

Basic literacy education

Basic literacy education is a programme meant to provide an opportunity for the acquisition of the skills of reading, writing and numeration at basic levels, in a particular language, local or foreign. Basic literacy is delivered within six to nine months and completers are expected to learn the equivalent of what children will learn in lower primary classes or Standard 1 to 3. The three prevailing forms in Africa are identified as follows:

Traditional
Seeks to teach the so-called 3Rs (reading, writing and numeracy) using the recall and rote memorisation method of formal primary school, without clearly defined objectives. In this type of programme there are major problems which include that the methods and content of learning tend to be similar to those of formal primary schooling. This creates a serious difficulty since the approaches to the teaching of children and adults differ markedly (Knowles, 1980; Indabawa, 2000). Another major problem is that of inadequate allocation of funds, especially by government or its agencies (Afrik, 2000). Yet another problem is the purpose or goal that basic traditional literacy seeks to achieve, that is, to retain and reinforce the status quo (Filson, 1991; and Youngman, 2000). This is a problem because the desire of many adult learners is to seek to change their external and often oppressive conditions of underdevelopment (Freire, 1972; Indabawa, 1991).

Functional
This is based on teaching occupational groups through their everyday economic activity. For example, farmers, fishermen, hunters, traders etc. are taught through their occupation to read and write as well as to improve their trades and occupations.

This was introduced as an Experimental World Literacy Programme by UNESCO in collaboration with the UNDP between 1967 and 1973. Its target was to reach one million adults, 'but only 120 000 actually attained literacy' (Agun, 1980: 20). One of the major factors given to explain the failure of that experiment is the high cost of planning and implementation, although the potential benefits of the experiment in terms of providing job-related skills, innovations and competencies to learners were not in any doubt.

Consciousness/awareness-raising
This is the form that the Brazilian adult educator, Paulo Freire, popularised through his works and practices (Indabawa, 1991). It seeks to build literacy skills by raising the consciousness of the learners about the dehumanising conditions of life imposed on them by their oppressors in society. This form has been tried in many parts of Africa, including Guinea Bissau, Ghana and Burkina Faso (Indabawa, 1993). Although it promises good results, not many countries are interested in experimenting with it, due largely to its strong political implications. Evidence exists to confirm that non-radical governments and regimes exploit the prevailing state of widespread adult illiteracy among the people to keep them unaware of bad governance and other problems in society.

Empowerment potential
Together these three forms of literacy have the potential to provide literacy and numeracy skills, information, communication, awareness and change in behaviour and attitudes.

Post-literacy education

This programme runs for one to two years and draws participants from among those persons who have become successfully literate after participating in basic literacy programmes. Here, learners are introduced to subjects that are equivalent to those acquired in upper primary school, that is, Standards 4 to 6 or 7. Usually, only about 10–20% of learners from the lower level move to this level in most developing countries, especially in Africa (Indabawa, 1991; and Mpofu, 1995). This low rate of transition is partly due to the low rate of completers of programmes and the usually small size of such programmes. At this stage, learners in many parts of Africa are also introduced to second languages, including English, French and Arabic. Apart from the low participation rate, post-literacy programmes are also faced with lack of sufficient funding and other material support.

Empowerment potential
Knowledge of subject matter and opportunity for advancement of educational career.

Remedial education

Remedial education is given to persons who have partially completed or dropped out of a course of education at primary or post-primary levels. Learners are enrolled to offer them an opportunity to remediate their initial deficiencies. Remedial programmes last for one to two years. This is popular especially in Southern and West African countries. It allows secondary school leavers who have not achieved the requirements for entry into tertiary education programmes to improve their grades and in this way secure the credits needed. In some cases, the existence of remedial programmes has tended to undermine commitment to learning for many secondary school students who know that they have the option to go to a second-chance institution. This problem was faced in Namibia, where it was found that numerous learners were keen to join the Namibian College of Open Leaning (NAMCOL), a remedial distance education institute, after failing in secondary school (Indabawa et al., 2000).

Empowerment potential
An improved chance of participating in further education or of securing employment.

Income-generating/vocational education

This is a type that pays attention to the provision of vocational skills in order to help learners gain opportunities to earn basic or additional income. It is popular in Nigeria, especially with women who are attending basic literacy programmes in the Women Centres managed by the thirty-six State Agencies for Mass Education and coordinated by the National Commission for Mass Literacy, Adult and Non-formal Education. It runs for six to nine months and is usually delivered through the mother tongue. One of its problems is that the vocational skills taught are generally gender-biased and stereotyped. Some of these skills are cooking, sewing, knitting, and embroidery. Newer and more marketable skills such as basic computing, which can be delivered in women's post-literacy classes, are not currently being offered. Another problem is that most of the time-adequate facilities for effective operation are lacking, and consequently, only a select number of women in urban centres are catered for.

Empowerment potential
Generation of employable skills, better income and higher standards of living.

Continuing education

Private providers mainly offer this form of adult education programme to people in professional occupations seeking information, knowledge, skills and techniques relating to their professions. Notable providers include the Central African Correspondence College (CACC), International Correspondence School (ICS), etc. Participants pay fees and obtain various qualifications that will help them gain promotion at work. Some of the problems of continuing education programmes in Africa are a lack of defined standards or uniformity and proper coordination.

Empowerment potential
Better performance of tasks and the possibility of greater efficiency and promotion at work.

Extra-mural/coaching education

This type normally offers coaching for those who are preparing to sit for external public examinations. It is widely patronised in Africa because passing external examinations through residential secondary programmes has tended to be problematic. Providers are both private and public institutions. In Nigeria, Ghana, Sierra Leone and The Gambia, university departments of extra-mural studies play major roles in providing this educational service. One of the problems of this form of adult education service is the high cost. It also encourages rote learning and orientation towards passing examinations rather than the acquisition of important life skills and competencies.

Empowerment potential
Better chance of passing examinations and joining the further education and employment ranks.

Leisure education

This is a trade mode of adult education that is not widely practised in Africa because it

is considered a luxury. Through it, learners acquire skills for using non-work time fully and productively. Learners learn games such as horse-riding, racing and various athletic activities, usually on the field.

Empowerment potential
Efficient use of time and the possibility of social interaction with others.

Liberal education

Here, learning is meant to allow the acquisition of the modern skills of debate on political, social, economic or cultural issues, as well as writing skills that can be used in popular news media for the defence of the rights of the oppressed and minorities. This type also involves learning about and assisting security agencies in civil defence work; supporting the elderly; and caring for children and people in need. Providers are usually private and voluntary parties seeking to improve the level of the civilised mode of the community.

Empowerment potential
Enlightenment on human rights issues and readiness to protect the rights and duties of citizenship.

Agricultural extension education

This is a support type of adult education activity meant to assist people engaged in farming and other agricultural work who can benefit from new ideas, information, innovations, techniques and equipment. Learners are taught application skills in order to improve current practice. Generally, providers are government agencies located under ministries of agriculture, rural development or education. Some civil society groups such as farmers' associations may also be providers, usually in collaboration with a relevant government department.

Some of the difficulties of this type of adult education work include the inadequacy of facilities and extension agents, and the lack in the visible impact of the intervention in terms of farmers' productivity or efficiency.

Empowerment potential
Improved productivity, prospects of higher income and a better standard of living.

Distance/correspondence education

This is more a mode of delivery than a programme of adult education. It is a system through which learners register for and pursue different types of educational programmes, particularly higher education, through the distance mode. Higher or tertiary education can be delivered through the face-to-face or regular mode, or through the distance mode. Distance education was previously known as correspondence education, in which learners interacted with their tutors via the post. In order to widen access to education, this mode has become widespread. Besides the University of South Africa (UNISA), the mother of distance education in Africa, there are now many other distance education universities in Africa, notable of which are the Open University of Tanzania, the Zimbabwe Open University and the recently inaugurated Open University of Nigeria. In addition, almost all conventional universities in Africa now have a distance education unit on the side through which they offer some of their programmes. Notable examples of such units include the Centre for Continuing Education at the University of Botswana; the Centre for External Studies at the University of Namibia; the Institute of Distance Education at the University of Swaziland; the Institute of Extra-Mural Studies at the National University of Lesotho; and the relatively new Centre for Continuing Education at the National

University of Science and Technology in Zimbabwe. Many people who would otherwise not be able to enrol in regular tertiary education programmes do so through these institutions. Learners are enrolled in these programmes and they follow instruction through open modes of delivery via receipt of printed course materials and through radio or television programmes. In addition, learners converge (usually two times a year) on a vacation school that runs for several (normally two) weeks to allow for face-to-face contact between lecturers and students (Mpofu, 2004). Learners also gather once or twice a year to sit for prescribed examinations. At the end of the programme, learners acquire certificates, diplomas and degrees equivalent in status to those of the regular students. These adult education programmes are characterised by flexibility in their mode of delivery and perhaps in respect of the students who enrol in them. Normally, the clientele for distance education programmes are working adults who are unable to register and follow residential higher education programmes.

Empowerment potential
Opportunity for access to higher education and training, and prospects for better employment and income.

Worker/labour education

This type of adult education takes place within the workplace or outside it, but is essentially for workers. The focus is on union, labour and industrial relations matters. Workers are given skills of negotiation and engagement with their employers. They are also given instruction about society, politics, social relations and the economy, and the place of workers in relation to these. Providers are either owners of industry or workers' organisations. In some cases, for example in Kano, Nigeria, during the time of the Peoples Redemption Party's (PRP) government (1979–1983), the government provided a workers' literacy programme in all state and industrial establishments. The goal was to help eradicate adult illiteracy among workers (Indabwa, 1988).

Empowerment potential
Improved skills of negotiation, organisation and a better place in society for workers.

Higher/tertiary adult education

This type of adult education work is done at the level of post-secondary education institutions, colleges and universities across Africa and outside. Some refer to it as university adult education. It is done through departments known variously as adult education, continuing education, non-formal education or extra-mural studies. Learners who pursue training at this level acquire various professional qualifications in adult education, ranging from certificates through to doctorate degrees. The academic departments that offer these programmes are also engaged in research work, producing reports and books that seek to extend the knowledge base in adult education and at the same time improve practice in the field. The academic staff of these departments is also involved in various community service support activities, collaborating with governmental and non-governmental organisations.

Although these units are growing in number, there is a need for more and more, especially in French-speaking parts of Africa, where reports indicate that there are relatively few (Afrik, 2000), essentially because extension and extra-mural programmes are features of the English education system. There is also the need to provide them with adequate funds, facilities and equipment for them to continue to work more effectively.

Empowerment potential
Opportunity for advanced training and development, and prospects for better employment and income.

☒ ACTIVITY

1   Describe two adult education programmes operating in your community and show three specific ways in which learners will acquire empowerment skills through any of them.
2   Suggest solutions to some of the problems of basic and post-literacy education programmes in your country.
3   Adult education cannot empower everyone. Do you agree? State reasons for your answer.

ADULT EDUCATION FOR DISADVANTAGED GROUPS

Now that adult education programmes have been identified and described, which of them are most capable of empowering people? To a degree, all adult education programmes have the potential for empowering those who seek and use them to overcome their powerlessness. However, the choice of which one is most suitable remains the main task of those who need to be empowered. As already indicated, most programme providers think that their programmes are in the best interests of those targeted for them, often without consultation with the particular adult learner concerned. Adult learners are in fact the best judges with regard to which adult education programmes are best suited to their needs. Nevertheless, specific suggestions may be made about the features of empowering adult education for dis-empowered groups, for instance, women.

Adult education programmes for women must seek to meet the following conditions (Bhasin, 1992; Stromquist, 1988):

- Offer opportunities for joyful learning that releases women's creativity and make them feel energetic.
- Provide opportunities for them to clarify their vision of sustainable development and a society of hope and common goals.
- Seek to assist women to acquire new skills of justice, equality, honesty, truthfulness and solidarity.
- Affirm and increase women's self-confidence and respect.
- Help women develop analytical and questioning minds and a scientific understanding of realities around them.
- Provide the chance for women to be able to challenge oppression and domination.
- Employ participatory methodologies.
- Enable women to discover knowledge for themselves, knowledge that will enable them to enter the market economy in more advantageous conditions than before.
- Give women skills and knowledge capable of emancipating them from unequal labour and social relations.
- Offer knowledge and skills components that will enrich their reproductive, productive and emancipatory capabilities.

Given the above criteria, it is possible to argue that any adult education programme or activity may empower or disempower, depending on the goals that are built into it. While some programmes may be meant to reinforce existing conditions of inequity (that is, unfairness), others may be meant to rectify these. However, checking inequity through educational programmes is not generally an easy task since historically, the system of education (including adult education) in Africa is part of the colonial and neo-colonial experiences. The agents and facilitators of the system will resist any changes designed to make the system more responsive to local needs and aspirations.

The policy makers in post-colonial African nations may be ignorant of the need for change of the education system. Some of them may be indifferent to it since they are its products. Another obstacle to the possibility of changing the system is that resources may be insufficient to develop programmes and implement them effectively. Also, public attitudes to efforts directed at the transformation of adult education may be indifferent or negative due to ignorance or lack of sufficient mobilisation on the issue.

Disadvantaged groups of people such as the poor, women, and the disabled may be even more difficult to mobilise and involve in the process of change. Nevertheless, the task is not impossible, and unless the education system is reformed in its goals, form, content and method, it will be difficult to use adult education as a tool for the empowerment of the powerless in African societies.

Whatever steps are taken to offer adult education programmes for the empowerment of the people, those who are directly affected, namely, the disadvantaged groups, need to be fully involved. In addition, there is need for collaboration and coordination among the various role players such as government agencies, civil society, non-governmental organisations, community leaders and organised youth and adult groups.

⊞ ACTIVITY

1 **What three key questions would you ask a potential participant in an empowering adult education programme?**
2 **Indicate how answers to such questions would assist you to plan suitable**

programmes for disadvantaged women farmers in the community.

ISSUES AND PROBLEMS IN EMPOWERMENT

In providing and implementing adult education programmes for empowerment, numerous issues and problems will arise that may challenge these efforts. Everyone involved in such efforts should expect challenges of one kind or another. Outlined below are potential problem areas to any effort of empowerment involving adult education in Africa. The list is not exhaustive. Also, there is no formula for dealing with these challenges. However, an appreciation of possible challenges on the part of adult educators will go a long way in sensitising them for the formidable task of empowerment via adult education.

Consensus on the conception of empowerment, its processes and objectives

Conceptions of empowerment and how it can be achieved will be as many as the people who claim to be engaged in empowerment activities. There is a need for a common workable definition of empowerment among all concerned to help guide programmes and activities. Similarly, efforts should be made to ensure that there is some uniformity in respect of the processes and methods of empowerment programmes, so that they do not cancel out one another.

Methods and techniques for instructional delivery

Utilising oppressive instructional techniques that are inconsistent with empowerment may compromise the process of empowerment. All instructors need to adopt instructional techniques that seek to transform the learners from dependent to independent personalities. *The Psychology of Adult Learning* (Fasokun, Katahoire and Oduaran, 2005) in this series provides more details on the importance of using instructional techniques that are congruent with the self-concept of the adult learner.

Language of instruction

The continent of Africa is second to none with regard to the multitude of languages in use. Without any doubt, the mother tongue is preferable at the basic levels. A transition to second languages, such as French and English, Arabic or German, can be done at post-literacy and higher levels (Ouane, 1989, 2003; and Obanya, 2003).

Funding

Funding for programme planning, delivery, monitoring and evaluation is generally inadequate. Adult education and training are generally appendages in organisations whose mainstream activities do not involve providing adult education programmes. In such organisations, annual allocations for adult education and training programmes range from 1–10% of the annual budgets (Mpofu and Amin, 2004). There is a need for the provision of adequate funding for education in general, and for adult education in particular.

Development of materials needed for pedagogical processes

This is a perennial issue for adult education provision in Africa. It is difficult to develop and produce relevant materials for formal education, let alone non-formal education – the Cinderella of education. Nevertheless, current efforts to develop appropriate learners' and instructors' materials for adult education should be sustained and expanded to include materials with a strong empowerment slant.

Role of the media in mobilisation and delivery of programmes

Where it is available, the media should be used for mobilisation so as to generate awareness and support for programmes, as well as to encourage learners to enrol in them. It is also possible (in some parts of Africa) to use the media (print, electronic, radio and television) for the delivery of lessons to learners in various parts of the communities.

Commitment to change

A programme that offers genuine opportunities for empowerment to its clientele is not likely to receive the blessing of everyone in the community. As Julius Nyerere once said 'Politicians … do not always welcome real (empowering) adult education' (1982: 41). It is, therefore, not uncommon for community leaders and other significant groups in the community to strongly oppose a programme that seems perfectly suited to the needs of its clientele. It is imperative for planners of empowerment programmes to get all interested parties (including the target clientele) on board in the early stages to avoid opposition or passive resistance at the implementation stage, when resources have already been expended and committed.

Flexibility

As adult educators we tend to fall in love with our own methods. Just because one group seems to favour a particular method does not give the tutor the right to expect subsequent groups to do likewise. Facilitators should be willing to change with the

tide. Through refresher courses, facilitators should learn about varieties of methods, techniques and approaches and apply them as appropriate.

Place of learning

The norm in adult education classes in Africa is that basic facilities, infrastructure and equipment are not up to standard. Sometimes there is very little that facilitators can do about this. However, facilitators should learn to improvise in order to complement existing support services. A little imagination can transform a somewhat unfriendly environment into a very pleasant learning environment. Besides, the learning atmosphere is the sole responsibility of the tutor. Notwithstanding the lack of sophisticated facilities and equipment, the teacher should strive to create a very friendly atmosphere that is conducive to learning.

Timing of learning

The scheduling of classes can play a very big role in a person's decision to participate or not. There are two issues involved here.

Firstly, certain times of the year may be inconvenient for many in some communities due to the need to work in the fields or to undertake some other important seasonal task.

Secondly, certain times of day may be inconvenient for some. In most communities in Africa, women are not expected to be walking around at night, as it may be dangerous to do so.

In each case, suitable times must be found for programme delivery, otherwise learners will fail to take full advantage of the programmes on offer. It will be helpful to consult the learners or their representatives in deciding on suitable times and timetables. The learners' convenience has to be given due regard.

Assessment

This is a very delicate issue. The wrong form of assessment can easily derail a good empowerment programme and lead to exactly the opposite of what was intended. Although the final outcome is important for adult learners, it is the criteria used to arrive there that may be inappropriate. Tests and examinations are known to threaten adult learners, and where they cannot be avoided, should constitute a very small portion of assessment.

As far as possible, assessment should be solely based on continuous activities that do not pose a threat to the fragile egos of disenfranchised people – the target of most empowerment programmes.

Costs

The target clientele for empowerment programmes consists of people who are normally unable to pay for the programmes that are meant to uplift them. Therefore, efforts must be made to ensure that financial costs for participants in these programmes are minimal.

Retention of skills

If the programme at hand is a direct response to the learning needs of the participants (which should be the case most if not all the time), the retention of the acquired skills and competencies is guaranteed as participants will certainly apply them in their everyday activities. Where the acquired skills do not quite fit into everyday activities, efforts must be made to create opportunities for the practise of such skills so that they become part of everyday life (Mpofu, 1997). For example, participants could be assisted to start income-generating activities that will require them to use the newly acquired skills. This will ensure that

the skills and competencies acquired by the learners become part of their everyday life.

⌗ ACTIVITY

Identify any other three issues or problems that can threaten the process of empowerment and indicate what you would do to counter them.

SUMMARY

This chapter has examined the process of empowerment through adult education programmes. The range of adult education programmes that can be used for empowerment include literacy and remedial education, income-generating and vocational programmes, continuing education, extra-mural/coaching, leisure education, liberal education, agricultural extension, distance education, worker/labour education, and higher education. Empowerment programmes in adult education have to contend with many issues, namely, choosing the language of instruction in a multilingual community, inadequate funding, lack of relevant resource materials, and lack of commitment to change. An appreciation of possible challenges will enable adult educators to appreciate the many rivers that need to be crossed in the course of empowerment.

KEY POINTS

- Empowerment is the process of changing the balance of power in favour of those who were previously disadvantaged in all respects.
- Traditionally women are among the most disadvantaged groups in society.
- If properly handled, adult education can

be a very effective tool for the empowerment of the disenfranchised in society.

⬚ ACTIVITY

Adult education is not a panacea for
empowerment. Do you agree? Explain your
answer.

FURTHER QUESTIONS

1 What do you consider to be the three
   major objectives of empowering adult
   education programmes in the community?
2 Who should take the initiative in the
   provision of empowering adult education? Why?

SUGGESTED READINGS

Bown, L. and Okedara, J. T. (eds.). 1981.
    *An introduction to the study of adult
    education: A multi-disciplinary and cross-
    cultural approach for developing countries.*
    Ibadan: University Press Ltd.
Bhasin, K. 1992 'Education for women's
    empowerment: Some reflections.' In
    Adult Education and Development, No. 39,
    pp. 11–24.
Omolewa, M. A. 1981. *Adult education prac-
    tice in Nigeria.* Ibadan: Evans Brothers
    Ltd.
Stromquist, N. P. 1988. 'Women's educa-
    tion in development: From welfare to
    empowerment.' In *Convergence*, Vol. 21,
    No. 4, pp. 5–16.

Chapter 7

Democracy and adult education

OVERVIEW

Democracy is a topical issue of discussion in the world and especially in developing countries. Democratic governance has been on the rise since 1950. According to UNESCO (2000: 32) 'there were 22 democratic nations in the world in 1950. The number increased to 119 in 2000, with 58 per cent of the world population residing in them'. However, liberal or plural democracy as practised in western European nations and the United States of America has not been fully institutionalised or practised in Africa. After gaining independence from colonial rule in the 1960s, most African nations tried to imitate the political systems of their colonising nations. These ranged from the British Parliamentary (Westminster) type, with a Prime Minister, to the Presidential system, with an Executive President as practised in France and the USA. However, due to the many problems associated with building new nations, many African countries have also experienced military rule and dictatorships. Military rule and dictatorships have been fraught with socio-economic problems and human rights abuses. In comparison, modern democracy seems to promise good governance and prosperity. Accordingly, more and more Africans have been agitating for democratic rule. Today, most African countries operate modern democracies with regular elections in which they elect their leaders and representatives. This chapter focuses on this important topic and the possible role of adult education in a democratic society.

LEARNING OBJECTIVES

By the end of this chapter, you should be able to:

1 Define democracy.
2 Describe the essential elements of democracy.
3 Identify and explain ways in which adult education can help to foster democratic practice.

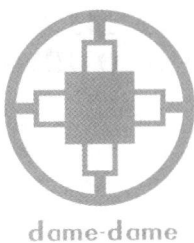

dame-dame

KEY TERMS

civil society organisations   Groups that
mediate between public and private
interests and try to influence government for the improvement of the life of
a nation.

democracy   A modern system of rule
or governance in which every eligible
member of the community has the right
to participate.

election   Periodic choice through a ballot
system whereby the elected representatives of the people hold political office
for a given time.

pluralism   In political terms, the existence
of a multi-party system of government.

BEFORE YOU START

**Is your country a democracy? Explain your
answer.**

THE MEANING OF DEMOCRACY

To some, democracy is simply a type or form of rule in society based on the freely given consent and wishes of the people, by the people and for the people through their active participation and involvement (Marrison, 1999). In this description, three essential components of democracy are evident, namely, rule, people and participation. To others, democracy means, 'the form of government in which power is in the hands of the people collectively and is administered by them or representatives elected by them. It is a political system where there is popular participation by the people in governance' (Johns Hopkins University, 2002: 4).

The three essential components of democracy, namely, rule, people and participation, are equally evident in this definition. Clearly, the concept of democracy can be seen from three perspectives:

1 Rule – a system of government in which everyone who is eligible can vote to elect its members.
2 People – a country that has a government which has been elected by the people of that country.
3 Participation – a system in which everyone is equal and has the right to vote and is thus part of the decision-making process.

In all cases, including Africa, the right to vote or to be voted for is only for those who are eligible as specified by the law. Eligibility is normally defined by age and citizenship, among other requirements. In most, if not all African democracies, a citizen has to attain the age of eighteen years to qualify as a voter.

ESSENTIAL COMPONENTS OF DEMOCRACY

Democracy, as a system of government, has many essential components. For the purpose of this chapter, eight are provided and explained briefly as follows:

Rule of law

No democracy can survive without the rule of law. In other words, democratic societies are guided by laws which seek to protect the basic rights and interests of individuals and groups. A major instrument of law in a democratic society is the constitution, a supreme legal guide and framework for individual and collective existence. Every member of the society is equal before the law and all persons have the right to be heard in different types of courts. For example, Ghana, Nigeria, Senegal, South Africa, Botswana, Namibia, Zambia, Malawi, Zimbabwe, Kenya, Tanzania and Mozambique are democratic nations where the rule of law exists. In these countries, everyone is equal under the law and can appear before a customary court, a magistrate's court, a high court, an appeals court or supreme court of the land to seek redress or answer to a summons. There are cases of manipulation when it comes to the implementation of the law in many parts of Africa. Where this occurs, it is mainly the fault of the implementers, not the system itself.

Freedom of choice

In a democratic society, every citizen has a right to choose the type of leaders they wish to see elected, provided they have met all the requirements for making such a choice. Generally, in African countries the vital requirements include citizenship, eligibility in accordance with voting age, and registration for an election. For example, one can, at an election, freely choose a particular person or a particular political party. It is also possible that a person can choose not to participate in the electoral process, although it is always better to participate rather than become part of 'the spectators' (Fanon, 1974). Participating in an election provides opportunities for the electorate to choose the candidates or political parties that are expected to meet the aspirations of the people in terms of good governance.

Elections

Under a democratic system of government, elections are conducted periodically to allow people to exercise the right to choose their own representatives. Generally, political parties offer a variety of programmes for the development of the nation, and certain members of these political parties stand for elections to serve in elective offices of the executive or legislative arms of government. For example, members of political parties stand for elections to offices of the president, vice president, members of the national assembly, members of the state (regional or provincial) assembly, and members of the local or district council, depending upon the structure that is in place in a particular country. Usually, elected representatives serve for three to five years before another election is conducted.

As indicated earlier, all eligible voters have the right to participate in the elections. Normally, elections are conducted by legally appointed bodies that are independent of the ruling government or any other political party's influence. These bodies have different names in some parts of Africa. For instance, in Mozambique the body is called the National Electoral Commission, whereas in Nigeria it is known as the Independent National Electoral Commission (INEC).

Elections are supposed to be conducted fairly and peacefully but in many parts of Africa, this has not been possible due to two main factors. Firstly, the voters are not usually properly informed or educated about how to participate in an election. Secondly, party or state officials often manipulate the way elections are conducted as well as the outcomes. This is generally done for selfish reasons and in order for some politicians to take advantage of the system. For example, in the last parliamentary elections held in Zimbabwe in 2000, and in the recent elections held in Nigeria and Rwanda in 2003, many allegations of irregularities, especially of intimidation of supporters of opponents and cheating at polling and counting centres were reported. This is why voter education is a very important adult education programme that will be needed in many parts of Africa for a long time to come.

Protection of citizens' rights

As already indicated, citizens in any society have rights that must be guaranteed by law at all times. Some of these rights are fundamental, for example, the right to life, to own property, to hold and express an opinion, profess a religious belief and seek redress in a court of law. All such rights are clearly listed in national constitutions. They are protected for all citizens by the government (using security agencies like the police and armed forces) and civil society organisations, such as human rights advocacy groups. In protecting citizens' rights, due process of the law must be followed. However, having these rights does not necessarily translate into realising them. For example, the right to own property was provided for all in South Africa after the elections of 1994. Laws were enacted to back this up. Nevertheless, many citizens are unable to realise this right because they are simply unable to buy property.

Existence of political institutions

Political institutions must exist in a democratic society. Such institutions include the three arms of government, namely, the executive, the legislature and the judiciary. The executive is responsible for running the civil administration. Leaders of this arm include the president, the vice president, governors (or premiers), and chairpersons of local councils and their deputies. The next arm, the legislature, makes laws for the good governance of the society. The leaders here include the president of the senate or the upper chamber (where applicable), the vice president, the speaker of parliament (or the house of representatives) and members of the national assembly. At the state or provincial level, there is the state or provincial assembly. Finally, there are local council legislative arms, with their leaders. The third arm, the judiciary, interprets the laws. The executing agencies here include the different courts of law as listed above.

Other political institutions are the political parties, examples of which include the African National Congress (ANC) of South Africa; the Tanzania African National Union (TANU) of Tanzania; the Kenya African National Union (KANU) of Kenya; the Botswana Democratic Party (BDP) of Botswana; the South West Africa Peoples' Organisation (SWAPO) of Namibia; and the National Council for Nigeria and Cameroon (NCNC). The rest include electoral agencies and civil society organisations such as pro-democracy groups, labour unions, religious organisations and student bodies. All of these play important roles in ensuring the existence or survival of a democratic system of government.

Popular participation

In a democracy, there must be the right to popular participation. This is necessary to allow adequate representation of different groups, opinions and interests. All persons and groups should be given the right to take part. No group should be denied this right. It is widely reported in some African countries that some disadvantaged groups, including women and ethnic minorities, are not given the full right to participate. This is usually on the basis of cultural constraints, such as the culturally prescribed dominance of men over women when it comes to contesting elections or holding high public offices. In respect of ethnic minorities, the exclusion is done to ensure the dominance of majority ethnic groups. This denial usually results in under-representation, which seriously undermines the democratic credentials of the government concerned. In a full democratic system, there is full representation of all groups in society, so that good governance is done in the interest of all persons.

Existence of civil society groups

These are groups that play important mediating roles in any democracy. The list of such groups includes labour unions, human rights groups, pro-democracy groups, religious bodies, non-governmental commonweal organisations, community-based organisations, student unions, women's groups, professional associations and environmental movements (Filson, 1991; Youngman, 2000; and Indabawa, 2001). These groups articulate group interests and try to protect them through debate, advocacy and engagement in governance activities. They influence public policy and reforms in order to improve society. Although 'their relationship to the state (i.e. government) may be … conflictual'

(Youngman, 2000: 202), the opinions and views of civil society organisations must always be sought and considered in nurturing the democratic systems in place in Africa. This is necessary because such organisations represent popular and informed interest groups in the society.

Diversity and pluralism

Africa is generally a diverse setting accommodating different people. These diversities and pluralisms must be accommodated in order to strengthen democracy and good governance. In particular, the existence of a multi-party system (that is a party system with more than one political party) must be allowed to cater for the wide-ranging interests, views and ideological positions of the people, as is practised in some African countries such as South Africa, Nigeria, Namibia, Kenya, Zambia, Malawi, Ghana and Botswana. For example, in 2003 Nigeria had more than thirty political parties, each with its own members and distinct agenda on how the country should be developed. This is better than forcing a one-party system on the people, as is the case in Uganda. A one-party state is a situation in which there is only one political party. Also, it is prudent to allow for diversity in terms of input into public policy through all arms of government: the executive, the legislature and the judiciary.

In addition, minority opinions need to be allowed and accommodated, because all persons and groups have something to contribute to the development of the society.

⚏ ACTIVITY

1 Identify the three most important components of democracy that ought to always be in place. State the reasons for your choice.

2 Briefly explain the key roles of the three arms of government in a democratic society.

DEMOCRACY AND ADULT EDUCATION

Adult education relates to democracy in many ways. In terms of the Hamburg Declaration from The Fifth International Conference on Adult Education (also known as CONFINTEA V), democracy and adult learning constitute some of the major challenges of the twenty-first century. CONFINTEA V considered democracy to be a means of active participation of citizens at local, national and global levels. Democracy is achieved through collective action, therefore, adult learning is both a tool for and an outcome of democracy. Specifically, the interplay of adult learning and democracy is manifested in three basic forms, described as follows:

1 Enhancing possibilities and the potential for self-determination, generation of participatory skills and raising informed citizens.
2 Generating social commitment to building a society that favours more liberty, gender equality, solidarity and equity.
3 Providing opportunities for every citizen to exercise her or his rights to participate fully in the construction of a more just society, to become involved in social decision-making and to train his or her capacity to work with others (UIE, 1997: 8).

Significantly, adult education can facilitate democratic practice in a more concrete manner through the provision of information and skills for participation in and the conduct of democratic elections.

Through adult education, learners can be taught democratic norms and methods of promoting its practice. Similarly, adult education can be used to promote democracy in society through instructional interventions by way of introducing elements of democracy in various programmes offered to different learning groups. For example, the basic concepts and practices of democracy, the rights and obligations of citizens, case studies on democratic practice, problems and prospects, can be taught in basic and post-literacy, extra-mural or continuing education programmes. However, this will depend on the willingness of the providers of the programmes, who often have to be convinced of the importance of inserting elements of democracy into their curriculum, since this has implications for the objectives, resources and facilities available to them. It is much easier to do this in state (government) sponsored programmes.

A second alternative strategy for fostering democracy through adult education is to mount specific programmes to teach elements of democracy to specialised groups. For instance, civil society organisations can teach their members. Similarly, the state (government) could also offer more content on democracy through civic or political education programmes. Although this approach is likely to be costly, it is also more likely to yield better results, since special attention will be paid to the subject matter (Indabawa, 2002).

A third strategy will be to ensure that adult education programmes are planned, delivered and implemented in a democratic way so that both the adult learners and programme providers, as well as delivery agents appreciate that democracy is in practice. In this regard, it is important to pay attention to consultation and needs identification in programme development, as well as the adoption of democratic approaches in adult teaching and learning. For instance, it is necessary to use participatory techniques, discussion, group work and mutual sharing of experiences between learners and facilitators, as well as among learners themselves.

A fourth strategy is to identify a critical issue in democracy and mount an adult education programme for its promotion. For example, elections are considered very important in any democracy but, in Africa, voters are hardly informed about the need for effective participation in the process. Therefore, voter education is an important adult education programme that can always be organised and delivered to help the democratic process. This is an essential intervention tool that most actors in elections, such as government and civil society groups, easily accept and invest in. However, a major problem is that those who organise and deliver such programmes hardly realise the need to adopt adult educational delivery strategies in their implementation. For this reason, the positive results are not easily noticed. In order to make voter education programmes more efficient the following schemata are proposed:

Action plan for voter education programmes in Africa

Objectives
- To help educate voters on better voting behaviour
- To promote greater participation in voting
- To reduce the incidence of electoral malpractice in an election
- To help minimise the violence in an election

Content
- What is democracy?
- What is an election?
- How should voting be done?
- Who is an eligible voter?

- Organising an election from national to local level
- An ideal election polling station
- Role of stakeholders, that is, electoral officials, police and security agencies, political party agents, traditional/community leaders, observers
- Counting of votes and declaration of election results
- Lodging complaints on the election results
- Any other suitable topic of interest

Administration and implementation
For optimum benefit, those who administer voter education programmes should include the following (on a proportional representative basis):

- Trained officials of the electoral body
- Trained representatives of all political parties
- Officials of a relevant local adult education government agency
- Officials of relevant civil society organisations
- Representatives of local traditional institutions

Funding
Voter education programmes should be funded adequately by government and interested donor bodies. Funding levels should be commensurate with the need for adequate facilities and material resources.

Training and delivery
All delivery agents should receive relevant training of at least one month ahead of the time of programme delivery. During such training, adequate emphasis should be placed on the best adult education delivery methods, strategies and techniques. The programme should be delivered uniformly for a period of at least one month prior to an election. Relevant units of tertiary educa-

tion institutions in the community should be involved in the design and delivery of this training.

Participants/beneficiaries
The participants and beneficiaries of the voter education programme should be drawn from among stakeholders such as election officials (especially those directly involved at the local level), security agencies, political party agents, and representatives of local community leaders, select youth group leaders and election observers.

Programme evaluation/review
After every election, an evaluation should be conducted on the voter education programme delivered, to help assess the success or otherwise of the entire programme. Where necessary, programme goals, processes or outcomes should be redefined accordingly. It is advisable that such a review be conducted by an independent team to be drawn from the staff of a relevant tertiary education department in the community.

Complementary popular media programme
While the internal voter education programme is in progress, the electoral commission should also ensure that a popular media programme on radio, television and local newspapers is mounted on the basic elements of the forthcoming election.

The above plan is only for voter education. However, it is also possible to plan and deliver adult and non-formal education programmes in such areas as human rights education (rights and obligation of citizens in a democracy), peace and conflict, culture and diversity, equal rights for all, fundamental freedom and democracy, the environment and sustainable development, as well as education for social and cultural democracy (Marrison, 1999; and

Hazoumê, 1999). Similarly, other issues that can be addressed include the rule of law, tolerance, operating political parties, conducting political meetings and other essential aspects of democracy. All that is needed is for responsible government agencies to make the first move and engage voluntary bodies to collaborate in the exercise. When the efforts of all parties involved in adult education delivery are coordinated effectively, the degree of impact of the programmes at hand will be better assessed or determined. If this could be done in all countries in Africa, then institutionalising democracy will be an easier task, and the benefits of good governance will be more widely realised in developing the various nations of the continent.

A fifth approach to use in promoting democracy through adult education is the development of a research agenda on adult education and democracy. The agenda should be pursued and implemented by researchers at universities and institutions of higher learning and by multi-disciplinary teams of researchers in continental organisations and institutions such as the Council for the Development of Economic and Social Research in Africa (CODESRIA); the new African Union (AU); the New Partnership for Africa's Development (NEPAD); the Economic Community of West African States (ECOWAS); the Southern African Development Community (SADC); UNESCO and other interested partners.

The outcomes of such research activities should be publicised through journals and books rendered in the major languages of communication on the continent.

⌗ ACTIVITY

1 Describe any two roles that adult education can play in promoting democracy in your community.

2 Plan a training schedule for a human rights education programme to be delivered to a group of thirty civil organisation leaders.
3 Identify five issues of democracy in which research is most needed. Explain why you consider these issues the most urgent.

SUMMARY

This chapter has explained the meaning of democracy and the ways through which adult education can promote democracy. Democracy is both a concept and a cultural practice involving the existence of willing and free consent, and the participation of the people in the governance of society. Democracy should seek to advance the best interests of all without any discrimination. There are eight basic elements of a democratic order, namely, rule of law; freedom of choice, elections; protection of citizens' rights; existence of political institutions; popular participation; existence of civil society groups; and diversity and pluralism. Several ways through which adult education can promote democracy in Africa have been outlined. They include organising adult education programmes around a critical issue in democracy and developing a research agenda on democracy in Africa. These approaches are not exhaustive. Many others can be added. Finally, the chapter has proposed a scheme through which voter education can be organised more efficiently. The scheme can be applied on any other issue of relevance to the promotion of democracy.

KEY POINTS

■ Democracy is about freedom of choice and the right of the people to participate in making decisions that affect their lives in the community.

■ Adult education can be a viable tool in enhancing democratic practice which, in turn, is likely to promote development in society.

■ A key strategy for promoting democracy is to model democratic practices on the way adult education programmes are implemented in the teaching and learning process.

■ There is a need for closer collaboration and partnership between government agencies and civil society groups that seek to promote democratic practice.

⊞ ACTIVITY

What is the most critical issue in democracy that is facing your community today? How would you go about addressing this issue?

FURTHER QUESTIONS

1 How would you counter cheating and other election malpractices such as intimidation, rigging and election fraud?

2 As a concept, democracy is different from democracy in practice. Do you agree? Explain your answer.

SUGGESTED READINGS

Hazoumê, M. L. 1999. *Africa and the democratic challenge: An essay in adult education for democracy and the culture of peace*. Hamburg: UNESCO Institute for Education.

Johns Hopkins University. 2000. *Basic facts on democracy and good governance*. Abuja: Johns Hopkins University/USAID.

Marrison, K. (ed.). 1999. *Education for human rights and democracy in Southern Africa*. Windhoek: UNESCO and Longman Namibia.

UNESCO Institute for Education. 1997. *Democracy and peace*. Hamburg: UIE.

Chapter 8

Health, HIV/AIDS and adult education

OVERVIEW

One of the challenges of survival for human beings is the number of risks faced on a daily basis, some natural and others created by human actions or inactions. A large number of people face the risk of contracting various types of diseases. Most diseases arise from the environmental conditions that people live in. This challenge is even more serious for Africa in the twenty-first century (Mazrui, 1996). People encounter the probability of taking on one disease or another through the food they eat, the water they drink, the air they inhale and the various interactions they engage in. Some diseases are fatal in their effect, leading to death, while others lead to severe deformities, such as the loss of human limbs. Some diseases are pandemic or epidemic, while others are restrictive in the way in which they spread.

This chapter deals with issues of health and examines some ways through which adult education can help us understand, act and mitigate the negative effects of diseases in Africa. In discussing health issues, more attention is focused on HIV/AIDS due to its magnitude and the social consequences thereof.

LEARNING OBJECTIVES

By the end of this chapter, you should be able to:

1 Describe the types of prevailing health problems in Africa.
2 Explain what HIV and AIDS are.
3 Explain how HIV develops into AIDS.
4 Explain the causes and impacts of HIV/AIDS in Africa.
5 Explain the prevention, care and management of HIV/AIDS in Africa.
6 Identify and examine possible roles of adult education in the prevention, care and management of HIV/AIDS, especially through government and non-governmental organisations.

dwennimmen

KEY TERMS

behavioural change   Change in the way people live their lives, particularly in order to help improve their conditions. For example, abstention from sexual intercourse by adolescents until lawful marriage, or the use of condoms in unregulated sexual engagements. These two measures can help reduce vulnerability to contracting HIV/AIDS.

denial   Refusal to accept the fact that something exists. For example, in some parts of the world, many people do not believe that HIV/AIDS exists. Denial prevents positive action for helping to reduce the spread of deadly diseases such as HIV/AIDS or the care of its victims.

HIV/AIDS (Human Immunodeficiency Virus/ Acquired Immune Deficiency Syndrome)   A killer disease that destroys the human body's systems of health and resistance.

preventive education   Education intended to stop something from occurring. For example, preventive education on HIV/AIDS is meant to help control the spread of the disease.

research   A systematic investigation of a phenomenon in order to understand it or draw conclusions and generalisations about its influence or impact. For example, research can be done on the effects of HIV/AIDS on the economy of a community.

stigma   A negative attitude towards the victims of certain problems, especially diseases such as HIV/AIDS, whereby the victims are socially isolated or rejected.

⌗ BEFORE YOU START

State the local name(s) of HIV/AIDS used in your community. Do(es) the name(s) indicate the seriousness of the disease? Explain your answer.

TYPES OF HEALTH PROBLEMS IN AFRICA

Although the types and effects of diseases vary across societies and countries, the patterns may be similar in their regional dimensions, as in the case of malaria or HIV/AIDS in Africa. In Africa, the most worrisome types of disease include malaria, tuberculosis, HIV/AIDS, cholera, ebola, malnutrition and kwashiorkor. Also, there are several other neglected, but debilitating diseases afflicting many people in Africa. These include elephantiasis, river blindness, trachoma, sleeping sickness and kala azar. The situation becomes critical when it is realised that millions of Africans lack access to medicines for diseases which have been neglected by researchers and funding agencies for many years. In addition, there are other numerous health risks that arise from socio-economic and culturally related disadvantages such as poverty or powerlessness. A case in point is the violence against women through domestic battering and female genital mutilation (Kisekka, 1992).

In light of all these challenges, it is imperative that all human beings and institutions have a clear and complete understanding of these diseases, as a basis for the prevention, cure, management and control of the diseases, and the care of their victims. Whereas some diseases such as river blindness are associated with the socially disadvantaged, others such as HIV/AIDS have no regard for social, economic, political or religious status, gender, colour, creed or race.

WHAT IS HIV/AIDS?

The Human Immunodeficiency Virus (HIV) is the major cause of the disease Acquired Immune Deficiency Syndrome (AIDS). AIDS develops over a period of time, taking on opportunistic infections such as tuberculosis or untreated sexually transmitted diseases in individuals, male or female. It is a potentially fatal disease in that it destroys the immune system in the body of an infected person.

The human immune properties protect the body system and protect it from attack through various diseases associated with human beings. Without the usual immunity, the body is at high risk of contracting or getting infected by any disease. Clearly, HIV/AIDS is 'a life-threatening disease' (Bwakirah, 2003: 84). As soon as the HI virus is contracted, it takes a period of two weeks to ten years to develop into full-blown AIDS. The disease passes through five basic stages as follows:

Stages of HIV's growth

1 **Contact stage:**
   Contact via portals of entry into the body for one to two weeks
2 **Nascent or early stage:**
   Human body asymptomatic for two to twelve weeks, without any real signs
3 **Stage of effect:**
   Weakening and breakdown of immune system, three to ten years
4 **Stage of fatal attack:**
   Opportunistic infections leading to full-blown AIDS, three to ten years
5 **AIDS**

Once AIDS takes full shape, it is difficult to cure. In fact, for now, there is no definite cure for the disease. In most cases, AIDS victims eventually die. The death of active individual members of families results in varying unpleasant and negative outcomes.

Why is HIV/AIDS a social problem?

HIV/AIDS is both a disease and a major social problem. It is a problem since individuals, families and communities are affected considerably by its processes and results. The processes involve considerable stress for the victims, who are also called *persons living with HIV/AIDS* (PLWA). The stress occurs largely because of unfavourable community attitudes towards HIV/AIDS and outright rejection of AIDS victims by members of the community. This has the unfortunate effect of discouraging victims from coming out into the open early on so that efforts can be made to contain the HIV infection before it degenerates into AIDS. Various costs such as loss of family income, reduced productivity in the workplace, cost of health care provision, and social-emotional stress to victims and their families are incurred as a result of HIV/AIDS. The costs of HIV/AIDS are not limited to individuals, families and communities. They also affect government and its agencies, particularly health institutions; other interested parties such as churches, mosques and other civil society bodies; and various non-governmental organisations. Meaningful socio-economic endeavours such as working, learning, and other productive activities are adversely affected or totally disrupted by HIV/AIDS. Family life and support (e.g. feeding, clothing, educating children), community group membership and many other civic roles that people perform as citizens are also negatively affected by HIV/AIDS. Furthermore, when victims die, they leave behind orphans who are vulnerable to social stigmatisation and various forms of discrimination in society.

CASE STUDY: STIGMA AND DENIAL IN SWAZILAND

In Swaziland these days, Saturdays are devoted to funerals, says Dorothy Littler of the Swaziland National Commission for UNESCO. Because HIV/AIDS is connected with sex, it represents a stigma. People avoid talking about it. Living in denial to keep the family from social condemnation is a norm, not an exception. It is common to hear a relative of a dead person at the funeral identify the cause of death as witchcraft or poison. While this could be due in part to the froth or salt found around the deceased's mouth in their last days, it is also motivated by a subconscious or conscious refusal to admit the terrible truth. Even the official cause of death is often explained as a 'long illness', or as pneumonia or meningitis if the person suffered severe headaches.

⊞ ACTIVITY

1 Think about a family that has lost a member due to AIDS. In your view, how does the community see and relate to them?
2 What advice would you give to a family who is discriminated against due to AIDS?
3 What advice would you give to those people who discriminate against others on account of HIV/AIDS?
4 What specific steps would you take to reduce incidents of HIV/AIDS denial and stigmatisation?

HIV/AIDS IN AFRICA

Causes

The spread of HIV/AIDS is caused by a number of factors. The primary factor is uncontrolled sexual activities, whether coercive (forced, e.g. through rape) or consensual, where two or more people agree to participate in sexual activities. Other factors include: the transfusion of contaminated blood in hospitals, use of unsterilised skin-piercing instruments, prevalence of untreated sexually transmitted diseases (STDs), low condom use, poverty, low level of literacy, poor health status, low status of women and stigmatisation of victims (UNESCO, 1994; and *Daily Trust*, 2003). Other variables that promote the rapid spread of HIV/AIDS are induced abortion, cultural sensitivity and reluctance to discuss sexuality issues, especially with adolescents and adults (particularly females), and the migration of sex workers (Adara, 2003). In addition, labour mobility was found to be 'an important factor in the spread of HIV as evidenced in several countries in sub-Saharan Africa including South Africa, Zimbabwe, Angola and Uganda. For example, in one town in Zimbabwe near [the] South African border with a large population of migrant workers, 7 out of 10 women attending antenatal clinics tested HIV positive in 1995' (Adara, 2002: 64, quoting FAO and UNAIDS sources).

A place which is largely populated by migrant workers is the perfect breeding ground for prostitution, which is undoubtedly the most certain way to contract and spread STDs and HIV/AIDS. Unfortunately, the infections are not confined to the migrant town. When the migrant workers move on to other places or return to their homes they take the STDs and HIV/AIDS with them, and spread it to other communities and/or to their own communities, particularly to their spouses. In this regard, HIV/AIDS becomes a socio-economic issue, as migrant workers and prostitutes are generally poor people who move from place to place in search of work and clients, respectively. Similarly, in this respect, HIV/AIDS becomes a gender issue on two accounts. Firstly, the prostitutes are generally women. Secondly, the spouses are mostly women who are often not in a position to deny their husbands (who have been away from home for a long time) their conjugal rights.

Nature and impacts

HIV/AIDS is a major disease that afflicts a large number of people in Africa and its spread and effects are increasing daily at an alarming rate. It has become a major health and social issue in Africa, attracting the attention of governments and their various agencies, as well as non-governmental and civil society organisations, the donor community and the larger society. However, HIV/AIDS is more than just a health problem. It has social, economic and political dimensions. Its negative effects are felt daily in the families and communities of victims. Public policy concerns and programmes are increasing as part of efforts to minimise its impact on society.

In a recent survey by UNAIDS (2003), it was found that there are now more than forty million people living with HIV/AIDS in the world. Seventy per cent of the total number live in sub-Saharan Africa. On a daily basis, about 8 000 people die from AIDS. As a result, more than thirteen million children are left behind as AIDS orphans. In Africa, twelve million people now live with HIV/AIDS.

Although HIV/AIDS spreads rapidly, a definite medical cure has not yet been found. In addition, medical services and anti-retroviral treatments remain

inaccessible to more than 95% of the HIV/
AIDS patients worldwide (UNAIDS, 2003).

AIDS has devastating effects on families, communities, on the economy, as
well as the social life of countries. In 2001
alone, 170 000 persons died of AIDS in
Nigeria (*Daily Trust*, quoting a USAID
report, 2003). In Botswana, there are already
signs of 'declining economic growth with
data showing that by 2015, the economy
will be nearly a third smaller than it would
have been if not for HIV/AIDS' (Spencer,
2003: 2). Some of the negative impacts of
AIDS are indicated by the fact that 'AIDS
attacks adults in their most productive years,
leaving behind not only dependent children but dependent ageing parents. It puts
incredible strain upon a glaringly inadequate health system. It prompts a decline in
agricultural production and threatens food
security. Education suffers, as the supply of
teachers shrinks, healthy children withdraw
from school to care for family' (Spencer,
2003: 1).

In addition to the above, there are also
other consequences including social and
economic disruption and the weakening
of family structures of support. There is
also the loss of income due to expenditure
on treatment, care and funeral costs,
particularly in non-Muslim parts of Africa,
where coffins and extensive ceremonies
are normal at burials. There is also the
expansion of extended families, given
that AIDS primarily affects adults of child-
bearing age.

Other consequences are the psychological vulnerability of orphaned children;
absenteeism and withdrawal from school by
affected children; a reduction in the number
of children who complete school; a decline
in the educational services including the
number of classes and schools; as well as a
decline in the quality of educational services provided.

Prevention, care and management

Prevention of HIV/AIDS can take many
forms. The best form of prevention is to
be as careful as possible about how one
lives one's life. Since HIV/AIDS is largely
caused by unprotected sexual activities,
abstention is worth considering. Safe sex
through the use of condoms is often recommended. Adolescents and adults are often
advised to either postpone sexual activities
until marriage or (where their cultures and
religion permit) practise safe sex with great
care. It is argued that it is safer for people to
forego sex until they are married to chosen
spouses. Once married, husbands and wives
should remain faithful to one another. All
major religions in Africa, Christianity, Islam
and traditional religion demand abstinence
from unlawful sexual indulgence, and commitment and faithfulness to one's spouse, at
all times.

Care and management are also important aspects of the HIV/AIDS pandemic.
Care is given to those who are victims
and those that are left behind, including
orphaned children, widows, parents and
relations. The best form of care that can be
given to persons living with HIV/AIDS is
to live with them as normal human beings.
Secondly, care and management are needed
in order to ensure that victims are given the
best medical attention possible. Here, the
role of government is essential since the cost
of providing anti-retroviral treatment is
high and may not be easily afforded by most
victims who are found to be mostly among
the poor and among disempowered women
(Medel-Añonuevo, 2002). Governments in
African countries must provide the policy
and health programmes to cover the need
for maximum medical care for victims.
Donor agencies, too, can help in this regard
(WHO, 2000).

In addition, the basic needs of people living with HIV/AIDS, especially the need for food and shelter, should be met by their families (where possible), communities, government or non-governmental organisations, severally or jointly. Victims and orphans deserve special attention in this regard. Similarly, love and affection should always be extended to victims and to those left behind since they also need empathy.

Because society still has deeply embedded negative attitudes to issues of HIV/AIDS, care and management are very difficult without the mobilisation of families and communities. This is necessary in order for them to appreciate the need to offer all forms of support. For this to be possible, various means and strategies have to be adopted. These will include massive use of the media, including radio, television and newspapers as a means of reaching the people. Mobilisation through media can also be more effective if local languages which people understand are used.

⌗ ACTIVITY

1 Discuss two major causes of HIV/AIDS in your community.
2 Identify ten problems faced by families of HIV/AIDS victims. Suggest possible solutions to each of the problems identified.
3 Which preventive measures would you recommend to stop the spread of HIV/AIDS in your community? State the reasons for your choice.
4 What roles do you think religious leaders and institutions should play in the prevention, care and management of HIV/AIDS in the community?

ROLES OF ADULT EDUCATION IN HIV/AIDS

Adult education can be used in numerous ways to help cope with the problems of diseases, especially with regard to HIV/AIDS in Africa. This is so because most of the victims of HIV/AIDS are adults from lower socio-economic backgrounds, whose educational needs may not be fully met through the formal education system (Indabawa, 2002). However, there is evidence from some parts of Africa that teachers who are educated also constitute a large percentage of the victims of HIV/AIDS. Non-sufferers of HIV/AIDS can also be reached through information dissemination and educational measures so as to help them protect themselves and others from the disease. Adult education can be used in the fight against the spread of HIV/AIDS in Africa through nine basic ways:

1 Promoting awareness of HIV/AIDS.
2 Promoting better ways for healthy living, especially through knowledge of basic hygiene, sanitation and disease.
3 Providing victims with skills to cope with HIV/AIDS.
4 Mobilising families and communities to understand and commit time, resources and efforts to the fight against HIV/AIDS.
5 Promoting behavioural and attitudinal changes among adolescents and adults in respect of sexuality and HIV/AIDS victims.
6 Providing strategies for the prevention, care and management of HIV/AIDS.
7 Promoting public awareness via the mass media to help reduce the spread of HIV/AIDS and to help generate favourable attitudes towards victims and orphans of HIV/AIDS.

8 Conducting research, especially on the best approaches for tackling the spread of HIV/AIDS and for counselling individual victims, families and communities.

9 Providing skills for the management of HIV/AIDS educational intervention strategies for community leaders, educators, donors, public policy makers and implementers, as well as civil society organisations, particularly religious bodies.

In order to use adult education to promote the reduction of the spread of HIV/AIDS in the ways indicated above, a number of approaches can be adopted. The approaches cover three essential areas as follows:

1 Provision of adult education programmes for the prevention of HIV/AIDS to adolescents, youths and adults, as well as to the delivery agents of adult education.

2 Enrichment of the content of existing adult education programmes with elements of HIV/AIDS issues, problems and concerns.

3 Conducting relevant research through higher educational institutions and agencies involved in teaching and research, in the specialised area of adult education and related fields, such as social welfare, extension education and community development, all of which deal with youth and adults.

In order to proceed with any of the three approaches, it is necessary to engage all concerned institutions, role players and stakeholders in the provision, planning and delivery of the programmes. Similarly, victims of HIV/AIDS and those they leave behind must be involved in determining what is taught and what works in this regard.

⌗ ACTIVITY

1 Identify and discuss two major roles of adult education in the understanding and prevention of HIV/AIDS in your community.

2 Describe how an organisation can use adult education to create awareness about HIV/AIDS in any community in Africa.

APPROACHES TO PROGRAMME CONTENT

Intervention pertaining to HIV/AIDS can be done through existing government-sponsored adult education programmes, non-governmental organisations and international partners as described below.

Existing government programmes

Existing government programmes usually come in the form of basic literacy or post-literacy services, health education and extension programmes. For example, literacy programmes offered at the basic level are meant to enable adults to read and write as well as be numerate in local languages. A few of the products of such programmes move on to the post-literacy level for the equivalent of formal primary education (Indabawa, 2001). For more details on adult literacy programmes, refer to Chapter 6.

The reason for the ease of intervention in these programmes is that, in large part, government is the major force of intervention for awareness on HIV/AIDS. The other types of basic literacy programmes, namely awareness-raising and functionally oriented, which can be reformed to infuse HIV/AIDS content, are not favoured by governments in most parts of Africa essentially for ideological reasons (Indabawa, 1991) and, as such, are generally unsuitable for intervention for the purposes of promoting HIV/AIDS awareness.

Health education programmes such as family planning, hygiene and sanitation are perhaps the most suited for HIV/AIDS interventions for the simple reason that relevant HIV/AIDS topics can be easily incorporated into the health subject matter at hand.

Local non-government bodies

Local bodies within the nation or in communities could develop their individual or joint adult education programmes for HIV/AIDS intervention purposes and ensure full implementation. Donors and international partners may assist them with funds or technical expertise (WHO, 1981). However, these bodies should work with the victims, their families and communities in order to develop intervention programme packages that will be acceptable and suitable to their clientele. The usual top-bottom approach through which intervention programmes are imposed should be discontinued as it often results in large and expensive efforts that do not help anyone in particular.

Intervention of international partners

In order to develop an Africa-wide agenda for adult education's response to HIV/AIDS, several bodies have to be involved at local, national and international levels. These will include institutions, role players and stakeholders, such as the United Nations and its agencies, such as UNAIDS, UNESCO, UNICEF and ILO; international and regional financial institutions, such as the International Monetary Fund (IMF), the World Bank and the Africa Development Bank (ADB); continental and regional bodies, such as the African Union (AU); the Economic Community of West African States (ECOWAS); and the Southern

African Development Community (SADC). Other interested development partners of Africa such as the Department for International Development (Dfid); the United States Agency for International Development (USAID); the Swedish International Development Agency (SIDA); and the Canadian Agency for International Development (CIDA), should also intensify their involvement. These bodies could develop joint action plans on adult education to address HIV/AIDS in Africa in collaboration with relevant local organisations. Also, each of these bodies may have an adult education for HIV/AIDS component in their education intervention and support programmes, as some of them, such as the Dfid and the World Bank, already have done.

While the UN agencies can concentrate on programme development and advocacy for policy reform regarding HIV/AIDS or the provision of support in terms of expertise and funding for HIV/AIDS adult education programmes, the other agencies may play a greater role in supplying funds, since not all African countries are able to provide adequate funds for adult education work (Afrik, 2000). The use of funds that may be supplied needs to be closely supervised to avoid wastage or misapplication as was witnessed during the five-year (1995–2000) support of over US$8 million for mass literacy work in Nigeria (Indabawa, 2001). The funds were provided by the United Nations Development Programme (UNDP), while three tiers of government in Nigeria provided their own counterpart cash contribution and offered administrative support through the use of existing adult education organs and their personnel. For more details on debt and adult education, which affects the supply of adequate funds for adult education work in Africa, see Chapter 9.

Whatever the form of intervention, using adult education to promote efforts aimed at the reduction of the incidence of HIV/AIDS will require attention to some key issues, such as:

- Language of teaching adults.
- Development of instructional materials.
- Extent of content infusion required, that is, how much of the curriculum should cater for HIV/AIDS in relation to other components.
- Time available for intervention.
- Methods and techniques of instruction.
- Training of instructors and facilitators.
- Involvement of community leaders and youth groups in mobilising and facilitating educational intervention.
- Evaluation of learning outcomes.
- Improvement and sustainability of adult education intervention programmes.

ACTIVITY

1 **Which intervention strategy do you think is best for Africa? State the reasons for your choice.**
2 **A local community-based organisation is in a better position to mobilise families to care for their HIV/AIDS victims than any other group. Do you agree? Explain your answer.**

RESEARCH IN ADULT EDUCATION FOR HIV/AIDS

Research is important for refining any activity or practice. New ideas, methods, approaches, techniques and intervention strategies are often generated through research. Research to support adult educational intervention for the prevention and management of HIV/AIDS in Africa is necessary. Fortunately, apart from Francophone Africa (where adult education studies

in higher education are not common), there are many higher education institutions on the continent that are engaged in the provision of teaching, research and community services in adult education. By the year 2000, there were more than fifty university departments of adult education and an array of other tertiary institutions engaged in adult education scholarship and activities in Africa (Oduaran, 2000).

In addition, there are numerous local, national and international agencies, including NGOs that are engaged in or interested in research and publication on adult education and HIV/AIDS. Two agencies are worth mentioning in this regard. The first is the UNESCO Institute for Education (UIE) in Hamburg, which promotes not only research in this and other areas but also the publication of the results. The other is the Institute for International Cooperation of the German Adult Education Association (IIZ/DVV) that promotes research in this area through its journal, *Adult Education and Development*.

The universities and other institutions of higher learning engage in research for two basic objectives. Firstly, research is undertaken by students in partial fulfilment of the requirements for the award of certificates, diplomas and degrees. The major problem with this type of research is the limited dissemination of the outcomes. Once the qualifications are awarded, copies of the projects, dissertations and theses are kept mainly in the university libraries. In this way, access to the results is limited (Indabawa, 1995; Afrik, 1997). However, this might be a blessing in disguise since recent trends show that lower-level research done in partial fulfilment of the requirements for the award of diplomas and bachelors and masters degrees is largely a replication of earlier works.

The second type of research done at institutions of higher learning is the scholarly work that academic staff do in order to extend the frontiers of knowledge and educational practice in their specialised areas. This type is also done in order for the staff to earn regular promotion across academic ranks. The major problem with this type of research is its short span and lack of adequate funds for meaningful longitudinal studies capable of achieving meaningful and tangible results. Sources of funding are limited and competition for scarce resources is often intense. In any case, there is very little interface between research undertaken for promotion at universities and the practice of adult education (Mpofu, 1997).

So, where does research in adult education for HIV/AIDS fall? In order to achieve reasonable results, research into adult education for HIV/AIDS should be conducted at both levels, namely by the students, especially post-graduate students and by academic staff. However, funding must be provided beyond the present feeble scales. More and more resources should be committed to this by the universities and local financial institutions as well. Similarly, the focus and methodology of such research should be reformed. Participatory approaches will be the most suitable to ensure the involvement of all stakeholders. Also, key areas of the impact of the disease should be targeted and the outcomes should be published and widely circulated in the form of books, journal articles and occasional publications and the findings should influence information, education and communication programmes.

Research conducted by adult education and undertaken in support of efforts aimed at tackling the problems of HIV/AIDS, should receive priority attention in the following areas:

- Awareness of the meaning of HIV/AIDS and its spread, as well as the need to curtail the disease's spread and effects.
- Information on better healthy living that is free of diseases, especially HIV/AIDS.
- Religion, culture and HIV/AIDS in Africa.
- Vulnerable groups and HIV/AIDS, that is, women, youth and children.
- Coping strategies for HIV/AIDS.
- Sexuality, behaviour change and HIV/AIDS.
- Mobilisation of families and communities for HIV/AIDS prevention.
- Approaches to the prevention of HIV/AIDS, and the care of HIV/AIDS victims.
- Use of the media through popular theatre, drama and shows to demonstrate how to control HIV/AIDS.
- Adult education research for HIV/AIDS, that is, justification and need, mode and methodology, funding and dissemination of results.
- Managing adult educational HIV/AIDS interventions and support.
- Adult education and the role of international, national and local players, stakeholders and institutions for the prevention and management of HIV/AIDS.

⧈ ACTIVITY

1 List three reasons why you think research is important in the understanding of and coping with the problem of HIV/AIDS.
2 Identify one area in adult education for HIV/AIDS that, in your view, is in urgent need of research. State the reasons for your choice. Formulate a researchable topic for the chosen area and explain how you would go about conducting the research.

SUMMARY

This chapter discussed the issues and problems of diseases in Africa, especially HIV/AIDS and how adult education can play positive roles in the understanding, prevention, care and management of the problem. Special attention was given to HIV/AIDS because of its seriousness as a large-scale social problem that has made a huge impact on the African peoples, society and economy. The spread of HIV/AIDS has reached alarming levels in Africa, with devastating effects for the most vulnerable groups, namely, the poor, women and children. Adult education programmes can be used to prevent the spread of the disease and to mitigate against its effects. This could be done either through the development of new programmes or through the infusion of relevant content elements into existing programmes. In the provision of such programmes, special attention must be paid to the pedagogical concerns of teaching methods and techniques, as well as instructional materials and timing. In addition, efforts must be made to involve the victims in determining the mode of intervention. In this process international, national and local agencies and institutions can play vital roles. Research on how adult education can help to address the problem is an essential tool of intervention in this important effort of ridding Africa of HIV/AIDS and other preventable diseases.

KEY POINTS

- Diseases are not just health problems, they also have social, economic and other dimensions.
- HIV/AIDS is an incurable condition with very serious negative implications for individuals, families and communities.
- It is possible to reduce the spread of preventable diseases in Africa (such as HIV/AIDS) if everybody acts positively towards the attainment of this objective.
- Adult education in its wider context can help in this process through the provision of information, knowledge and skills for victims, their families, as well as non-sufferers. This would help to reduce the spread of HIV/AIDS and at the same time equip the infected and the affected with coping strategies.
- Individuals, families, communities, governments and organisations have varying roles to play, either collectively or separately, in the fight to reduce the spread of diseases, especially HIV/AIDS.
- Africa's development is dependent upon healthy and disease-free peoples.

⌗ ACTIVITY

What, in your view, could have been done (and by whom) to avoid the critical state the African continent is in with regard to HIV/AIDS infection? Explain your answer. Is it too late to do that now? Explain your answer.

FURTHER QUESTIONS

1 Malaria is another disease that is killing many people in Africa. What could be done (and by whom) to reduce the incidence of malaria in society?
2 African governments have the capacity to prevent the spread of HIV/AIDS and malaria. The only thing missing is the political will to do so. Do you agree with this assertion? Explain your answer.

SUGGESTED READINGS

Allen, J. 2000. *Opening windows to a brighter world: A better future for girls and boys orphaned by AIDS.* Paris: UNESCO.

Medel-Añonuevo, C. (ed.). 2002. *Addressing gender relations in HIV prevention education.* Hamburg: UNESCO Institute for Education.

Van Dyk, A. 2005. *HIV/AIDS Care and Counselling.* Cape Town: Pearson Education.

Webb, D. 1997. *HIV and AIDS in Africa.* London: Pluto Press.

Chapter 9

Poverty, debt and adult education

OVERVIEW

In Chapter 1, it was indicated that poverty and debt are two of the most serious problems adversely affecting the pace of development in Africa. This chapter discusses poverty and debt, and their causes. The chapter also discusses the relationship between debt and poverty, and the role of adult education in alleviating this state of affairs.

LEARNING OBJECTIVES

By the end of this chapter, you should be able to:

1   Define poverty and identify some of its trends and causes.
2   Describe debt and its trends in Africa.
3   Suggest the ways in which adult education can alleviate poverty and debt in Africa.

dame-dame

KEY TERMS

creditor nation   A nation that gives loans to other nations.

debt   A sum of money owed, which has to be repaid on agreed terms.

debt rescheduling   A system through which the repayment period of a particular debt is re-arranged to allow more time for its redemption.

foreign/external debt   Debt owed to external bodies, institutions or countries.

hunger   Lack of food, sometimes leading to malnutrition, especially among children and particularly in drought-affected areas.

income   The amount of money one earns or gets from an economic activity or job. Income of people in developing countries is generally low.

internal/local debt   Debt owed to local banks, financial institutions or contractors. Repayment of such debt is made in local currency, but it is usually added to the total debt of a nation.

poverty   Inability to secure the basic necessities of life such as food, shelter, education and health.

⊞ BEFORE YOU START

1   From your perspective, what would you define as poverty?
2   In your experience, what does *debt* mean?
3   Are there any differences between debt and poverty? Explain your answer.

WHAT IS POVERTY?

In a broad sense, poverty is an individual's inability to meet the basic needs for food, shelter, education and health. Poverty can be explained from two perspectives, namely, absolute deprivation and relative deprivation (Wallace and Wallace, 1985). From the perspective of absolute deprivation, poverty means the complete absence of basic necessities such as food, shelter, clothes and health care. People who do not know where their next meal is going to come from are considered to be absolutely poor. From the perspective of relative deprivation, poverty is a relative state in that it is based on what has been determined to be the normal standard of living for a particular community rather than on the deprivation of essentials. Whereas absolute deprivation is based on the essentials of life, relative deprivation is based on an official poverty line that may be unrealistic for the community. For example, it is considered normal in urban centers to own a television set. People who cannot afford television sets would therefore be considered relatively poor. Yet, these people would not be considered absolutely poor because they have life-sustaining essentials such as food, shelter and health care. In the relative sense, poverty is contextual in that a person who is poor in one setting may be considered reasonably well-off in another. The poor of the urban areas could be considered affluent in the rural areas.

Whatever it is termed, poverty is real in Africa. The people who lack the basic essentials of life and those who fall below the norm of their society are essentially the same. They are hungry, they lack shelter, they are sick, they are unable to go to school, they do not have jobs, they are uncertain and fearful about the future, and they lose their children to all sorts of illnesses due to unclean water, powerlessness and lack of freedom or representation (World Bank, 2002). The poor can hardly benefit from or contribute maximally to the development of the society in which they live (Indabawa, 1991). In short, they do not participate fully in the life of their societies. Poor people have been described as 'all the losers of the world, who live in sub-human conditions' (Rahnema, 1993: 158; Oyen, 2002: 21).

The next section seeks to link the concept of poverty to its manifestation or the ways in which poverty can be seen in practical terms.

APPROACHES TO POVERTY

Laderchi et al. (2003) examined the concept of poverty from four approaches, namely, the monetary, the capability, the social exclusion and the participatory. As the name suggests, the monetary approach places more emphasis on income as a measure of poverty. It links poverty with a 'shortfall in consumption (or income) from the poverty line' (Laderchi et al., 2003: 6). The capability approach considers poverty as 'the failure to achieve certain minimal or basic capabilities, where basic capabilities refer to the ability to satisfy certain crucially important functioning up to certain minimally adequate levels' (Sen, cited in Laderchi et al., 2003: 14). A person should be capable of achieving a 'good life', otherwise that person is poor (Laderchi et al., 2003: 17). Like the first, the second approach faces the limitation of arriving at operational measures that generate an inordinate number of methodological choices and problems.

The third approach sees poverty as the social exclusion of people who do not fit into the norms of industrial societies, are unprotected by social insurance and are considered social misfits. The list of such people can include the handicapped, drug users, delinquents, and the aged, among others (Laderchi et al., 2003). It refers to people who are generally marginalised and deprived in society. Like the two previous approaches, which are externally imposed, and as such do not take the views of the poor into consideration, the third also lacks a clear definition and acceptable scales of measuring exclusion.

Finally, the participatory approach, which is built on the poor's perspective of the meaning and magnitude of poverty (Chambers, cited in Laderchi et al., 2003: 23), views poverty as what the poor feel and accept as their state of being and demands the participation of all to evolve and implement a poverty reduction strategy, as initiated by the World Bank and the International Monetary Fund (IMF). The key targets here are the enhancement of material well-being, namely physical and social security, and freedom of choice and action.

Manifestations of poverty

Poverty manifests itself in many forms. Generally, the poor are 'the weak, the hungry, the sick, the homeless, the beggar, the mad, the enslaved and the exiled' in society (Rahnema, 1993: 158). The World Bank (2001) has characterised the poor as

people who live without fundamental freedoms of action and choice. They often lack adequate food and shelter, education and health, deprivations that keep them from leading the kind of life that everyone values. They also face extreme vulnerability to ill health, economic dislocation, and natural disaster. And they are often exposed to ill treatment by institutions of the state (or government) and society and are powerless to influence key decisions affecting their lives.

Perceptions of poverty may differ across cultures or times, but its description seems to indicate the commonality of hopelessness. In a study conducted by the World Bank on The Voices of the Poor that involved 60 000 women and men in sixty countries, a man in Kenya was asked to describe his level of poverty and he said, 'Don't ask me what poverty is because you have met it outside my house. Look at the house and count the number of holes. Look at the utensils and the clothes I am wearing. Look at everything and write what you see. What you see is poverty' (The World Bank, 2001: 3).

The poor live in abject conditions below the poverty line and are defined as 'those who spend less than one United States dollar per day' (World Bank, 2001). On average, this amount cannot pay for one full plate of food for an adult anywhere in Africa. It is very common in Africa for a family of five members to live on less than US$1 a day, a sum which is barely adequate for one meal. Yet, for people to function normally, it is expected that they should feed three times a day. However, some scholars feel that in fact, the amount of US$1 per day is inadequate to explain the poverty situation in Africa. A higher amount, for example US$3 per day, would change the number of people living in poverty from 'a marginal minority' to that of a 'structured majority'. In any case, opinion on the extent of poverty will always differ according to the perspective one takes (Reddy and Pogge, 2002).

Global trends in poverty

The global rate of poverty has continued to remain very high. For example, in 1998, there were more than 1.2 billion persons who were living below US$1 per day or the poverty line. Of the total, 2.0% were in Europe and Central Asia, 0.5% in the Middle East and North Africa, 6.5% were in Latin America and the Caribbean, 43.5% were in South Asia, while East Asia and sub-Saharan Africa had 23.2% and 24.3%, respectively (World Bank, 2001: 4). From these figures, it can be seen that Africa had the second highest number of poor people who lived on less than US$1 per day. Significantly, although there are no accurate statistics to rely on, poverty is found to be more prevalent among the rural populations and among women (Dfid, 2000).

Whereas poverty is falling in other parts of the world, it is rising in South Asia and sub-Saharan Africa (World Bank, 2001). This is in spite of the application of numerous strategies and several efforts by the United Nations, international donor agencies and individual countries, aimed at reducing, minimising or eradicating poverty. There is still a need for interventions that effectively reduce the worst kinds of poverty to the barest minimum, particularly in Africa and parts of Asia and Latin America (Oyen, 2002). There is also a need for an effective assessment of poverty eradication projects and programmes worldwide. This is important because the actual impact of the billions of dollars spent on development assistance remains largely unknown to many (Baker, 2000).

As part of efforts to intensify the search for a positive response to the problem of global poverty and to guarantee significant and measurable improvement in people's lives, the United Nations established the Millennium Development Goals (MDGs) in September 2000. The goals are geared towards reducing poverty by 50% by the year 2015. This goal is complemented by the following seven targets (World Bank, 2002):

1. The attainment of universal primary education for all.
2. The enhancement of gender equity in respect of access to primary and secondary education.
3. The reduction of under-five child mortality rates by two-thirds.
4. The improvement of maternal health by three-quarters.
5. The combating of HIV/AIDS and malaria.
6. The attainment of environmental sustainability through the curtailment of natural resource waste.
7. The establishment of a global partnership for development.

Another complementary effort is the New Partnership for Africa's Development (NEPAD) that pays attention to Africa using broad universal collaboration with the international community (Akwekwe, 2002; Diescho, 2002).

ACTIVITY

1. **Identify five poor families in your community and classify them according to whether they are 'absolutely' or 'relatively' poor. Explain your classification.**
2. **Which approach do you consider most suitable for tackling poverty in your community?**
3. **State three reasons why you consider that particular approach the best for your community.**

THE CAUSES OF POVERTY

Poverty, like other social problems in society, has many causes. The most familiar causes and the major contributory factors include the following (Williams, 1979; Okwuosa, 1994; Omolewa, 1997; World Bank, 2001; and Aliyu, 2002):

1. Lack of income and assets with which a person can secure basic necessities such

as food, education (including basic literacy), health, shelter and clothing. In this case, assets include capacity for labour; skills and health; land; access to roads and other physical infrastructure; and access to credit and other financial services or contacts helpful in terms of political or social influences.

2 Lack of opportunity to participate in those institutions of state and society that make decisions about the lives of people, leading to powerlessness. For example, the poor and especially women are hardly ever represented in African parliaments, top government decision-making positions or even in managerial posts in industry.

3 Vulnerability to conditions of shock or inability to cope with them. For example, uncertainty about rainfall; living in over-crowded environments that are prone to threat and dangers; precarious employment conditions; high risk of contact with preventable epidemic diseases such as malaria, tuberculosis and HIV/AIDS; arbitrary arrest or ill treatment by state agents; and violence, particularly against women.

4 Low productivity due to low capacity utilisation of existing industrial or manufacturing companies; lack of local or foreign capital; political instability; breakdown of family or social values; and inability to harness local resources for development.

5 Unemployment due to lack of skills (for example, 70% of unemployed youth in Nigeria are unskilled); inability to explore informal opportunities for self-employment; inappropriate skills generated from formal educational institutions and programmes (for instance, of the 1 110 000 graduates produced in Nigerian tertiary institutions in 1997, only 100 000 secured formal jobs); and retrenchment of

workers due to rationalisation and restructuring.

6 High population growth with an average annual growth rate in Africa of about 3%, resulting in the overstretching of the use of basic social and physical infrastructure, especially health and educational services.

7 Adverse effects of globalisation on Africa's economies, especially through the impacts of the liberalisation of trade (via the World Trade Organisation's conventions) and the so-called African Growth and Opportunity Act (AGOA) signed between the USA and several African countries. Some of the effects of these measures have been the export of thousands of goods from the USA, in the hope that the African countries might also be able to export to the USA. Other adverse effects have been the free movement of capital in the face of a weak economic base and low level development of Information and Communication Technologies (ICT), hampered by unreliable electrical power supplies, poor telecommunication infrastructure and low levels of computer literacy across the continent.

8 Bad governance, arising from prolonged military rule in some parts of Africa and from white minority apartheid rule in several Southern African countries. Governance under these regimes was not sensitive to or committed to solving the major problems of society. In particular, little was done to address the problem of poverty. Where attempts have been or are being made to do so, poverty reduction programmes are usually poorly implemented or not sustained long enough to allow for the realisation of their maximum impact on people.

9 Corruption, which increases nepotism in public service and massive misappropriation of state resources meant to be

used to address people's needs for food, education, employment and health.

10 Negative attitudes of people towards innovative ways of generating income. For example, most rural people have resisted technological innovations that are intended to boost activities in agriculture and other small and medium enterprises. Similarly educated people have preferred 'white collar' jobs and responsibilities in government or industry, although opportunities for these are limited. Instead of self-employment or engagement in the vocational and informal sectors of the economy, many have chosen to remain unemployed.

11 Debt burden, which in most parts of Africa diverts resources meant for development to the repayment and servicing of foreign debt. For example, Nigeria's debt of US$14.28 billion in 1980 rose dramatically to more than US$30 billion in 2000. Clearly, debt has become a significant national burden that deprives schools, hospitals, and the transportation and power supply sectors, among others, of much-needed funds and thus contributes significantly to the worsening conditions of poverty.

12 Unequal distribution of wealth. Given that African countries have mostly adopted capitalism (sometimes referred to as a 'mixed economy') as an economic order, wealth is distributed unequally. Only a few people control resources and the means of generating wealth. This has created three broad classes in most of Africa: the rich, the middle class and the poor. The majority of the people have been denied access to wealth and resources, which is why they remain poor.

13 Poverty as an act of God. Some representatives of Christianity and Islam take poverty as an act of God on humanity.

It is He who gives to whom He wants. Consequently, many poor people believe that there is little anyone can do about their situation. According to them poverty is God's will (Lamb, 1987). However, there is no scientific basis for this. It is a matter of religious belief. Scholars consider this fatalism as a negation of human effort to overcome existential difficulties (Freire, 1972).

⊞ ACTIVITY

1 Which three of the above causes of poverty do you consider to be mostly responsible for poverty in your community? Give reasons for your choices.

2 Apart from the above, are there any other causes of poverty that you know of? List them and explain why you consider each of them a cause of poverty.

DEBT IN AFRICA

Debt is another major problem that hinders development in Africa. Debt is 'a sum of money that a country owes or the state of owing money' (Longman, 1994: 354). Debt is incurred by African countries from loans, advances, repayable grants and facilities secured from wealthy nations or international financial institutions, such as the World Bank and the International Monetary Fund (IMF). Debts are accumulated through borrowings that have not been repaid over a long period of time. The initial loans are taken supposedly in order to carry out developmental projects that will promote growth, especially the provision of infrastructure such as roads, communication facilities, transport (air and sea), machinery, equipment and services that are considered to be vital for national economic development.

Long-term loans are mostly secured from local and foreign sources by various governments in Africa. Externally, such loans are usually secured from such sources as multilateral financial institutions, including the World Bank and the IMF, the Paris Club and the London Club. Most of the loans are procured from the Paris and the London Clubs of creditor European nations (Obadan, 1996).

The simple logic behind the procurement of the loans and grants is that the money would be used to generate wealth that would boost the economy, and thus enable the country to repay the debts with ease. However, due to the misapplication and mismanagement of funds, the anticipated growth has not materialised. Africa abounds with tales of how government officials have diverted aid money meant for development projects to their personal bank accounts in Europe. Consequently, the development projects on whose account the funds were procured do not thrive and eventually collapse, placing the government in a worse off financial situation than before. Hence, most African governments are simply unable to repay the loans, and therefore remain indebted to creditor nations and institutions for long periods. The volume of both the principal loan and the interest on the initial loan increases periodically. Therefore, many African nations are only able to pay the interest on their huge loans, and have to make arrangements to reschedule the burden of repaying the principal or main loan. In effect, this means that they are trapped into paying enormous amounts of money in interest only to international financial institutions without actually reducing their external debt. This in turn has the effect of increasing their debt. The table on page 126 provides information on the debt profile of Africa in 2001.

The table shows that Africa's total debt was US$258 277 billion in 2001. Projections indicate that the amount is much higher today. Although some African countries have debts of less than US$8 billion, eight of Africa's major countries are among the thirty-four most heavily indebted countries in sub-Saharan Africa (Kanbur, 2000). The eight countries can be grouped into two. Firstly, there are those that have debts of US$8 to 16 billion. These include Angola, the Democratic Republic of Congo (DRC), Ethiopia and Morocco. The second group consists of four countries with external debts of US$16 to 30 billion plus. These are the Republic of South Africa, Algeria, Egypt and Nigeria. On the whole, the most heavily indebted countries are also the most populous, and they seem to have higher adult illiteracy rates, high rates of the prevalence of preventable diseases such as malaria and HIV/AIDS, and higher degrees of poverty.

▦ ACTIVITY

1 **Differentiate between internal and external debts in Africa.**
2 **Explain how debt affects the provision of adult education programmes in the country.**

DEBT AND POVERTY

In Africa, debt and poverty have a reciprocal cause and effect relationship. Generally, it is the poor countries that seek loans and grants as part of efforts to dig themselves out of poverty. Due to the misapplication and mismanagement of those funds, these countries find themselves with a much bigger burden of poverty than they were in before they sought the loan. And, in a bid to rid themselves of this burden they seek more aid and loans, in this way increasing the load even further. Before long the debt is so big that it becomes a contributing factor towards poverty. The existence of huge debts in African countries means that governments have to make substantial provisions for debt repayment in their annual budgets. Consequently, the little funds available for developmental purposes have to be reduced considerably, thereby accentuating poverty among the people. For example, since 1999, Nigeria has had to provide US$1.5 billion annually to service foreign debt (Nigerian Economic Summit Group, 2000). For sub-Saharan Africa, it has been reported that between 1990 and 1993 'the region transferred US$13.4 billion annually

1	Algeria	30 665 billion	28	Libya	No debt
2	Angola	12 173 billion	29	Madagascar	4 394 billion
3	Benin	1 649 billion	30	Malawi	2 444 billion
4	Botswana	548 million	31	Mali	3 201 billion
5	Burkina Faso	9 907 billion	32	Mauritania	2 489 billion
6	Burundi	1 119 billion	33	Mauritius	2 482 billion
7	Cameroon	9 829 billion	34	Morocco	No data
8	Cape Verde	244 million	35	Mozambique	8 208 billion
9	Central Africa Republic	921 million	36	Namibia	No debt
10	Chad	1 091 billion	37	Niger	1 659 billion
11	Comoros	203 million	38	Nigeria	30 315 billion
12	Democratic Republic of Congo (DRC)	12 929 billion	39	Rwanda	1 226 billion
13	Congo	5 119 billion	40	Sao Tome & Principe	246 million
14	Côte d' Ivoire	No data	41	Senegal	3 861 billion
15	Djibouti	288 million	42	Seychelles	2 457 billion
16	Egypt	31 964 billion	43	Sierra Leone	1 243 billion
17	Equitorial Guinea	306 million	44	Somalia	285 million
18	Eritrea	No data	45	South Africa	628 million
19	Ethiopia	10 352 billion	46	Sudan	16 843 billion
20	Gabon	4 425 billion	47	Swaziland	251 million
21	Gambia	477 million	48	Tanzania	7 603 billion
22	Ghana	6 884 billion	49	Togo	329 million
23	Guinea	3 546 billion	50	Tunisia	11 078 billion
24	Guinea Bissau	1 653 billion	51	Uganda	3 935 billion
25	Kenya	7 010 billion	52	Zambia	No data
26	Lesotho	692 million	53	Zimbabwe	415 million
27	Liberia	2 103 billion			
GRAND TOTAL = US$258 277 billion					

Table 9.1: Africa's debt profile in US$ in 2001

to external creditors. This is four times as much as governments in the region spent on health services. In fact, it is more than their combined spending on health and education' (Oxfam, 1995: 2).

In the late 1990s and the year 2000, African countries transferred huge proportions of their annual national income to creditors in compliance with debt service agreements. The remaining funds were undoubtedly insufficient or unavailable for the development of infrastructure, agriculture, education, health, water, environmental management and for other vital national needs.

The debt situation in Africa has become self-perpetuating. In order to service their foreign debts, more and more countries have sought assistance from the World Bank and the IMF (Youngman, 2000). These bodies have granted loans on the strictest conditions which have threatened the sovereignty of some of the countries. Since the early 1980s, lending has been made on condition that the governments adopt economic structural adjustment programmes (SAPs). This was the case in Nigeria, Ghana, Zambia and Zimbabwe in the 1980s. Essentially SAPs prescribe drastic changes in the economic policies of the countries concerned. The prescriptions include 'the removal of restrictions on foreign investment and trade, the promotion of exports, the privatisation of public enterprises, the reduction of government spending, the removal of price controls, the imposition of wage restraints, and currency evaluation' (Youngman, 2000: 69).

The adoption of the SAPs by most African countries has entailed, among other things, the reduction of government spending on the social development sector, particularly education and health; and the suspension of subsidies, including those on school fees and medical fees. This further curtailed access to education for the chil-dren of the poor. It also meant that hospital services and drugs became luxuries and that most adult education programmes moved beyond the reach of the poor – the very people who needed them most.

In other cases, international financial institutions and creditors impose fiscal policies and even take full control of and supervise the operations of the debtor nation's central bank. For instance, this was the case in the Democratic Republic of Congo during the regime of Mobutu Sese Seko in the 1980s. This undoubtedly compromised the sovereignty of that country. Similarly in the 1990s, facilities provided by the World Bank to several African countries were tied to the procurement of Western technologies and equipment, thereby promoting the consumption of Western products instead of the development of local products. This practice inhibits local initiatives in this direction and increases unemployment since local African industries cannot compete with the cheaper, more easily available imported goods.

In addition, the structural adjustment programmes opened up Africa's economies to the capitalist economic systems of Western Europe and North America and brought them under the control and manipulation of the institutions they borrowed from. The SAPs also brought with them liberalisation that allowed Western nations to export all sorts of luxury goods and services into Africa. This was legitimated by the provisions in the conventions of the World Trade Organisation (WTO), as well as the African Growth and Opportunity Act (AGOA). As a result, many local industries in Africa had to close. The closures resulted in the retrenchment of workers and escalated unemployment. In these and other subtle ways, the debt owed to international financial institutions and creditor Western nations has contributed significantly to the creation of conditions that have aggravated the poverty situation in Africa. The measures introduced to 'curtail waste and reduce costs' have largely made the poor poorer and the rich richer. In this way, the income gap between and within groups and nations has widened. In fact, the entire process has sometimes been termed the 'recolonisation of Africa' (Bonger, 1999; Buthelezi, 1999).

▦ ACTIVITY

What do you consider the five major factors that are responsible for the external debt crisis and poverty in Africa? Explain your answer.

POVERTY, DEBT AND ADULT EDUCATION

From the above analysis, it is evident that poverty and the debt crisis in Africa adversely affect adult education in two ways. Firstly, publicly funded adult education programmes become fewer as the government diverts funds meant for them to more urgent and pressing issues, such as servicing the foreign debt. Secondly, the remaining unsubsidised programmes move out of the reach of the poor. This section examines how adult education can contribute towards the alleviation of this state of affairs in Africa.

Poverty and adult education

Specifically, poverty has long been identified as a contributory factor to the lack of adequate educational provision in Africa. Firstly, many poor countries are unable to provide adequate schools and other educational facilities. Secondly, many poor people cannot afford the cost of educating their children, let alone themselves. Either way, it is the poor who are affected; their

areas are not provided with adequate educational facilities, and they cannot afford the necessary fees. For this reason, it is the majority of the poor who are illiterate (Ampene, 1980; Duke, 1988; Omolewa, 1997; Indabawa, 2000). Illiteracy limits people's capabilities to take part in or benefit from development. It has long been found that widespread adult illiteracy is one of the major problems that hampers the development of the African continent, which in the year 2000 had 40% of the over one billion non-literates worldwide. (Indabawa, 2001). Therefore, the eradication of adult illiteracy is instrumental in development and in the reduction of poverty. Literacy programmes, when properly developed, planned and introduced, are ready tools for this purpose, bringing many benefits to the people. For instance, Omolewa (1997: 11) has stated that

literate people are often healthier, and, a healthy community will reduce its expenses on health care. Literacy can also produce a more active economy with higher revenues and taxes contributed to the state. Literacy can provide the means of becoming better informed in the history, culture, religion and politics of the people. Literacy can be an effective instrument of assisting a people to even recognize the elements of poverty and the indicators for measuring [it].

In Africa, literacy has in many contexts on several occasions been used as an instrument for income generation, health education, safe motherhood, popular awareness, socio-economic reintegration, and engagement in the informal sector of the economy. Notable cases have been reported in Mali, Nigeria, Swaziland, Zimbabwe, Sierra Leone and Kenya (Ben-Barka, 1985; Indabawa, 1988; Karagu and Otiende, 1996; Omolewa, 1997; Mpofu, 1997; Sesay,

1999; Biswalo and Baartjies, 2001; David, 2001).

Literacy is not the only tool that can be used for the alleviation of poverty. Poverty alleviation can also be approached through the use of other adult education programmes, especially those that will provide skills with which people can earn a living or improve their conditions. The alternatives include continuing education and continuing professional education; civic, popular or political education; agricultural extension education; health and population education; workers' education; nomadic and migrant people's education; women's education; peace education; distance and open learning programmes and vocational education (Akinpelu, 2002). Such programmes can reach all people who experience one disadvantage or another and whose educational needs cannot be catered for under the formal system of education, due to its restrictive nature.

The providers of these types of alternative education vary widely. They include government or its agencies and civil society organisations, such as churches, mosques, trade unions, human rights advocacy groups, pro-democracy movements, individuals, corporate bodies and international development agencies. In Africa, literacy and popular education programmes are generally government-sponsored. Other providers tend to engage in adult education programmes that are consistent with their organisational goals. It is very rare to find adult education programmes that have been deliberately planned to help alleviate poverty. In most cases, poverty alleviation is expected to be a spin-off from the attainment of other educational goals. This is a gap that needs to be addressed in Africa given the scale of the problem of poverty. All concerned parties should mount specific adult education programmes towards alleviating poverty. Chapter 6 of this book contains suitable examples of potential adult education programmes that can be used or adapted for this purpose. Also, poverty alleviation policies of governments and international bodies such as the World Bank should have a specific education component to ensure that suitable adult education programmes are provided to meet the needs of the diverse groups of people experiencing poverty in Africa. The World Bank in particular needs to invest more in the education of adults beyond its current low level of interest (Oxenham, 1999).

Similarly, funds should be set aside to cater for research on poverty alleviation. The results of such research should be used in the practice of adult education where it is intended for poverty alleviation. Implied here is a need for effective monitoring and coordination of efforts, especially those of government and non-governmental organisations across the continent.

Debt and adult education

The degree of indebtedness of a country has a direct impact on whether or not adult education programmes are funded and if so, how they are funded. Since African countries have huge debts to repay, it is likely that state-sponsored adult education programmes will continue to be underfunded. The whole education sector suffers the same fate, as it cannot be prioritised in nations that are indebted. This is partly due to the creditors' conditions that usually limit any serious commitment to the social sector, particularly education and health. To many creditors, education and health are regarded as wasteful channels for using scarce resources in Africa, particularly since the returns on investment in these areas are long term and do not promise any immediate gains. It is largely for these reasons that fiscal allocation is often limited only to the provision of basic education and health.

Basic education, which receives the lion's share of the education budget, covers up to nine years of primary and junior secondary school. Relatively less attention is paid to higher levels. A glimpse at the formal education statistics of any African country will show a pyramid-shaped enrolment profile. The funding situation is worse for adult basic education. A very tiny portion of the government education budget is spent on adult basic education. The spending pattern is similar in the health services sector. Basic health services receive more attention than tertiary health services, hence Africans are sometimes shipped out of their countries for specialised treatment.

Advancement in most Western nations can be traced to their levels of education. This suggests that advancement in Africa will only occur if African governments pay more attention to education beyond the basic levels. Investment in tertiary health services is also vital since the types of diseases faced by people in Africa require more than basic health services. Basic health services have proved to be inadequate in the face of increasing HIV/AIDS cases 'that affect adults in their most productive years, leaving behind not only dependent children but [also] dependent aging parents'. Clearly, there is a need to go beyond basic education. To this end, it has been argued that 'without significant debt relief, there is little money for prevention, education, research, and medication for HIV/AIDS' (Spencer, 2003). Besides the HIV/AIDS scourge, the African continent has to contend with the rising incidence of malaria and malnutrition. Compounding the glaringly inadequate health systems is the declining agricultural and food security situation in Africa, at a time when there is a rapid increase in the population. More investment in secondary and tertiary health services will go a long way to alleviating the many health problems on the African continent. Therefore, as part

of debt management, African countries must convince their creditors of the need for investment beyond the basic levels in health and education.

More investment in adult literacy education, for example, would take such programmes beyond the acquisition of skills pertaining to reading, writing and arithmetic, the so-called 3Rs. For instance, incorporating an awareness-raising component into such programmes would help adult learners (and through them the larger society) appreciate the implications of the debt burden in Africa.

⚏ ACTIVITY

1 **Describe an adult education programme that can help alleviate the poverty problem of your country.**
2 **Describe how debt owed by your country has affected the education sector, particularly the adult education sub-sector.**
3 **Discuss how adult education can be used to raise public awareness about the issue of the debt burden in Africa.**
4 **State three ways in which poverty affects adult education in your country.**

SUMMARY

This chapter examined the concepts of poverty and debt, how they affect adult education, and, in turn, how adult education affects them. Poverty can simply be described as a person's inability to secure basic needs such as food, shelter, education, and health, among other necessary requirements of normal life. The majority of people in Africa (especially women) are poor and live below the poverty line, spending less than US$1 per day. African countries are heavily indebted to creditor institutions and Western nations to the tune of more than US$258 277 billion. Given the decline in the economies of African countries and the mounting annual interest accruing on the existing loans, this figure is expected to continue to rise annually. Both poverty and debt limit the possibility of rapid development in Africa. When people are poor and the debt is high, only a small amount of funds will be made available for the provision of infrastructure, food, education, health and housing.

Adult education is affected by poverty and debt. For example, there is a correlation between poverty and adult illiteracy. Huge debts in African countries limit the extent to which adult education programmes for poverty alleviation can be provided. As part of efforts to alleviate poverty and to reduce the debt burden several African countries accepted conditional aid packages, which seem to have made the poverty and debt situations worse than before. For example, structural adjustments programmes that were forced upon African countries (as part of the conditions for aid and loan packages) imposed restrictions on government spending in health and education, thus eliminating subsidies for the poor in those two sectors.

There is need for debt relief in Africa, without which African governments will find it hard to initiate and implement programmes that will seriously address poverty in their countries. Creditors need to pay attention to this, and African negotiators need to convince creditors of the importance of offering relief in respect of debt management.

KEY POINTS

- Poverty simply means a state in which a person is unable to meet basic needs.

- Most Africans (particularly women) live on less than US$1 per day.
- Africa's indebtedness to creditor institutions and Western nations is likely to become worse, largely because of the decline in the economies of African countries.
- Both poverty and debt adversely affect development in Africa because, as a consequence, only a small portion of the annual budget will be made available for poverty alleviation and development activities.
- Poverty is closely linked to adult illiteracy, in that wherever there is poverty there is adult illiteracy, and vice versa.
- The debt situation in Africa limits funds which could be made available for adult education programmes and that are aimed at poverty alleviation.
- Structural adjustment programmes which have been forced upon African countries (as part of conditional aid packages) impose restrictions on government spending in the social development sector, therefore worsening the plight of the poor.
- Debt relief in Africa is a necessary condition for poverty alleviation and development.

✖ ACTIVITY

African countries do not need loans and grants to rid their people of poverty. Do you agree with this assertion? Explain your answer.

FURTHER QUESTIONS

1 African nations have vast natural resources and wealth. How and why have they become indebted?

2 How can African countries reduce the debt owed to creditor institutions and nations?

SUGGESTED READINGS

Filson, G. C. (ed.). 1991. *A political economy of adult education in Nigeria.* Ibadan: Ibadan University Press.

Indabawa, S. A., Oduaran, H. A., Afrik, T. and Walters, S. (eds.). 2000. *The state of adult and continuing education in Africa.* Windhoek: Department of Adult and Non-formal Education, University of Namibia.

Sachs, W. 1993. *The development dictionary: A guide to knowledge and power.* London: Zed Books.

Youngman, F. 2000. *The political economy of adult education and development.* London: Zed Books.

Chapter 10

Globalisation and adult education

OVERVIEW

Globalisation is a major development that no nation should ignore, especially the countries of Africa. This is due to the many implications of the concept, its practices and impacts, both positive and negative, on human development. Globalisation's impacts are particularly relevant to education in general and adult education in particular. This is especially because globalisation will affect all aspects of our lives, with serious implications for lifelong learning. Globalisation relates to knowledge, educational reform and transformation, citizenship, work, language, information and communication technologies, leisure, democracy, politics, economics and social interaction within and across societies. A general survey of the literature indicates that there is growing interest in what globalisation is, how it works, and the practical implications thereof (Mpofu, 1996; Mittleman, 1997; Kosgaard, 1997; Walters, 1997). This chapter explains the meaning of *globalisation* and considers the alternative conception, *Africa and globalisation*, as well as *adult education and globalisation*.

LEARNING OBJECTIVES

By the end of this chapter, you should be able to:

1 Define globalisation.
2 Discuss globalisation and adult education.
3 Discuss the implications of globalisation for adult education in Africa.

dwennimmen

KEY TERMS

globalisation   The increasing interdependence and interconnectedness of people of the world. It is a process whereby the economy, culture, technology and governance of countries are integrated.

social problems   Challenges that arise as a result of interaction among people, for example, when HIV/AIDS is contracted through unprotected sex. Other notable examples in Africa are poverty, inequality, criminality and war.

BEFORE YOU START

Which three features of globalisation are most visible in your country? Explain.

THE MEANING OF GLOBALISATION

Globalisation is yet to be defined in a commonly acceptable way. Almost everyone defines the concept in forms that suit their own purposes. However, globalisation, just as development, has been viewed mainly as an economic concept (Oduaran, 2003). To many, globalisation is the unification of the world into one entity, a common village for all without borders. However, we will attempt to provide some commonly used definitions to foster a common understanding of the concept.

A common but narrow definition of globalisation considers it as 'a term that captures (the) multiple changes taking place in the world economy, triggered by the dramatic impact of computer generated information technology in production' (Oduaran, 2003: 16). This definition tends towards the economic dimension of the concept. There are three key indicators of the economic dimension of the concept, namely, immediate movement of capital (especially money and material resources) across countries; production of goods and services on a global scale by multi-national corporations that seek markets, higher economic returns and cheap labour; and an increase in the ratio of world trade.

Globalisation, seen from the above perspectives, necessarily leads to the following outcomes which affect adult education policies and practices (Schugurensky, 1997):

- Integration of national economies into common markets and trading blocks;
- Concentration of capital at the global level, thereby making multi-national corporations more powerful;
- Widening the technological gap between more developed and less developed countries of the world;
- Reduction in the role of the government and its agencies, especially in regulating economic and social matters, allowing greater dominance of the market;
- Increased flexibility in terms of production and the use of labour; and
- Growing social and economic polarisation, leading to an increase in world poverty.

Available data indicate that globally more than 1.3 billion people survive on less than US$1 per day. There is evidence that 'today, the assets of the world's 358 billionnaires exceed the combined annual incomes of countries accounting for half or 45% of the world's peoples' (Schugurensky, 1997: 27).

This polarisation is shown in the increasingly uneven distribution of global income. Seventy-five per cent of the world's income goes to the developed world where only 15% of the population reside, while less than 5% of the world's income goes to over 56% of the world's population who live in developing countries (Oduaran, 2000).

A much broader definition of globalisation comes from Johnston (cited in Oduaran, 2000: 271), who defines globalisation as 'the increasing interdependence and interconnectedness of people of the world in their quest to improve the general condition of life for all human beings'. A similar explanation of the term is provided by the UNDP (2003: 17) when it refers to globalisation as 'the growing interdependence of the people of the world, a process of integrating not just the economy but culture, technology and governance'.

Although there is increased interdependence among the nations of the world, globalisation represents the ideological practice of global political, economic, social and cultural dominance of the world by developed countries, which is accelerated by the increasing use of new information communication technologies. This phenomenon has many impacts, some of which are positive, such as the rapid growth of the world economy (although this has largely been for the benefit of the rich nations and individuals). Other impacts are negative, such as the use of information communication technologies to spread and impose programmes, cultures and ideas that are inimical to local values and norms, especially to the peoples of Africa. For lack of a better term, this conception of globalisation has been referred to as 'neo-liberal' (World Social Forum, 2004).

Although Africa is not culturally homogenous, there are many common cultural values shared around the continent. For example, sexual permissiveness is considered a taboo. However, through the Internet, pornographic sites are posted from worldwide sources. These sites are widely patronised by young Africans in Internet cafes (shops where commercial Internet services are provided) now found in most African cities. The cafes are fast becoming 'sexual cinemas'. This development is seen to be encouraging sexual permissiveness among young Africans and may partly contribute to the rise in child pregnancies and the spread of HIV/AIDS.

In spite of their culturally negative effects, the new information technologies can also help to promote a positive understanding of other people's way of life. In this sense, cultural diffusion can become a way of learning and gaining new experiences. In particular, Africans who go on to study or live in other parts of the world can easily learn about these new societies on the Internet. This may reduce the incidences of 'culture shock' that people widely encounter all over the world.

Basically, globalisation is an old phenomenon that has been in existence since at least the sixteenth century. However, what appears to be new in globalisation are its contemporary structures and features

(Oduaran, 2003), as well as the resultant impacts on people and nations worldwide.

THE ALTERNATIVE CONCEPTION OF GLOBALISATION

Not all are in agreement with the inevitability of neo-liberal globalisation (globalisation as dominated by advanced, industrialised or capitalist nations of the world). To some, the dominant type of globalised economy will not benefit all world nations evenly since there are already in existence factors that place some countries' economies well ahead of others. In particular, the nations of the Northern Hemisphere stand to gain more than countries in the Southern Hemisphere which are generally poor and as such have very low economic bases.

A leading group of those who think of alternative versions of globalisation is the World Social Forum (WSF), which is a platform that seeks to promote a global agenda that 'engages in building a planetary society centred on the human person. It is an open meeting place of groups and movements of civil society opposed to neo-liberal globalization, coming together to pursue their thinking, debate ideas democratically, formulate proposals and share experiences in order to enhance networking for effective action on globalization issues and concerns' (World Social Forum, 2004: 1).

The Forum emerged from a meeting held in Porto Alegre, Brazil, that was attended by some 20 000 participants from 117 countries in January 2001. On that occasion, the Forum adopted a fourteen-point Charter of Principles in respect of globalisation. Subsequent annual meetings of the Forum have taken place to assess the impact of activities carried out in five priority areas of concern, namely, 'Democratic, sustainable development; principles and values, human rights, diversity and equality; media, culture and alternatives to accommodation and homo-genisation; political power, civil society and democracy; and democratic world order, combating militarization and promoting peace' (WSF, 2004: 2). These activities were promoted through conferences, seminars and workshops focused on four thematic areas, as follows: 'Production of wealth and social reproduction; access to wealth and sustainability; asserting civil society and the public realm; and political power and ethics in the new society' (WSF, 2004: 3).

Africa was identified as one of the five regional forums of the WSF. Essentially, the African Social Forum strengthens and con-solidates the WSF in order to help achieve faster progress in terms of set goals. The African Social Forum met in Addis Ababa, Ethiopia, in January 2003 and adopted an agreed set of regional objectives and a methodology of operation. The objec-tives are intended to enhance the potential of African nations as they participate in the current neo-liberal globalisation. The objectives are also intended to put African nations in a better position to work out alternative strategies of local development in partnership with regional and interna-tional partners.

Features of globalisation

The features of globalisation vary widely. According to Watson (cited in Oduaran, 2003: 16), there are ten main features of glo-balisation. Nine of them are outlined below:

1   The growth of multi-national corpora-tions (that is, big companies that have a network of branches throughout the world, such as Shell Petroleum, Merrill Lynch and UBS Securities).
2   The increase in the international division of labour with some areas of commerce monopolised by some multi-national corporations.
3   The dominance of market forces (as is often prescribed by the World Bank and the International Monetary Fund) rather than government control through national planning.
4   The growth of finance and telecommuni-cations which link banks, stock markets, companies and organisations together in a global network, thereby making the movement of capital or money easier across national boundaries.
5   The rise in internal and external migra-tion of people across national boundaries for purposes of seeking employment and job opportunities.
6   The growth of the media through sat-ellite to enable programmes to be transmitted around the world, thereby accelerating considerable cultural diffu-sion and influence.
7   Rapid development of civil society and non-governmental organisations assuming responsibilities of advocacy for social, economic and political reforms.
8   Shrinking space across borders (that is, communication and the flow of ideas and capital are no longer restricted through rigid government control).
9   Shrinking time (that is, information, ideas and influences on cultures and other practices move without regard to time).

IMPACT OF GLOBALISATION

Globalisation, like any other developmental phenomena, has a variety of impacts, both positive and negative. These will depend on what types of benefits or disadvantages are experienced by individuals, groups or nations within the competitive interna-tional framework that has been created by globalisation. Hallak (2000: 24–25) identified three basic consequences of globalisation as follows:

1 The geographical consequences, especially the erosion of the capacity for independent action of national governments, requiring them to surrender some of their powers, authority and sovereignty to regional groups, such as the European Union (EU), the Economic Community of West African States (ECOWAS) and the Southern African Development Community (SADC). These are some of the negative impacts. On the other hand, flexible border controls allow greater mobility of people, goods and services across nations, thereby enhancing the potential for employment and income generation, and enhanced economic prosperity.
2 The cultural impacts which generate two contradictory phases of standardisation and diversification. Standardisation refers to cultural habits leading to similarities in behaviour in different societies. Diversification refers to the tendency of globalisation to stimulate the assertion of cultural identity by different ethnic groups. Diversification leads to the preservation of the multiple facets of society. There is also the possibility of globalisation tending towards encouraging the rise of isolated societies covered by traditional, local, regional or ethnic groups.
3 The segmentation of countries and societies as beneficiaries of globalisation. Here, three distinct participants in globalisation emerge, namely,
    a. those who globalise, that is, the advanced nations that lead with regard to capital and resources, as well as information generation and utilisation;
    b. those who are globalised, generally the information poor; and
    c. those who are left out of the entire process particularly with regard to its potential benefits.
In this respect, most of Africa falls under categories 'b' and 'c' above.

▦ ACTIVITY

1 **Identify and explain two ways through which your country has benefited from globalisation.**
2 **Identify two ways through which your country has been adversely affected by globalisation.**

GLOBALISATION AND AFRICA

Africa is a continent of many problems but with considerable prospects for growth and development. It has huge untapped natural resources – untapped largely due to low technological capacity. Africa also has large numbers of highly trained human resources, many of whom live and work outside the continent. With the emergence of globalisation, concerns have been expressed about whether Africa, in its present condition, can take full advantage of its resources and compete favourably with other nations. Many problems have been identified and debated by different African scholars, most notably Oduaran (2000; 2003) and Walters (1997). Oduaran and Walters, among others, have shown that Africa currently faces many challenges and problems that can hinder the continent's active participation in globalisation. Some of these are stated as follows:

High level of poverty. Many people in Africa live on less than US$1 per day. In many countries, the poverty level is up to 50%. Despite the interventions of governments and international donors through poverty reduction policies, programmes and efforts, the level of poverty has not been substantially reduced over the years. In addition, Africa's huge external debt burden which stood at $258 billion in 2001 increases the scale of poverty being experienced by its people. Therefore, poverty is a significant limiting factor in the continent's participation in globalisation, since with less capital and financial resources, Africa remains less competitive than other parts of the world.

Civil and military conflicts. These types of conflicts, sometimes expressed in full scale and prolonged wars resulting in a huge loss of lives, property and time, are some of the factors which disempower nations from active participation in globalisation. In fact, available data show that in 2000 about 7.3 million people were made refugees in Africa through conflicts in countries such as Angola, Sudan, Liberia, Sierra Leone, Democratic Republic of Congo, Rwanda, Burundi, Ethiopia and Eritrea (Oduaran, 2003).

Spread of epidemic but preventable diseases. The most prevalent epidemic diseases in Africa are malaria and HIV/AIDS. With respect to HIV/AIDS, Africa was reported in 2003 to be 'by far the region worst-affected with an estimated 26.6 million people living with the disease' (UNAIDS/WHO, 2003: 7). It was reported that Southern Africa alone contains about 30% of the world's population of people living with HIV/AIDS (UNAIDS, 2003).

Therefore, apart from the waste of scarce resources invested in health care and other social services, Africa also loses active citizens who might play vital roles in global competition. Further, life expectancy has been lowered to about 47 years, one of the lowest compared to other parts of the world.

Low levels of technology and industrialisation. Africa lacks the necessary technology that will promote effective production of goods and services to allow it to compete in the global market of quality goods. Yet several African countries are signatories to conventions governing world trade, an example of which is the African Growth and Opportunity Act (AGOA) entered into with the United States of America for the free flow of raw materials and manufactured goods to and from Africa (Bugaje et al., 2000).

Poor infrastructure. Africa lacks the physical infrastructure, especially roads, electricity power supply and telecommunication, to facilitate the easy flow of manufactured products for the global market.

Environmental degradation. Currently, Africa faces several threats to its environment and sustainable development. For example, the Sahara desert has encroached on more than 600 000 square kilometres of Africa's landmass. This is apart from other adverse effects on the environment such as increasing deforestation, oil spillage and industrial pollution, depletion or scarcity of water, and poor urban planning and development policies. All these factors affect Africa's natural resource base and position in a globalised world, making the continent less competitive in the global market place.

Adult illiteracy. This is a major problem that limits considerably the process of providing African working people with skills. In 2003, the illiteracy rate in Africa was reported to be about 43% with a gender disparity rating of 33% male and 53% female (UN, 2003). People who are illiterate are unlikely to take full advantage of globalisation as its distinguishing features include knowledge and information flow, dissemination and utilisation. African women are even more likely to be excluded from the benefits of globalisation, given their relative disadvantage in terms of literacy.

Low levels in the provision and use of Information Communication Technologies (ICTs). Africa's ICT usage capacity was reported to be less than 0.1% of the world population of users (Oduaran, 2003). The problem of very low computer usage, as well as difficulties of connectivity with the Internet can be attributed to a severe shortage of electrical power and the lack of telephone facilities across the continent. It is clear that if a nation cannot use ICTs effectively, its participation in globalisation is also affected adversely.

Negative sociocultural practices. For example, rejection or resistance to innovations, norms and practices are manifested in low support or participation in education and training. Similarly, poor attitudes, especially those of community leaders, and difficulties in mobilising them and their people to take an active part in using innovative technologies are major hindrances.

Poor capital base. Most African nations have dwindling economies with a very poor capital base. Even where loans are secured for the development of the national economies from international financial institutions, such as the World Bank and the International Monetary Fund, it is often difficult to operate the structural adjustment programmes prescribed as the prerequisite for economic growth. This problem is made worse by the inability of many nations to tap their natural resources effectively due to poor technological capacities.

Poor leadership and bad governance. In addition to the above factors, Africa also seems to face the problem of a lack of effective political leadership. Many leaders are alleged to be corrupt and not supportive of true democratic governance. In this regard, too many of Africa's leaders tend to be self-serving. Such leaders have been unable to raise the necessary morale and discipline among the people, yet these are essential requirements for successful global competition.

The problems listed above directly affect the ability of Africa to compete favourably in the globalised economy. Therefore, facing these problems as challenges and solving them are necessary steps towards attaining a state in which African nations will fully benefit from globalisation. Africa's poverty has to be tackled, diseases need to be brought under control and stopped from spreading, adult illiteracy needs to be reduced to tolerable levels, conflicts must be minimised, infrastructure and technological bases need to be improved, environmental degradation must be halted, and investment in ICT and its optimum application in the workplace and the socio-cultural arena must be promoted.

Another important strategy for preparing Africa for participation in globalisation is the intensification of the use of education and training programmes. Education, in all forms, needs to be promoted for maximum impact (Oduaran, 2000). Education in general and adult education in particular can lay down a solid foundation for Africa's meaningful participation in globalisation.

▦ ACTIVITY

1 **Which three problems mostly limit Africa's benefits from globalisation? Explain your choices.**
2 **How can adult education be used to counter these problems, and thus enhance Africa's benefits from globalisation?**

GLOBALISATION AND ADULT EDUCATION

A careful look at the features of globalisation reveals that already major social, economic and political changes are occurring across the world with considerable implications for people's cultures, education and training. As UNESCO (1993: 98) pointed out, 'all countries of the world can only benefit from knowing more about the cultural premises of each other's education'.

It is also clear that workers who move to other countries need to learn new skills, languages and other competencies that will help them fit into their new societies. Employers need new information, knowledge and the skills of communication for conducting business. Members of civil society and non-governmental organisations and groups also require re-education of some sort in terms of how to bargain and succeed in their advocacy roles. They also need to learn about ways of reaching out to diverse target groups and to those from whom they seek compensation for violations or infringements of individual rights and freedoms. Similarly, they need skills of mediation between international and local private sector operators on one hand, and governments that are responsible for regulation and control on the other, especially regarding labour and migration issues, problems and concerns.

Almost everybody needs to acquire the newer skills of Information Communication Technologies, especially the use of computers and the Internet in business, popular enlightenment, administration, law enforcement and education. All these are open channels that express the need for various forms of adult education and training for different groups of people, especially the adults and youth who are increasingly engaged in global labour mobility and migration.

Adult education is lifelong in nature. In this regard, it seeks to offer or generate learning which develops the 'human potential through a continuously supportive process which stimulates and empowers individuals to acquire all the knowledge, values, skills and understanding [needed] throughout lifetimes, and to apply them with confidence, creativity and enjoyment in all roles, circumstances and environments' (Longworth and Davies, cited in Oduaran, 2000: 270).

Adult lifelong education can be used to re-equip Africa to take an active part in globalisation in the following ways:

- Generating awareness by educating all actors in globalisation, especially about the nature, objectives, structures and processes of globalisation. This could be done by incorporating elements of globalisation and how it affects people in the curricula of educational programmes (Oduaran, 2000).
- Strengthening lifelong education programmes through allocation of the required levels of funds and facilities for optimum and effective operation. Particular attention should be paid to basic education programmes in both the formal and adult non-formal education sectors.
- Using social action community development programmes to help 'ease the pains of transition from local realities to the global ones' (Oduaran, 2000: 277).
- Collaboration among African scholars to develop relevant research and knowledge bases to enhance Africa's competitiveness in the area of globalisation. It is important for Africa to package and sell its positive values and practices of kindness, support, resilience and persistence in the face of extreme adversities.
- Initiating scholarly debates and dialogues in Africa in order to help facilitate

'understanding of the forces of globalization and how best a balance can be struck
in the interest of all' (Oduaran, 2000:
277).

- Enhancing links between African
  scholars and those scholars in other parts
  of the world through higher education
  linkages and the networking of staff and
  students.
- Intensifying the provision of workplace
  education on globalisation to workers,
  especially so that they can understand
  the meaning, implications and impact of
  globalisation on their lives as producers
  of wealth.
- Increasing the level of financial support for the development and delivery
  of women's vocational education programmes, thus ensuring that women are
  given opportunities to acquire modern
  skills that offer alternatives to traditional
  jobs and social mobility.
- Developing supplementary learning
  materials to serve the needs of adult
  learners and their facilitators in basic literacy, post-literacy, civic and continuing
  professional education programmes.
- Initiating seminars and workshops for
  managerial and other technical-level personnel of private sector establishments.
  This will help generate ideas about the
  best practices that can be adopted to suit
  African conditions.
- Investing in computer education in
  government agencies and in the private
  sectors of the economy, so that these
  skills can be applied for rapid communication.

⌗ ACTIVITY

Adult education is better suited than formal
education to counter the problems that
limit Africa's benefits from globalisation.

Do you agree with this assertion? Explain
your answer.

SUMMARY

This chapter examined the concept of
globalisation, and appraised some of its
features and impacts. Most definitions
of globalisation emphasise the economic
dimensions of the term. However, even in
its broader sense, globalisation is characterised by inequity between the developed
and the less developed countries, with the
former reaping the most benefits, mostly
at the expense of the latter. To counter neo-
liberal globalisation which is dominated
by the developed nations, a new movement, the World Social Forum (WSF), has
since 2001 been working on an alternative
global agenda that will cater for the needs
of all nations, strong and weak, from both
the North and the South. Africa is not posi-
tioned to gain much from globalisation due
to the existence of many problems, such
as poverty, disease, adult illiteracy and the
low level of the use of information and
communication technologies. To be more
competitive in the global era, Africa needs
to redress some of these problems. However, Africa is not just a continent full of
problems. It has considerable human and
material resources promising tremendous
advantages if they are fully exploited and
utilised properly. Adult education, especially
in a broad lifelong learning perspective,
can be used to help Africa become more
competitive in the global arena and in
this way gain more from globalisation. To
this end, all the support necessary must
be provided for all forms of learning and
training programmes. This would help
ensure that people gain the skills, values
and behaviour that will equip them to meet
the requirements of a global world. Also,
it is imperative that Africa invest more in

computer education and the use of ICTs in order to be on par with the main actors in the globalisation process, namely, countries from the North.

KEY POINTS

- The current practices in globalisation are neo-liberal and, as such, more favourable to the developed nations.
- A new movement of those opposed to neo-liberal globalisation, has, since 2001, been working under the auspices of the World Social Forum (WSF) to formulate an alternative global agenda that will cater for the needs of all nations, that is, the developed and the less developed.
- Africa cannot compete effectively in the global arena due to the prevalence of poverty, disease, adult illiteracy and the low-level use of information and communication technologies.
- To be more competitive globally, Africa needs to solve these problems.
- Notwithstanding the existence of these problems, Africa has considerable human and material resources that can give it a competitive edge if these resources are fully exploited and properly utilised.
- Adult education, particularly in a broad lifelong learning perspective, can help Africa become more competitive and therefore gain more from globalisation.
- All forms of adult learning and training programmes must be given the necessary support in order to ensure that the peoples of Africa gain the skills and values which they need in order to compete effectively in the global arena.
- There is a need for more investment in computer education and ICTs as part of efforts to make Africa more competitive.

▓ ACTIVITY

Identify an adult education programme known to you and indicate how you would incorporate elements of globalisation into its content and process.

FURTHER QUESTIONS

1 What would you do to mobilise community support for globalisation in Africa?
2 What should Africa do to solve the many problems that are affecting its meaningful participation in the globalisation process? Explain your views.
3 Can the World Social Forum develop an alternative global agenda that is more helpful to Africa? Explain your answer.
4 African governments should be more concerned with the provision of food, security, basic education and health services to the nation than with the procurement of computers and computer education. Do you agree? Explain your answer.

SUGGESTED READINGS

Bhola, H. S. 1997. 'Education of adults in the age of globalization: Lifelong and full-scale.' In *Issues in the education of adults,* Vol. 8, No. 15, pp. 53–69.

Oduaran, A. 2003. 'Order out of chaos: Repositioning Africa for globalization through lifelong learning.' *International journal of adult and lifelong education,* Vol. 1, No. 1, pp. 11–25.

Walters, S. (ed.). 1997. *Globalization, adult education and training: Impacts and issues.* London: Zed Books.

Chapter 11

Adult education and the environment

OVERVIEW

Human survival largely depends on the factors of the environment. By *environment* is meant the total surroundings in which people live. The environment covers a wide range of components, but the most important include the planet Earth; land and land-related resources such as plants, food, fuels and animals; air; water; and shelter. Almost all life-related activities are affected by these components of the environment. These components are used to foster human progress and meaningful existence. In fact, the environment largely defines human, social, cultural, economic, political and religious activities, particularly in Africa where most people live directly from the environment. However, in using the vital resources of the environment, human action or inaction sometimes generates many problems. Some of these are natural, others are human-made (Jauro, 1996).

This chapter discusses the environment and these related key issues. It also examines the role of environmental adult education for the generation of sustainable development in Africa.

LEARNING OBJECTIVES

By the end of this chapter, you should be able to:

1 Define environment, environmental education, environmental adult education and sustainable development.
2 Identify and discuss at least three key issues in environmental adult education.
3 Describe the principles, approaches and methods applied in environmental adult education.
4 Analyse the role of environmental adult education for the generation of sustainable development in Africa.

KEY TERMS

environment   Everything around us,
including plants, air, water, land, life,
conditions, circumstances and events.

environmental education A process
through which people learn about environmental issues, particularly how to
solve present and future environmental
problems.

environmental adult education   The
deliberate involvement of adults and the
youth in the community in tackling environmental problems and issues.

sustainable development   Continuous
progress that is aimed at meeting the
needs of today while ensuring that
future generations can also meet their
needs based on available environmental
resources.

BEFORE YOU START

In small groups, discuss the kinds of environmental adult education programmes
you are aware of in your community.

DEFINITION OF CONCEPTS

In this section, three main concepts are defined, namely, *environment, environmental education* and *environmental adult education*. It is hoped that this will provide an informed basis for the analysis of the implications of these concepts for practical actions, plans and programmes.

What is the environment?

It is important to start this discussion with a definition of the environment. This is so because, without a grasp of the concept, the attempt to link any type of education to it may not be clearly understood. Put simply, the environment is 'everything around us, plants, air, land, life, etc.' (Pacha, 2000: 2). From this notion, it will be evident that anything that can be identified with the surroundings constitutes an element of the environment. However, some of these elements may be more important than others. For example, some of the most essential elements are life (human and animal), air, water and land, and all the resources associated with these. They are basic elements because human survival is in jeopardy without them.

The environment has also been defined as the totality of external surroundings, including conditions, circumstances and events (Hawes and Hawes, 1982). Therefore, as indicated above, the constituent parts of the environment are many and vary widely according to circumstances. Human beings and animals, as well as the flora (plants) and fauna (animals) are central to any discussion of the environment because all the defined circumstances, conditions or events affect them, directly or indirectly, and in positive or negative ways.

Regardless of how the environment is defined, what is important is for us to ensure that all existing environmental resources and conditions are used in ways that will not adversely affect the quality of life and growth of all inhabitants within it (World Bank, 2003).

What is environmental education?

The interest in environmental education as a concept has intensified since the intervention of the United Nations Educational, Scientific and Cultural Organisation (UNESCO) in 1987, which followed the convening of two joint conferences with the United Nations Environmental Programme (UNEP) held at Tblisi, Georgia (Clover, 2003). Later on, Agenda 21 of 1992 emphasised the need for educational programmes that promote education, public awareness and training on the environment to be provided by governments, educational institutions, industry, employers and workers' organisations (Gagliardi and Alfthan, 1994). Since then, successive attempts to clarify the meaning of environmental education have been intensified. Broadly, environmental education is defined as 'a permanent process through which individuals gain awareness of their environment and acquire the knowledge, values, skills, experiences and also the determination which will enable them to act individually and collectively to solve present and future environmental problems' (ICAE, 2003: 107).

Environmental education has been described as 'education about environmental issues: awareness raising, promotion of ecology-sensitive practices and skill training, [all] involving teaching about the environment' (Belanger, 1996: 23). Environmental education is also known as 'ecological education' (Hautecoeur, 2000).

Environmental education has been considered mainly as the concern of formal schools, especially primary and secondary, where selected elements of the content of environmental education are infused into science, mathematics and literary instruction. Also, through these means 'significant space has been given to environmental education in the official curriculum [with progress] noted and some impact observed including some spillover effects in the community: in agricultural practices, health, hygiene [and] the use of scarce reserves of wood' (Bélanger, 1996: 2–25).

However, it has been found that this approach limits the impact of environmental education to a schooling system that is not inclusive of all people. In fact, millions of children, youths and adults who have no access to formal education cannot take advantage of environmental educational experiences delivered in schools. Yet, there is evidence that major links exist between the poor (most of whom lack access to formal education) and environmental problems (Mabogunje, 1996). Poverty has a direct impact on environmental health, livelihoods and vulnerability to environmental hazards (World Bank, 2003). Besides the limitations of environmental education in schools, such as the exclusion of those who have no access to formal education, there are other problems associated with current practices in environmental education. These include the limited use of practical exercises and the failure to relate education to local issues; emphasis on the educational aspects while ignoring the surrounding environment; and failure to involve the whole community. Due to these limitations, the adult education option becomes more relevant and critical in serving the needs of the poor in society (Bélanger, 1996).

It has also been observed that 'to rely on youth education and wait for the next generation is indeed unthinkable: the ecological risks are too immediate, without involving adults (and to rely on children), has proved to be ineffective' (Bélanger, 1996:

26). This is especially true for Africa, where environmental issues and problems are compounded by poverty and educational inequity. What then is environmental adult education?

What is environmental adult education?

It is difficult to arrive at a generally acceptable definition of environmental adult education. This is so for many reasons, one of which is that until the time of the Fifth International Conference on Adult Education (CONFINTEA V), organised by the UNESCO Institute for Education in Hamburg in July 1997, adult education had hardly received the desired attention in the effort towards promoting environmental education (UNESCO Institute for Education, 1997). Also, adult education lacks clear methodology, does not attract sufficient positive attitudes, understanding and support from policy makers, and there is insufficient in-depth research by scholars. In addition, adult education lacks adequate and relevant instructional materials and support for learning. However, in spite of this difficult situation, adult education is fast emerging as a significant way of pursuing education for environmental sustainability and development.

Consequently, environmental adult education is conceived and practised as the sharing of knowledge and information; the generation of skills and competencies; the raising of awareness; and the mobilisation of adults and the youth in the community for tackling environmental problems and issues. It also stresses the need for practical action in solving environmental problems and for creating a better and more sustainable environment for human development. Therefore, environmental adult education particularly focuses on understanding the sources of environmental problems in order to take steps to deal with them through practical efforts. (Clover, 2003; UIE, 1997).

⌗ ACTIVITY

1 Why do you think it is important for us to know the meaning of *environment, environmental education* and *environmental adult education*?
2 What are the limitations of environmental education, and how can they be countered?

ENVIRONMENTAL ISSUES AND PROBLEMS

Africa, just as other continents on earth, faces many environmental problems and challenges. As already indicated, this arises partly due to natural and human actions or inactions. According to the United Nations Environmental Programme, the following have been identified as Africa's current environmental problems and challenges:

■ Deforestation. Only 20% of forest cover remains and the effect of this varies widely. For example, of the Côte d'Ivoire's original forest cover of 8.5 million hectares, only 1.5 million hectares remain. Forests are used as wood for energy and for commercial agri-business commodities.
■ Desertification. To date, the Sahara desert has encroached on more than 600 000 square kilometres.
■ Overgrazing speeds up desertification.
■ Pressures of increasing population.
■ Emerging lack of water or what has been described as 'hydric stress', especially in the Maghreb, the Sahel and southern parts of Africa where reports indicate that more than 300 million people live without access to good drinking water

and 350 million live without efficient sanitary facilities.
■ Plunder of fish resources by fishing fleets from outside the continent leading to more than a 50% drop in fish stocks in some parts of Africa.
■ Poorly controlled urban development. There is a general trend to desert the rural areas. It has been estimated that by 2015 more than 46% of Africans will live in cities.
■ Industrial pollution, especially in oil-drilling zones such as the Niger Delta in Nigeria.
■ Failure to implement conventions duly signed by many African countries on pro-environment policies, plans and programmes.
■ Failure to properly fund ministries of environment that exist in more than fifty nations of Africa, thereby leading to their inability to tackle most environmental problems.

In addition to the above problems and challenges, there are many others, such as famine, drought and oil spillage which are not fully appreciated nor adequately addressed through meaningful policies, programmes and strategies. These problems negatively impact on the lives of millions of Africans (Oduaran, 2003).

However, African countries are reported by the United Nations Environmental Programme (UNEP, 1997: 1–8) to have placed priority rating on seven areas of concern in environmental policies and programmes since the adoption of Agenda 21 of 1992:

1 Land degradation and desertification, as these relate to food security and sufficiency;
2 Protection and sustainable use of forests;
3 Effective management and protection of biodiversity;

4 Issues of water resources, including the problem of water scarcity and efficient management;
5 Pollution problems, particularly those affecting fresh water resources as well as urban, coastal and marine areas;
6 Climate problems, including drought and climate change; and
7 Demographic change and population pressure on natural resources and in urban areas.

In order to translate policies into practical action to protect and promote the environment, many plans, projects and programmes have been undertaken, some by individual countries and others jointly, since environmental problems are the common concern of all (Bélanger, 1996). The varied impact of these efforts have been assessed variously by different interest groups (ARD, Inc, 2002). However, Africa has considerable natural and human resources that necessitate positive action for environmental protection and sustainable development. Africa has rich biodiversity and forests as indicated in the following examples:

Western Africa
The relic blocks of forests left at Gola in Sierra Leone, at Sapo in Liberia, and at Tai in Côte d'Ivoire are the last remains of the structurally complex and species-rich forests of the upper Guinea zone, and as such are of global importance. Some areas such as Fouta Djallon, Mount Nimba, and Loma at the head of major watersheds in Western Africa (the Niger, Senegal and Gambia rivers) encompass areas of exceptional biodiversity.

The Congo
This area constitutes the second largest primary tropical rainforest area in the world. It has the lowest population density in Africa but the highest level of urbanisation (52%). One of the main economic activities is forest exploitation; others include mining, gas and oil exploration and related industrial activities, although the environmental problems of the sub-region are less severe compared with others on the continent. A future developmental challenge is to keep the primary forest intact while drawing benefits from its local use.

Islands of the Indian Ocean
The biodiversity of some of the island countries of the Indian Ocean are of global significance. The diversity of landscapes in Madagascar and the variety of its flora and fauna have put this country on the list of the environmental priorities of the world. Most of these species are found in the remaining forest areas.

It has been estimated that there were about 11.2 million hectares of eastern rainforest in the past, reduced to 7.6 million hectares by 1950. The main causes of the deforestation are slash-and-burn agriculture and the cutting of wood for fuel to sustain the growing population. The population is still rural, surviving by subsistence agriculture. Madagascar and parts of Southern Africa were the home of the giant ostrich or elephant bird, a huge 3-metre-tall flightless creature whose eleven known species have long been extinct. The mummified bodies and gigantic eggs of this bird have been found in the Madagascar swamps. Their demise was probably caused by human activities.

THE GLOBAL RESPONSE

In response to numerous global environmental problems and in order to help solve, reduce, manage or control their negative effects, the United Nations Organisation convened a World Conference on Environment and Development in June 1992. It was held in Rio de Janeiro, Brazil, and delegates came to the world assembly from more than 170 countries (Apel and Camozzi, 1996). At the end of the conference, which is also known as the Earth Summit (Clover, 2003), an Action Plan called Agenda 21 was adopted (Gagliardi and Alfthan, 1994).

One of the far-reaching recommendations of the Rio conference was the need for more attention to the provision of education and enlightenment opportunities on environmental issues and problems for the peoples of the world, especially in developing countries (Apel and Camozzi, 1996). This form of support for environmental sustainability is to be provided by governments through educational institutions and agencies. Similarly, the private sector and civil society and non-governmental organisations, especially workers' organisations and communities, as well as all interested groups, should take active part in providing educational programmes for the people. This is necessary since environmental issues and problems are the concern of all sectors of society.

It is for this reason that adult education in its widest ramification is considered to be a significant tool of intervention. Adult education will help to save the environment and promote sustainable development (Clover et al., 2000). It is common knowledge that access to opportunities for formal education remains insufficient and limited. Therefore, not all individuals can use formal education as a means of promoting environmental sustainability (Bélanger, 1996).

Ten years after the Earth Summit, a follow-up global meeting referred to as the World Summit on Sustainable Development (or Rio+10), was held in 2002 in Johannesburg. The meeting attracted wider international participation and re-emphasised the need for world nations to take more vigorous action in order to achieve the earlier goals of Agenda 21 of the 1992 Rio meeting.

ACTIVITY

1 What seven areas of concern that African countries have reported as priorities for environmental policies and programmes since the adoption of Agenda 21 of 1992 are being actively addressed in your country?
2 What were the implementations recommended for global environmental problems at the Earth Summit held in Rio de Janeiro, Brazil in 1992 being undertaken in your country?

ADULT EDUCATION AND THE ENVIRONMENT

While it has been observed that environmental adult education initiatives are taking place in many parts of the world (Clover, 2003), the areas of concern vary according to circumstances. In developing countries, particularly in Africa, environmental adult education seeks to cover the major items that will enable people to acquire and use knowledge and skills that will help protect the environment and promote sustainable development. According to Indabawa (2000), Bélanger (2003), and Clover (2003), some of the most pertinent ones include the following:

■ Raising consciousness or awareness about environmental issues and problems and how to deal with them.
■ Providing information about environmental issues, problems and challenges.
■ Providing skills and competencies on how people can safeguard their immediate and wider environment through practical action and decision-making.

- Encouraging the understanding and practical use of positive and diversified environmental practices.
- Drawing on peoples' indigenous knowledge and equipping them with skills for conserving and protecting the environment.
- Facilitating effective participation in the management of natural resources.
- Involving community leaders and youth in designing and implementing pro-environmental educational programmes.
- Engaging leaders of civil society, community-based and non-governmental organisations.
- Mobilising religious leaders to help raise awareness of environmental problems and the need for individual and collective positive action.
- Paying attention to local environmental issues while learning from others.
- Involving women and all those who live and maintain daily links with the immediate environment.

While it is important to identify issues and areas of concern for environmental adult education, the exercise is futile unless these are put into practice in real educational experiences.

There are many illustrations of relevant educational experiences from all over the world. Let us cite the specific example of the Friends of the Environment Association (FEA) in Alexandria, Egypt (Zahra, 2000) as follows:

CASE STUDY: EGYPT'S ENVIRONMENTAL EDUCATION INITIATIVE

The Association was founded in 1990 at Alexandria, Arab Republic of Egypt. Basically, it seeks to halt the deterioration of the environment through the protection, resto-ration and improvement of the natural and human-made environment in Alexandria. It approached the task through participatory education and the training of its target groups especially to help them realise the preservation of Alexandria's ecosystems.

In translating its participatory approach into practical terms, the Association identified various environmental issues and problems. Then it defined their major implications, especially for sustainable development. It also decided to focus on eleven target groups and drew select numbers of them, namely, school pupils, adult learners and university students; teachers; police officers; journalists; radio and television workers; private sector employees; housewives; lawyers; members of non-governmental organisations; government employees; and industrialists.

In delivering the environmental adult education content, the Association employed the method of awareness-raising, education and training, changing behaviour, learner-participation and advocacy. The Association also used a variety of open learning channels to reach the target audience. In particular, it adopted modes and techniques of lectures, seminars, publications of basic information brochures, video shows, workshops and discussion sessions, exhibits, festivals and competitions, press campaigns, peaceful marches and demonstrations, negotiation and the filing of law suits against persons, groups or institutions that engaged in environmental violations or infringements.

The positive impacts of these efforts are many. For example, from the lawsuit instituted against the government of Alexandria in 1991 for donating a public square to the World Health Organisation, the Association generated 25 million Egyptian pounds of government allocation for repairs to the infrastructure of the violated public square. This helped to reduce noise levels from 105 to 55 decibels. The Association's case on pollution against some factories located near certain poor districts is another successful case of legal intervention to save the environment.

⊞ ACTIVITY

1 Bearing in mind the example of the case study on page 153, identify two key issues in your immediate environment and show how best they can be addressed.
2 Who would you engage to undertake an environmental adult education plan in your community? State the reasons for your choice.

APPROACHES TO ENVIRONMENTAL ADULT EDUCATION

Environmental adult education is governed by a number of principles, and can be conducted through different methods and approaches. Some of the most important principles, methods and approaches are examined here.

Principles

The most noticeable principles that guide environmental adult education activities are indicated by Clover et al. (2000) in what follows:

■ A deliberate reconnection with the rest of nature through the human emotions and senses;
■ Identifying and critically examining the sources of current social and environmental problems so as to plan appropriate responses to them;
■ Initiating environmental adult education

efforts within our immediate daily experiences, location and context;
■ Taking personal responsibility for our actions in order to commit ourselves to the recreation of a healthy planet for all species both for the present and the future;
■ Planning appropriate educational responses outside the traditional hierarchical models of educational programmes delivery; and
■ Involvement of all people in the educational undertaking and not leaving it to teachers and learners, given that we are all poets, storytellers, songwriters and more, with the endowed capacity to contribute to environmental sustainability and development.

By keeping to these principles, the development and implementation of environmental adult education programmes and plans will be easier, and the achievement of set targets will be assured. Where programmes are imposed by authority figures, such as government or other sponsors, without due attention to local conditions or social structures it is difficult to accomplish the desired objectives of protecting and promoting the environment for development. It should be emphasised that the necessary factors for success are the principles of consultation and involvement by all.

Methods

The methods and techniques of delivering environmental adult education vary according to needs and conditions. There are broadly two sets of methods that can be applied. These are the traditional teaching and learning techniques, and the non-traditional or open modes. As indicated in the case study of Alexandria's Friends of the Environment Association, the goals of environmental education are not necessarily achieved through teaching, reading and writing only; a variety of other methods may be more important (Zahra, 2000). The open methods include the use of lectures, film shows, problem-solving workshop sessions, advocacy, negotiation and even peaceful protests against acts capable of retarding environmental sustainability and development.

The essential features of the open modes include encouraging participatory engagements, discussions, dialogue and consultation among participants in programmes or with partners. These features complement the limitations of the traditional teaching and learning modes, where the dominance of the teacher could limit the possibility of active participation. It is also possible that creativity and independent initiatives for positive action may be limited as well (Freire, 1972; Indabawa, 1991).

Approaches

Currently, there are three basic approaches to providing environmental adult education. The first is to provide full academic courses or programmes on the environment in formal educational institutions, either through related subjects such as biology and geography, or the other physical sciences. For example, in most African countries, the subject elementary hygiene has long been part of the basic education curriculum. Similarly, some universities in Africa offer diploma and degree programmes in environmental studies, although this is not uniformly practised. One of the many limitations of this approach is that the knowledge of the environment acquired tends to be mostly theoretical and not action-oriented for application in the solving of immediate environmental problems. Therefore, the practical application of knowledge and competencies gained

through formal education are more likely to be applied indirectly, since the holders of qualifications may occupy positions of responsibility in environmental or related areas.

The second approach is to infuse basic elements of information on the environment into the curriculum or content of formal or nonformal education programmes. The amount of content covered in this approach is usually limited since the main content of the programme, for example in basic literacy, has to be covered as well. Therefore, only a small percentage of the time and resources for teaching and learning will go to environmental education. Clearly, this approach limits the degree of the infusion. In addition, there are also difficulties such as developing appropriate learning materials to specifically cover aspects of the environment in the content of learning. The training of the right type of facilitators is yet another difficulty of this approach.

The third approach is to design special environmental adult education programmes or to form an association or group to promote environmental education activities. In this regard, we have already indicated the example of Friends of the Environment Association in Alexandria, Egypt. Another example is Greenpeace, which is an international non-governmental organisation engaged in the promotion of awareness on environmental issues and problems. One of the problems of this approach is that the coordination of the efforts of various groups engaged in environmental adult education programmes is often difficult. As a result of this, scarce resources may be wasted or efforts duplicated. Also, it might be difficult to assess the overall impact of these types of interventions.

The choice of any approach is largely determined by the nature of individuals, groups or institutions involved. However, whatever approach is adopted, it is necessary to ensure that a proper link is established with the task of protecting the environment and the sustainable development of the immediate community as well as the larger society. Paying primary attention to the immediate environment and communities always leads to positive outcomes as shown by the example of an environmental adult education project conducted in Burkina Faso, described in the following case study (Filson and Renaud, 1997).

CASE STUDY: CHANGING ENVIRONMENTAL PRACTICES

In an effort to eliminate the root causes of environmental destruction, the Centre Écologique Albert Schweitzer used environmental adult education as a tool to change household practices and habits in Burkina Faso. Through collaboration with local organisations, the Centre's staff was able to encourage women to use solar cookers and so change their cooking habits in order to reduce the use of wood for cooking, a major cause of deforestation in Africa.

Initially, the women were sceptical about this simple but novel energy-saving cooking technology. Through persistent encouragement, however, they became willing to try and through practise the new habit became acceptable to them. But how did this happen in practical terms?

The women approached the solar oven and put their hands into it. Some went on their knees and looked for the fire under the solar oven box. After some demonstration, they began to accept the innovation, tasted the cooked food and admitted that it was good, although some of them still felt it was impossible to cook food without fire. From then on, most women in the target community changed their cooking habits and adopted the solar option, especially because it was faster and more efficient. Women could now return home from the markets or other economic or social undertakings and begin cooking much later than they had previously done.

The replication of this experience in many parts of Burkina Faso not only helped to popularise solar cooking but it also contributed to a drastic reduction in deforestation and associated problems caused by it in the country.

As far as environmental adult education is concerned, each of the approaches mentioned above can be applied. Special environmental adult education programmes can be developed in tertiary educational institutions. Already, elements of environmental education are found in many adult education diploma and bachelors' degree programmes in some African universities. For example, courses such as these are offered in the Bachelor of Education (Adult Education) programmes at Ahmadu Bello University, Zaria, Nigeria, and at the University of Namibia, Namibia. Elements of environmental studies are also taught in many adult secondary and other equivalent programmes. Similarly, the infusion of the content of environmental studies into various non-formal adult education programmes, especially basic and post-literacy programmes sponsored by the government, has become commonplace in Africa. However, these interventions are generally regarded as inadequate given the enormity of the environmental problems being faced in Africa (ICAE, 2003). Therefore, more efforts are required to address the problem.

▦ ACTIVITY

1 In your own words, describe one principle, one method and one approach to environmental adult education.
2 Which method or approach would you choose to solve a particular environmental problem in your community, and why?
3 Examine one problem of each method and approach discussed above, citing relevant examples within your community.

ROLE OF ENVIRONMENTAL ADULT EDUCATION

As already indicated, one of the goals of environmental education, whether provided in formal or nonformal education programmes, is to help promote sustainable development. Sustainable development is defined as development that is aimed at meeting current needs, while ensuring that future generations can also meet their needs based on available environmental resources. Therefore, environmental adult education will help to promote the possibility of knowledge, values and skills which can help sustain natural and human resources within every environment. Environmental adult education is capable of creating the necessary conditions for responsible environmental behaviour. This can and has been done through the provision of knowledge with regard to relevant environmental concepts, environmental problems and issues; the creation of concern for the quality of the environment; awareness and competence about action strategies for the resolution of environmental issues; belief in the fact that individual and collective effort and actions can make a difference; commitment to action; and gaining as well as using

experience in action-based approaches (Husen, 1994).

Environmental adult education is also capable of promoting sustainable development through popularising local environmental issues and establishing links with global issues. In a study conducted in twenty-one countries involving 262 science teachers, six major global environmental problems associated with sustainable development were identified. The problems were world hunger and food resources; population growth; air quality and atmosphere; water resources; and human health and diseases (Husen and Postlethwaite, 1994).

All these issues should constitute part of the content elements of environmental adult education. On the other hand, these problems can be addressed more meaningfully at local level. In the end, understanding these issues and taking collective action to help solve them or to minimise possible damage that may occur, will be an important contribution to sustainable development in society. However, the issue is whether, as presently undertaken, environmental adult education programmes address these problems. If they are not fully addressed, then a reform of the curriculum is necessary, although as already pointed out, environmental adult education may also be conducted through means other than just teaching and learning. For instance, advocacy in favour of healthy environmental living and on the need to protect and promote environmental sustainability is effective in many countries of the world. In this respect, the role of non-governmental organisations is essential in that they play significant functions complementary to the efforts of governments and related agencies.

However, environmental adult education cannot support sustainable development effectively if it continues to face major problems itself as an area of practical activity. According to one of the workshop groups of CONFINTEA V, some of the major problems include the following (UNESCO Institute for Education, 1997: 13):

- Government policies for the promotion of environmental adult education are still unfavourable, especially in terms of clarity and the commitment of funds for its active implementation;
- Environmental adult education is less developed than formal education;
- Teaching in environmental adult education tends to be limited to transmission of knowledge, rather than critical examination of environmental problems;
- Practical solutions are not usually promoted in environmental adult education; and
- Contents of teaching and learning are hardly adequately linked to the immediate environment of the participants.

⊞ ACTIVITY

1 Describe the relationship between environmental adult education and sustainable development in your own words.
2 List five major problems that environmental adult education in your community faces in its efforts to create change, and suggest possible solutions to them.
3 Suppose you are appointed as the environmental adult education officer of the a mining or oil company in your area. Which problem would you consider to be the most important for the company's environmental adult education programme, and why?

SUMMARY

This chapter discussed the environment and the role of environmental adult education in the promotion of sustainable development. The environment is simply everything around us, including plants, air, land and life. Environmental education in formal schools and current government environmental policies and programmes have not been sufficient or effective in tackling the many environmental problems in society. To remedy this situation, the content of programmes needs to be reformed to allow for the inclusion of relevant local and global environmental issues and problems. There is also need to adopt open modes in delivering environmental education programmes. These open-mode type campaigns and advocacy are more relevant to the logistics of environmental adult education programmes.

In many ways, environmental adult education can help the process and outcome of efforts towards sustainable development in the community. However, the many obstacles militating against the effective planning and delivery of environmental adult education programmes need to be solved. Environmental adult education will succeed best when emphasis is placed on practical action and collective responsibility to environmental issues in the community. Therefore, the roles of civil society, community and religious leaders, as well as non-governmental organisations cooperating with relevant government agencies, are necessary factors for the success of environmental adult education programmes.

KEY POINTS

- The environment is everything around us, including plants, air, land, and life.
- Environmental education in schools and in government environmental policies and programmes have not been very effective in tackling the many environmental problems of society.
- To remedy this situation, there is a need for environmental adult education programmes that are adaptable to open-mode type campaigns and advocacy.
- To help the process and outcome of efforts in the community towards sustainable development, the many obstacles militating against the effective planning and delivery of environmental adult education programmes must be solved.
- Environmental adult education will be more effective when there is emphasis on practical action and collective responsibility for environmental issues in the community.

▦ ACTIVITY

Identify three major environmental problems in Africa and indicate ways in which they can be tackled through environmental adult education initiatives.

FURTHER QUESTIONS

1 Knowledge of the environment and environmental issues is a must for all adult educators. Do you agree? Explain your answer.

2 How would you go about generating funds from the environment in order to promote the sustainable use of the environment in your community?

3 What specific roles would you recommend for traditional and religious leaders in the community to help raise awareness about environmental issues and the need for collective action?

4 What type of environmental adult education programme would you propose for the solution of problems associated with refuse waste disposal in your community? Give reasons for your choice.

SUGGESTED READINGS

Apel, H. and Camozzi, A. 1996. *Adult environmental education: A handbook on context and methods.* Bonn: IIZ-DVV (Supplement to *Adult Education and Development* No. 47).

Filho, W. L. et al. (eds.). 1996. *A sourcebook of environmental education: A practical review based on the Belgrade Charter.* London: The Parthenon Publishing Group, Inc.

International Council on Adult Education. 2003. *Agenda for the future: Six years later – ICAE Report.* Toronto: ICAE.

Hautecoeur, J. (ed.). *Ecological education in everyday life.* Hamburg: UNESCO Institute for Education.

UNESCO Institute for Education. 1997. *Adult environmental education: Awareness and environmental action.* Hamburg: Unesco Institute for Education.

References

Adara, O. 2002. 'Pedagogical issues and gender concerns on HIV/AIDS education'. In *Education sector's response to HIV/AIDS in Nigeria*, eds. C. Hubert et al., pp. 61–78. Abuja: UNESCO.

Afrik, T. 1998. 'International input in adult education research in Africa'. In *Retrospect and renewal: The state of adult education research in Africa*, eds. M. A. Omolewa, E. E. Osuji and A. Oduaran, pp. 13–22. Dakar: UNESCO-BREDA.

Afrik, T. 2000. 'Significant post-independent developments in adult and continuing education in Africa'. In *The state of adult and continuing education in Africa*, eds. S. A. Indabawa, A. Oduaran, T. Afrik and S. Walters, pp. 19–30. Windhoek: Department of Adult and Non-formal Education, University of Namibia.

Agun, I. 1980. 'General mobilization for mass literacy'. In *Towards the national mass literacy campaign*, pp. 19–33. Lagos: Federal Ministry of Education.

Ahmadu, W. H. 2002. 'The new partnership for Africa's development (NEPAD): A neo-colonial agenda'. Available at http:/www.amanaonline.com/Articles/art_204.htm

Ajayi, A. 1981. *West African traditional religion.* Ado Ekiti: Omolayo Standard Press & Bookshop Ltd.

Akinpelu, J. A. 1987. 'Relevance in education: An inaugural lecture', University of Ibadan. Ibadan: University Press.

Akinpelu, J. A. 1990. 'Adult literacy and national development'. In *Literacy Voices,* Vol. 1, No. 1, pp. 3–13.

Akinpelu, J. A. 2002. *Philosophy and adult education.* Ibadan: Stirling-Horden.

Aksornkool, N. 2001. *Gender and post literacy: A non-formal education approach to HIV/AIDS prevention.* Paris: UNESCO.

Aliyu, A. 2002. 'Poverty in Nigeria: Factual dimensions and existing policy responses'. Paper presented at the All Stakeholders National Workshop on Nigeria's Poverty Reduction Strategy, Abuja, 5–6 February.

Allen, J. 2000. *Opening worlds to a brighter future: A better future for girls and boys orphaned by AIDS.* Paris: UNESCO.

Allport, G. W. 1971. *Die Natur des Vorurteils.* Cologne.

Ampene, E. K. 1980. 'The fruits of literacy'. In *Adult education in Nigeria,* December, pp. 1–8.

Anderson, C. A. and Bowman, M. J. 1966. *Education and economic development.* London: Frank Cass.

Apel, H. and Camozzi, A. 1996. *Adult environmental education: A handbook on context and methods.* Bonn: IIZ/DVV (Supplement to *Adult Education and Development,* No. 47).

Archer, D. and Cottingham, S. 1996. 'Action research report on REFLECT: The experiences of three REFLECT pilot projects in Uganda, Bangladesh, El Salvador', Serial No. 17. London: Overseas Development Administration.

dwennimmen

ARD, Inc. 2002. *Nigeria environmental analysis. Final report.* Burlington, VT: ARD Inc.

Assimang, M. 1989. *Religion and social change in West Africa: An introduction to the sociology of religion.* Accra: Ghana University Press.

Assimang, M. 1990. 'Women in Ghana: Their integration in socio-economic development.' In *Research Review*, NS, Vol. 6, No. 1.

Baker, J. L. 2000. *Evaluating the impact of development projects on poverty: A handbook for practitioners.* Washington, DC: The World Bank.

Barry, I. 'Women, literacy and social change: The case of the "Guilentico Women's Group" in Gongore.' In *Adult Education and Development*, No. 55, pp. 197–220.

Bélanger, P. 1996. 'Learning environment and environmental education'. In *The Sahara is coming*, ed. A. Ngaba-Waze, pp. 23–30. Hamburg: UNESCO Institute for Education.

Ben-Barka, L. A. 1985. 'Training in Malian rural women: Its impact on cash income and on improvement in standard of living: The CMDT case.' A report submitted to the University of Southern California.

Bettleheim, C. 1968. *India independent.* New York: MR Press.

Betts, J. 2002. 'Literacies and livelihoods: The Dfid Kathmandu Conference.' In *Adult Education and Development*, No. 58, pp. 61–66.

Bhasin, K. 1992. 'Education for women's empowerment: Some reflections.' In *Adult Education and Development*, No. 39, pp. 11–24.

Bhola, H. S. 1983. 'Non-formal education in perspective.' In *Prospects*, Vol. 13, No. 1, pp. 45–53.

Biswalo, P. L. and Baartjies, Z. 2001. 'Women's need for credit in order to participate in income-generating activities: Swaziland case study.' In *Adult Education and Development*, No. 57, pp. 89–106.

Blaug, M. 1972. *Introduction to the economics of education.* London: Penguin.

Bonger, T. 1999. 'Structural adjustment in Uganda and implications for rural poverty.' In *Journal of Economic Development for Southern Africa*, Vol. 1, Nos. 6 & 7, pp. 39–83.

Bown, L. and Okedara, J. T. (eds). 1981. *An introduction to the study of adult education: A multi-disciplinary and cross-cultural approach for developing countries.* Ibadan: University Press Ltd.

Bugaje, U. et al. (eds.). 2000. *On industrial development of the Northern States of Nigeria.* Abuja: National Development Project.

Burchfield, S. A. 1997. *An analysis of the impact of literacy on women's empowerment in Nepal.* Washington, DC: Academy for Educational Development.

Buthelezi, S. 1999. 'Development or re-colonisation: International finance and the developing world'. In *Journal of Economic Development for Southern Africa*, Vol. 1, Nos. 6 & 7, pp. 9–38.

Brookfield, S. D. 1994. *Understanding and facilitating adult learning.* Burkingham: Open University.

Bwakirah, C. 2002. 'Psycho-social and care issues in HIV/AIDS education.' In *Education sector's response to HIV/AIDS in Nigeria,* eds. C. Hubert et al., pp. 79–85. Abuja: UNESCO.

Carp, A., Peterson, R. and Roelfs, P. 1974. 'Adult learning interests and experiences.' In *Planning non-traditional programs: An analysis of the issues for post-secondary education,* eds. K. P. Cross, J. P. Valley et al., pp. 11–52. San Francisco: Jossey-Bass.

Carron, G., Mwiria, K. and Righa, G. 1989. *The functioning and effects of the Tanzanian literacy programme.* IIEP Research Report, No. 93. Paris: International Institute for Educational Planning.

Cawthera, A. *Let's teach ourselves: The operation and effectiveness of a peoples's literacy movement.* Manchester: Centre for Adult and Higher Education, University of Manchester.

Chebanne, A., Nyati-Ramahobo, L. and Youngman, F. 2000. 'Adult literacy and cultural diversity in Botswana.' A paper presented at the Fifth Botswana Annual National Literacy Forum (BANALF), June.

Chlebowska, C. 1992. *Knowing and doing: Literacy for women.* Paris: UNESCO.

Christenson, J. A. and Robinson, J. W. 1980a. *Community development in America.* Ames, IO: Iowa State University Press.

Christenson, J. A. and Robinson, J. W. 1980b. 'In search of community development.' In *Community development in America,* eds. J. A. Christenson and J. W. Robinson, pp. 3–17. Ames, IO: Iowa State University Press.

Child, H. 1968. *The history of the amaNdebele.* Salisbury: Government Printer.

Clover, D. E. 2003. 'Environment and adult education.' In *ICAE: Agenda for the Future: Six years later – ICAE Report,* pp. 114–115. Toronto: ICAE.

Clover, D. E., Follen, S. and Hall, B. L. (eds.). 2000. *The nature of transformation: Environmental adult education.* Toronto: University of Toronto and ICAE.

Collins, R. 1974. *Conflict sociology: Toward an explanatory science.* New York: Academic Press.

Comings, J. P. et al. 1998. *A comparison of impact from schooling and participation in adult literacy programs among women in Nepal.* Boston: World Education.

Coombs, P. H. and Ahmed, M. 1974. *Attacking rural poverty: How non-formal education can help.* London: Johns Hopkins University Press.

Daily Trust. 2003. 'HIV/AIDS increasing rapidly in Nigeria – USAID.' In *Daily Trust,* 16 September, p. 33.

David, M. D. 2001. 'The Zimbabwe literacy campaign: Problems and ways forward.' In *Adult Education and Development,* No. 57, pp. 123–128.

Delors, J. et al. (eds.). 1998. *Learning: The treasure within.* Paris: UNESCO.

Dexter, E. R. et al. 1998. 'Maternal schooling and health related language and literacy skills in rural Mexico.' In *Comparative Education Review,* Vol. 42, No. 2, pp. 130–162.

Dfid. 2000. *Poverty elimination and the empowerment of women: Strategies for achieving international development targets.* London: Dfid.

Diescho, J. 2002. *Understanding the new partnership for Africa's development* (NEPAD). Windhoek: Namibia Institute for Democracy.

Duke, C. 1988. 'Adult education and poverty: What are the connections?' In *Adult Education and Development,* No. 30, pp. 39–49.

Durkheim, E. 1984 [1893]. *The division of labour in society,* transl. W. D. Halls. London: Macmillan.

Ekwekwe, E. 1986. *Class and state in Nigeria.* Lagos: Longman.

Europa Publications. 2001. *A political chronology of Africa.* London: Europa Publications.

Evans, D. R. (ed.). 1994. *Education policy formulation in Africa: A comparative study of five countries.* Technical Paper No. 12. Washington, DC: USAID.

Fanon, F. 1974. *The wretched of the earth.* London: Penguin.

Fagerberg-Diallo, S. 2002. 'Learning to read woke me up: Motivations and constraints in learning to read in Pulaar (Senegal).' In *Adult Education and Development,* No. 58, pp. 45–60.

Federal Ministry of Education (Nigeria). 2000. *Comprehensive education analysis project.* Abuja: Federal Ministry of Education.

Federal Republic of Nigeria. 1989. *National policy on education.* Lagos: NERC Press.

Filson, G. C. (ed.). 1991. *A political economy of adult education in Nigeria*. Ibadan: University of Ibadan Press.

Filson, L. and Renaud, P. 1997. 'Femmes et formation en gestion appliquée (FEFGA).' Project pilote au Burkino Faso. Évaluation finale. Washington, DC: World Bank.

Freire, P. 1972a. *Cultural action for freedom*. London: Penguin.

Freire, P. 1972b. *Pedagogy of the oppressed*. London: Penguin.

Freire, P. 1974. *Education: The practice of freedom*. London: Penguin.

Freire, P. 1985. *The politics of education, power and liberation*. London: Bergin & Garvey.

Gaborone, S. S. M. 1980. *The evaluation of farmer education at Impala short course*. Gaborone: Institute of Adult Education.

Gagliardi, R. and Alfthan, T. 1994. *Environmental training: Policy and practice for sustainable development*. Geneva: ILO.

Gajanayake, S. and Gajanayake, J. 1995. *Community empowerment: A participatory training manual on community project development*. New York: PACT.

Gann, L. G. and Duignan, P. 1970. *Colonialism in Africa, 1870–1960*. Vols. I and II. Cambridge: Cambridge University Press.

Garrido, J. G. 1992. 'Open and non-formal education: New paths for education in a new Europe.' In *Comparative Education*, Vol. 28, No. 1, pp. 83–89.

Grandreams. 1996. *The pocket English dictionary*. London: Grandreams Ltd.

Groener, Z. 2000. 'The political and economic contexts of adult education and training in South Africa.' In *The state of adult and continuing education in Africa*, eds. S. A. Indabawa, A. Oduaran, T. Afrik and S. Walters, pp. 161–177. Windhoek: Department of Adult and Nonformal Education, University of Namibia.

Gordon, M. 1964. *Assimilation in America*. New York: Oxford University Press.

Haladu, A. A. 1995. 'Community development efforts in Nigeria.' In *Theory and practice of adult and community education*, eds. I. Bio and M. B. Shitu, pp. 70–75. Lagos: Text and Leisure Publishers Ltd.

Hall, S. 2000. 'Rassismus als ideologischer Diskurs'. In *Theorien uber Rassismus*, ed. N. Räthzel, pp. 7–16. Hamburg: Argument.

Hallak, J. 2000. 'Globalisation and its impact on education'. In *Globalisation, educational transformation and societies in transition*, eds. T. Mebrahtu, M. Crossley and D. Johnson, pp. 21–40. Oxford: Symposium Books.

Hamidullah, M. 1981. *Introduction to Islam*. Lagos: Islamic Publications Bureau.

Hautecœur, J. (ed.). 2000. *Ecological education in everyday life*. Hamburg: UNESCO Institute for Education.

Hawes, G. R. and Hawes, L. S. 1982. *The concise dictionary of education*. New York: Van Nostrand Reinhold Company.

Hazoumê, M. L. 1999. *Africa and the democratic challenge: An essay in adult education for democracy and the culture of peace*. Hamburg: UNESCO Institute for Education.

Hugkuntod, U. and Tips, W. E. J. 1987. 'Planning and implementation of non-formal education projects in rural Thailand'. In *International Review of Education*, Vol. 33, No. 1, pp. 51–73.

Hunt, E. K. and Sherman, H. J. 1981. *Economics: An introduction to traditional and radical views*. New York: Harper and Row.

Husen, T. and Postlethwaite, T. N. (eds.). 1994. *The international encyclopaedia of education*, 2nd edn. London: Pergamon.

Hutchinson, J. and Smith, A. (eds.). 1996. *Ethnicity*. Oxford: Oxford University Press.

ICAE. 2000. 'Damascus Declaration – Seizing the moment: A call for action on literacy and adult education for all.' In *Adult Education and Development*, No. 55, pp. 7–13.

ICAE. 2003. *Agenda for the future: Six years later – ICAE Report*. Toronto: ICAE.

Imam, A. 1990. 'Gender analysis and African social sciences in the 1990s.' In *African development*, Vol. 15, Nos. 3 & 4, pp. 1–17.

Imoagene, O. 1990. 'Predicting success in a developing society.' An inaugural lecture, University of Ibadan. Ibadan: University Press.

Indabawa, S. A. 1988. *A study of the 1982–1992 National Mass Literacy Campaign in Kano State*. Unpublished MEd thesis, Ibadan: University of Ibadan.

Indabawa, S. A. 1991a. *Themes in adult and non-formal education.* Lagos: Text and Leisure Publishers Ltd.

Indabawa, S. A. 1991b. 'The political determinants of mass education in some African countries.' In *Readings in education for all,* eds. I. A. Kolo et al., pp. 29–43. Lagos: Text and Leisure Publishers Ltd.

Indabawa, S. A. 1993a. 'On colonial adult education and the underdevelopment of Africa.' In *African Asssociation for Literacy and Adult Education Journal,* Vol. 7, No. 2, pp. 12–22.

Indabawa, S. A. 1993b. *Women in development: A comparative study of access to Western education in Kano and Oyo states of Nigeria, 1976–1991.* Unpublished PhD thesis, University of Ibadan.

Indabawa, S. A. 1995a. 'Literacy and development in the developing world: A critique of the position of the German Adult Education Association (DVV).' In *Kano Journal of Educational Studies,* Vol. 1, No. 2, pp. 81–92.

Indabawa, S. A. 1995b. 'On the trends of adult education research in northern Nigeria.' In *Journal of Education in Africa,* Vol. 5, No. 1, pp. 83–92.

Indabawa, S. A. 2000a. 'Language and literacy. Some thoughts on implications for policy and practice in Africa.' In *Language and development in Southern Africa: Making the right choices,* eds. R. Trewby and S. Fitchat, pp. 178–188. Windhoek: Gamsberg Macmillan.

Indabawa, S. A. 2000b. *Teaching methods and techniques I, II and III.* Windhoek: Centre for External Studies, University of Namibia.

Indabawa, S. A. 2000c. 'Diversity of non-formal education provisions in Namibia.' In *The state of adult and continuing education in Africa,* eds. S. A. Indabawa, A. B. Oduaran, T. Afrik and S. Walters, pp. 233–242. Windhoek: Department of Adult and Non-formal Education, University of Namibia.

Indabawa, S. A. 2001. 'Education for civil society in Africa: An agenda for the 21st century.' In *Africa in the new millennium: Challenges and prospects,* eds. E. Maloka and E. le Roux, pp. 114–130. Pretoria: Africa Institute of South Africa.

Indabawa, S. A. 2002. 'Non-formal education and HIV/AIDS.' In *Education sector's response to HIV/AIDS in Nigeria,* eds. C. Hubert et al., pp. 48–62. Abuja: UNESCO-Nigeria.

Indabawa, S. A., Mpofu, S. T., Avoseh, M. B. M. and Ramananandan, K. 2000. *Report of the University of Namibia panel on the recognition of the Namibian College of Open Learning's Certificate in Education for Development.* Windhoek: University of Namibia.

Indabawa, S. A., Oduaran, A. B., Afrik, T. and Walters, S. (eds.). 2000. *The state of adult and continuing education in Africa.* Windhoek: Department of Adult and Nonformal Education, University of Namibia.

International Bureau of Education. 1990. *Bulletin of the International Bureau of Education,* No. 254. Geneva: International Bureau of Education.

Jarvis, P. 1990. *An international dictionary of adult and continuing education.* London: Routledge.

Jauro, A. 1996. 'Cooperation between Africa and Europe on environmental education: The case of the Lake Chad Basin.' In *The Sahara is coming,* ed. A. Ngaba-Waye, pp. 47–52. Hamburg: UNESCO Institute for Education.

Jellema, J. and Hernendez, M. M. 2002. 'Empowerment of women in Cuba: Experiences of the Sofia Mentor programme'. In *Adult Education and Development,* No. 59, pp. 43–58.

Johns Hopkins University. 2002. *Basic facts on democracy and good governance.* Abuja: Johns Hopkins University/USAID.

Johnson-Bailey, J. 2001. 'The road less walked: A retrospective of race and ethnicity in adult education.' In *International Journal of Lifelong Education,* Vol. 20, Nos. 1 & 2, pp. 89–99.

Kabuga, C. 1982. 'Why andragogy?' In *Adult Education and Development,* No. 19, pp. 53–60.

Kanbur, R. 2000. 'Aid, conditionality and debt in Africa.' In *Foreign aid and development: Lessons learnt and directions for the future,* ed. F. Tarp, pp. 409–422. London, New York: Routledge.

Karugu, A. M. and Otiende, J. E. 1996. 'Women's and men's informal sector enterprises in Nairobi, Kenya.' In *Adult Education and Development,* No. 47, pp. 143–156.

Kassam, Y. O. 1988. 'Literacy and development: What is missing in the jigsaw puzzle?' In *Adult Education and Development,* No. 31, pp. 125–137.

Kim, K. D. 1973. 'Toward a sociological theory of development: A structural perspective.' In *Rural Sociology,* Vol. 38, No. 4, pp. 462–476.

Kisekka, M. N. (ed.). 1992. *Women's health issues in Nigeria.* Zaria: Tamaza Publishing Company Ltd.

Knowles, M. 1980. *The modern practice of adult education: From pedagogy to andragogy.* Eaglewood Cliffs, JNJ: Cambridge.

La Belle, T. 1983. 'Goals and strategies of non-formal education in Latin America.' In *Comparative Education Review*, Vol. 20, pp. 328–345.

Laderchi, C. R., Saith, R. and Stewart, F. 2003. 'Does it matter that we don't agree on the definition of poverty? A comparison of four approaches.' Working Paper No. 107, Queen Elizabeth House, University of Oxford.

Lamb, D. 1987. *The Africans.* New York: Vintage Books.

Lind, A. 1996. *Free to speak up: Overall evaluation of the National Literacy Programme in Namibia.* Windhoek: Gamsberg Macmillan.

Lind, A. and Johnston, A. 1990. *Adult literacy in the Third World: A review of objectives and strategies.* Stockholm: Swedish International Development Authority.

Lindeman, E. C. 1989. *The meaning of adult education.* Montreal: Harvest House Ltd.

Liveright, A. A. and Haywood, N. (eds.). 1968. *The Exeter papers: Report of the First International Congress on the Comparative Study of Adult Education.* Brookline: Centre for the Study of Liberal Education for Adults.

Loehlin, J., Lindzey, G. and Spuhler, J. M. 1975. *Race differences in intelligence.* San Francisco: W. H. Freeman.

Longman. 1994. *Dictionary of contemporary English.* London: Pearson Education Ltd.

Ludwig, S. 2002. 'Uganda's exemplary fight against AIDS.' In *Adult Education and Development,* No. 58, pp. 89–95.

Lummis, C. D. 1993. 'Equality.' In *The development dictionary: A guide to knowledge as power*, ed. W. Sachs, pp. 38–52. London: Zed Books.

Mabogunje, A. 1996. *Environmental challenges of sub-Saharan Africa.* Lagos: Malthouse Press Ltd.

McGivenny, V. and Murray, F. 1991. *Adult education in development: Methods and approaches from changing societies.* Leicester: NIACE.

Macmillan. 2000. *The Macmillan encyclopaedia.* London: Macmillan.

Macropedia. 1973. *Encyclopaedia Britannica.* London: Macropedia.

Marrison, K. (ed.). 1999. *Education for human rights and democracy in Southern Africa.* Windhoek: UNESCO and Longman.

Marx, K. 1967 [1867]. *Capital: A critique of political economy*, transl. S. Moore and E. Aveling. New York: International Publishers.

Mazrui, A. A. 1996. 'Africa in the twenty-first century: Problems and prospects.' An annual distinguished lecture, delivered at the Institute of Governance and Social Research, Jos, Nigeria.

Maslow, A. H. 1970. *Motivation and personality.* New York: Harper and Row.

Medel-Añonuevo, C. (ed.). 2002. *Addressing gender relations in HIV preventive education.* Hamburg: UNESCO Institute for Education.

Medel-Añonuevo, C. and Mitchell, G. (eds.). 2003. *Citizenship, democracy and lifelong learning.* Hamburg: UNESCO Institute for Education.

Midzi, D. 2001. 'The Zimbabwe literacy campaign: Problems and ways forward.' In *Adult Education and Development*, No. 57, pp. 123–128.

Mittelman, J. H. 1996. 'The dynamics of globalization.' In *Globalization: Critical reflections*, ed. J. H. Mittelman, pp. 1–19. London: Lynne Rienner Publishers.

Merriam, S. B. and Brockett, R. G. 1997. *The profession and practice of adult education: An introduction.* San Francisco: Jossey-Bass Publishers.

Miles, R. 1999. *Rassismus: Einfuhrung in die Geschichte und Theorie eines Begriffs.* Hamburg: Argument.

Mills, C. R. 1956. *The power elite.* New York: Oxford University Press.

Mitchell, G. (ed.). 1979. *A new dictionary of sociology.* London: Routledge & Kegan Paul.

Mpofu, S. T. 1995. 'Evaluation of the Government Literacy Campaign in Zimbabwe.' In *African Asssociation for Literacy and Adult Education Journal*, Vol. 9, No. 1, pp. 25–34.

Mpofu, S. T. 1996. 'The women's movement and current trends of globalisation: A case of women's agencies in Zimbabwe'. In *Convergence*, Vol. 29, No. 4, pp. 58–66.

Mpofu, S. T. 1997. 'The fallacies of literacy campaigns: Reflections on the Zimbabwe National Literacy Campaign.' In *Zimbabwe Journal of Educational Research*, Vol. 9, No. 1, pp. 18–43.

Mpofu, S. T. 1998. 'The research–practice interface in adult education.' In *Retrospect and renewal: The state of adult education research in Africa*, eds. M. Omolewa, E. E. Osuji and A. Oduaran, pp. 23–29. Dakar: UNESCO-BREDA.

Mpofu, S. T. 2000. 'The state of adult literacy education in Zimbabwe.' In *The state of adult and continuing education in Africa*, eds. S. Indabawa, A. Oduaran, T. Afrik and S. Walters, pp. 183–193. Windhoek: Department of Adult and Nonformal Education, University of Namibia.

Mpofu, S. T. forthcoming. 'The challenges facing distance education in Southern Africa.' In *Making distance education work: Understanding learning and learners at a distance*, ed. S. J. Levine. LearnerAssociates.net

Mpofu, S. T. and Amin, M. 2004. *A survey of perceptions, delivery systems and funding of adult learning in Namibia*. Windhoek: Department of Adult and Basic Education, Ministry of Education, Sport and Culture.

Muller, J. 2000. 'From Jomtien to Dakar: Meeting basic learning needs of whom?' In *Adult Education and Development*, No. 55, pp. 29–57.

Nafukho, F., Amutabi, M. and Otunga, R. 2005. The foundations of adult education. Cape Town: Pearson Education SA.

The New Internationalist Publications Ltd. 2001. *The World Guide*. London: The New Internationalist Publications Ltd.

Nigerian Economic Summit Group. 2000. *Report of the Seventh Nigerian Economic Summit*. Ibadan: Spectrum Books Ltd.

Nyerere, J. K. 1974. *Freedom and development: A selection from writings and speeches, 1968–73*. New York: Oxford University Press.

Nyerere, J. K. 1982. 'Adult education and development.' In *Adult Education and Development*, No. 19, pp. 37–45.

Nyirenda, J. E., Indabawa, S. A. and Avoseh, M. B. M. (eds.). 1999. *Developing professional adult education programmes in Namibia*. Windhoek: Department of Adult and Nonformal Education, University of Namibia.

Obadan, M. 1996. *The Nigerian economy and the external sector*. Lagos: Malthouse Press Ltd.

Obanya, P. 2003. 'The place of language in literacy and basic education.' In *Towards a multilingual culture of education*, ed. A. Ouane, pp. 215–228. Hamburg: UNESCO Institute for Education.

Oduaran, A. B. 1991. 'Concepts and principles.' In *Fundamentals of adult education*, eds. E. T. Ehiametalor and A. B. Oduaran, pp. 1–21. Benin: Nigerian Educational Research Association.

Oduaran, A. B. 1994. *An introduction to community development*. Benin: University of Benin Press.

Oduaran, A. B. 2000. 'Globalisation and lifelong education: Reflection on some challenges for Africa.' In *International Journal of Lifelong Education*, Vol. 19, No. 3, pp. 266–280.

Oduaran, A. B. 2002. 'Learning to live and living to learn in the 21st century. An inaugural lecture'. University of Botswana.

Oduaran, A. B. 2003. 'Order out of chaos: Repositioning Africa for globalisation through lifelong learning.' In *International Journal of Adult and Lifelong Education*, Vol. 1, No. 1, pp. 11–25.

Oduaran, A. B. and Eheazu, B. A. (eds.). 1986. *Issues in Nigerian adult and community development education*. Benin: Nigerian National Council for Adult Education.

Okafor, S. O. 1981. *Indirect rule: The development of Central Legislature in Nigeria*. Lagos: Nelson Africa.

Okedara, J. T. 1981. 'Terminologies and concepts in adult education.' In *An introduction to the study of adult education: A multi-disciplinary and cross-cultural approach for developing countries*, eds. L. Bown and J. T. Okedara, pp. 9–31. Ibadan: University Press.

Okraku, O. 1988. 'Literacy and development.' In *Adult Education and Development*, No. 31, pp. 133–136.

Okwuosa, E. A. 1994. *Options of socio-economic systems for African society*. Zarai: Ahmadu Bello University Press Ltd.

Omolewa, M. A. 1981. *Adult education practice in Nigeria*. Ibadan: Evans Brothers Ltd.

Omolewa, M. A. 1997. 'Literacy, income generation, and poverty alleviation.' In *CARESON Journal of Research and Development*, Vol. 1, No. 1, pp. 1–17.

Omolewa, M. 2001. 'The challenge of education in Nigeria. A university lecture'. University of Ibadan: University Press.

Omolewa, M. A. and Adekanmbi, G. (eds.). 1994. *University initiative in adult education*. Ibadan: University Press.

Opeke, R. O. 1991. 'Gender issues in comparative adult education: The African case.' Paper presented at the World Assembly on Comparative Adult Education, Ibadan.

Oppong, C. and Abu, C. 1985. *A handbook for data collection and analysis on seven roles and statuses of women.* Geneva: International Labour Organisation.

Ouane, A. 1989. *Handbook on learning strategies for post literacy and continuing education.* Hamburg: UNESCO Institute for Education.

Ouane, A. 2003. 'The impossible debate about the use of the mother tongues in education.' In *Towards a multilingual culture of education,* ed. A. Ouane, pp. 89–156. Hamburg: UNESCO Institute for Education.

Oxenham, J. 1999. 'Education for unschooled adults and the World Bank.' In *Adult Education and Development,* No. 52, pp. 103–108.

Oxfam. 1995. *The Oxfam poverty report.* Oxfam Publications.

Pachamama. 2003. 'Glossary.' Available at http://www.unep.org/geo2000/pacha/glossary.htm.

Peters, J. M., Jarvis, P. and Associates (eds.). 1991. *Adult education: Evolution and achievements in a developing field of study.* San Francisco: Jossey-Bass Publishers.

Pietermaritzburg Declaration. 2002. 'International Conference on Adult Basic and Literacy Education in the Southern African Development Community (SADC) region', University of Natal, Pietermaritzburg, South Africa, 3–5 December.

Rahnema, M. 1993. 'Poverty.' In *The development dictionary: A guide to knowledge as power,* ed. W. Sachs, pp. 158–176. London: Zed Books.

Reddy, S. G. and Poggy, T. W. 2002. *How not to count the poor.* New York: Bernard College.

Roberts, J. 1993. 'Production.' In *The development dictionary: A guide to knowledge as power,* ed. W. Sachs, pp. 175–191. London: Zed Books.

Rogers, A. 1992. *Adults learning for development.* London: Cassell.

Rogers, A. 2001. 'Afterword: Problematising literacy and development.' In *Literacy and development. Ethnographic perspectives,* ed. B. Street, 205–222. London: Routledge.

Rogers, E. 1983. *Diffusion of innovations.* New York: The Free Press.

Rose. P. I. 1974. *They and we.* New York: Random House.

Rostow, W. W. 1960. *The stages of economic growth: A non-communist manifesto.* Cambridge: Cambridge University Press.

Rushton, P. J. 1995. *Race, evolution and behaviour.* New Brunswick: Transaction Publishers.

Sachs, W. (ed.). 1993. *The development dictionary: A guide to knowledge as power.* London: Zed Books.

Salau, S. 1990. *A study of co-operative practices in Nigeria.* Zaria: ABU Press.

Sanders, I. 1958. 'Theories of community development.' In *Rural Sociology,* Vol. 23 (Spring), pp. 1–12.

Schugurensky, D. 1997. 'Forward to the past? Globalisation, neo-liberalism and adult education.' In *Issues in the Education of Adults,* Vol. 8, No. 15, pp. 23–51.

Sesay, S. B. 1999. 'The role of adult education in the socio-economic reintegration of ex-combatants in Sierra Leone.' In *Adult Education and Development,* No. 53, pp. 221–230.

Shitu, M. B. 1995. 'Political economy of community development in Nigeria.' In *Theory and practice of adult and community education,* eds. I. Bio and M. B. Shitu, pp. 56–63. Lagos: Text and Leisure Publishers Ltd.

Smith, C. A. 1965. 'Literacy and schooling in the development threshold: Some historical cases.' In *Education and economic development,* eds. C. A. Smith et al. Chicago: University of Chicago Press.

Spencer, L. 2002. 'The external face of injustice: AIDS, poverty and debt in Africa.' In *Africa Advocacy* No. 5 (March), pp. 1–4. Available at http://www.lwr.org/advocacy/africa/afadv5.pdf.

Spengler, O. 1980 [1918/22]. *The decline of the West,* transl. C. F. Atkinson. New York: Knopf.

Stromquist, N. P. 1988. 'Women's education in development: From welfare to empowerment.' In *Convergence,* Vol. 21, No. 4, pp. 5–16.

Stromquist, N. P. 2002. 'Poverty and schooling in the lives of girls in Latin America.' In *Adult Education and Development,* No. 59, pp. 15–34.

Stuart, J. (ed.). 1994. *Development in context, Book 1.* Windhoek: Longman Namibia Ltd.

Sweetman, C. 1998. *Gender, education and training.* Oxford: Oxfam.

Titmus, C. et al. 1979. *Terminology of adult education*. Paris: UNESCO.

Toynbee, A. J. 1962. *America and the world revolution*. New York: Oxford University Press.

Uche, G. 1993. *The practice of non-formal education in developing countries*. Hull: The University of Hull.

UNDP. 2001. *World development report*. New York: UNDP.

UNEP. 1997. *Global environment outlook. Global state of the environment report*. Nairobi: UNEP.

UNESCO. 1952. *International directory of adult education*. Paris: UNESCO.

UNESCO. 1993. *World education report*. Paris: UNESCO.

UNESCO. 1994. 'The impact of HIV/AIDS on education: A review of literature and experience.' Working Document. Paris: UNESCO.

UNESCO. 2001. *How to produce environmental education materials*. Tokyo: UNESCO Cultural Centre for Asia and the Pacific.

UNESCO. 2003. *World education forum: Final report*. Paris: UNESCO.

UNESCO Institute for Education. 1997a. *Democracy and peace*. Hamburg: UNESCO Institute for Education.

UNESCO Institute for Education. 1997b. *Adult environmental education: Awareness and environmental action*. Hamburg: UNESCO Institute for Education.

United Nations. 1963. *Community development and national development*. New York: United Nations.

United Nations. 1995. 'The Copenhagen Declaration and Programme of Action: Report of World Summit for Social Development', 6–12 March. Copenhagen: United Nations.

United Nations. 2003. *International covenant on economic, social and cultural rights*. Available at http://www.ohchr.org/english/law/pdf/cescr.pdf.

UN Foundation. 2003. 'The Global HIV/AIDS Crisis.' Available at http://www.unfoundation.org/media_center/publications/pdf/Global_HIV_AIDS_02.pdf.

Van der Zanden, J. W. 1972. *American minority relations: The sociology of racial and ethnic groups*. New York: Ronald Press.

Wagner, D. A. 1995. 'Literacy and development: Rationales, myths, innovations and future directions.' In *International Journal of Educational Development*, Vol. 15, No. 4, pp. 341–362.

Wallace, R. C. and Wallace, W. D. 1985. *Sociology*. Boston: Allyn and Bacon, Inc.

Walters, S. (ed.). 1997. *Globalisation, adult education and training: Impacts and issues*. London: Zed Books.

Walters, S. and Watters, K. 2000. 'From adult education to lifelong learning in Southern Africa over the last twenty years.' In *The state of adult and continuing education in Africa*, eds. S. A. Indabawa, A. Oduaran, T. Afrik and S. Walters, pp. 49–61. Windhoek: Department of Adult and Non-formal Education, University of Namibia.

Warren, R. L. 1978. *The community in America*. Chicago: Randy McNally.

Webb, D. 1997. *HIV and AIDS in Africa*. London: Pluto Press.

Weber, M. 1958 [1904]. *The Protestant ethic and the spirit of capitalism*, transl. T. Parsons. New York: Charles Scribner's Sons.

Weber, M. 1947 [1922]. *The theory of social and economic organization*, transl. and ed. A. M. Henderson and Talcott Parsons. New York: Oxford University Press.

Williams, G. 1979. *State and society in Nigeria*. Ibadan: Afrografika.

Williams, R. L. 1974. 'Scientific racism and IQ: The silent mugging of the black community.' In *Psychology Today*, Vol. 7, No. 12, pp. 32–41.

Wilmot, P. 1980. *Apartheid and African liberation*. Ile Ife: University of Ife Press Ltd.

World Bank. 2001. *Attacking poverty: World development report, 2000/2001*. Washington, DC: The World Bank.

World Bank. 2002. 'Understanding poverty. What is poverty?' Available at http://www.worldbank.org/poverty/mission/upl.htm.

World Bank. 2003. 'Environment'. Available at http://lnweb18.worldbank.org/ESSD/envext.nsf/41ByDocName/Environment.

World Health Organization. 1981. *Global strategy for health for all by the year 2000*. Geneva: WHO.

World Social Forum. 2004. 'Fórum social mundial.' Available at http://www.forumsocialmundial.org.br/home.asp.

Yahya, D. 1992. 'The crises of identity and choice: Colonial education in post colonial Nigeria.' In *Issues in Nigerian education*, eds. T. A. Adedoja et al., Vol. 1, pp. 1–15. Lagos: Text & Leisure Publishers Ltd.

Yoloye, E. A. 1987. 'Relationship between the work of teachers in non-formal settings and in schools.' In *International Review of Education,* Vol. 33, No. 3, pp. 339–350.

Youngman, F. 1998. 'Old dogs and new tricks? Lifelong education for all: The challenges facing adult education in Botswana.' Inaugural lecture, University of Botswana, Gaborone.

Youngman, F. 2000. *The political economy of adult education and development.* London: Zed Books.

Yusuf, K. A. 2003. 'Ethnicity, the media and nation building.' Paper presented at the 5th Commonwealth Editors Forum, held at Kandy, Sri Lanka.

Zahra, A. A. 2000. 'Addressing Alexandria's environmental problems.' In *Ecological education in everyday life,* ed. J. Hauteceur, pp. 150–158. Hamburg: UNESCO Institute for Education.

Zerger, J. 1997. *Was ist Rassismus?* Göttingen: Lamuv.

Index

dame-dame

religion 51
 and adult education 61–64
 components of 57–58
religious belief systems 58
religious communities 40–41
remedial education 85
research 105
Roman Catholic religion 41
rule of law 96
rural community 40
 and poverty 122

S

scientific stage, *see* positivistic stage
secular community 35, 41
sex 67, 69
sex roles 67, 69
sexually transmitted diseases (STDs) 108
sharia courts 35, 38
situational factors 75
skills, retention of 92
small community 40
social change 17
 conflict theories 23–24
 cyclical theories 20–22
 equilibrium theories 22–23
 evolutionary theories 18–20
social class 68–69
 and adult education 70–71
social context 5
social exclusion approach to poverty 120–121
socialism 17
social problems 135
sociocultural practices 141
Southern African Development Community (SADC) 37, 42, 102, 112, 139
state or government agencies, role of 47
stigma 105
 and denial 107
stigmatisation 107
structural adjustment programmes (SAPs) 127
sustainable development 31, 147

T

Tanzania National Literacy Campaign 7
technology
 African 26
 low levels of 140
theological stage 18
traditional basic education 84

transformation 9, 28
tribalism 51, 55
two-stage evolutionary theory 19

U

unemployment 119
UNESCOs Institute for Education (UIE) 63, 113, 139
United Kingdom's Department for International Development (DFID) 48
United Nations Children's Fund (UNICEF) 47
United Nations Development Programme (UNDP) 47, 112
United Nations Educational, Scientific and Cultural Organisation (UNESCO) 7, 48, 63, 102, 112, 113, 149
United Nations Environmental Programme (UNEP) 148, 150
United Nations Organisation 122, 152
United States Agency for International Development (USAID) 48, 112
upper class 70–71
urban community 39–40
urban development 150

V

village systems 40
vocational/occupational community 42
voter education programmes 100–102

W

water, lack of 150
West African Economic Community (ECOWAS) 42
Western Africa 151
women
 access to education 75, 77
 disempowerment of 82
 family roles 69–70
 globalisation 140–141
 male domination 24
 political change 28
 poverty 122
worker/labour education 87–88
World Bank 112, 121, 124, 129, 141
World Conference on Environment and Development (Earth Summit) 152
World Declaration on Education For All (EFA) 83
World Social Forum (WSF) 137–138
World Trade Organisation (WTO) 127

Z

Zimbabwe National Literacy Campaign 7